Adventures in
The Strand

ARTHUR CONAN DOYLE
AND THE
STRAND MAGAZINE

Arthur Conan Doyle in 1893 when he was 34. Photograph by Herbert Rose Barraud.

Adventures in
The Strand

ARTHUR CONAN DOYLE
AND THE
STRAND MAGAZINE

Mike Ashley

First published in 2016 by
The British Library
96 Euston Road
London NW1 2DB

ISBN 978 0 7123 0984 4

British Library Cataloguing in Publication Data
A catalogue record for this book is available from the British Library

Jacket designed by Rawshock Design
Type design by Geoff Green Book Design, Cambridge
Typeset by IDSUK (DataConnection) Ltd

Printed in Malta by Gutenberg Press

Contents

6   Contents

List of Tables and Charts

Acknowledgements

My thanks must go to Robert Davies, my editor at the British Library, for his help and guidance on this project, and to Sally Nicholls, whose help and advice on the illustrative material is always wise and sensible. I am extremely grateful to Phillip G. Bergem, who tirelessly read the first draft and provided invaluable advice on the inevitable errors and omissions. He also provided extremely helpful data on the American edition of *The Strand Magazine*, which I adapted for Appendix 2. My thanks to Jon Lellenberg for steering me through the necessities of copyright criteria and for his help and advice on archives and sources for Arthur Conan Doyle material. Thanks also to Randall Stock for his evaluation of the dates and contradictions in Doyle's diaries.

For access to the Arthur Conan Doyle papers at the British Library, London [Reference Add MS 88924], I must thank Helen Melody and Rachel Foss. Where comments are extracted from letters made available by the British Library they are noted as [BL] in the footnotes.

For access to the Arthur Conan Doyle Letters to Herbert Greenhough Smith held in the Albert and Shirley Small Special Collections Library at the University of Virginia, Charlottesville, Virginia [Call Number, MSS 10547-d], I must thank Penny White, Reference Coordinator. Where comments are extracted from these letters they are identified in the footnotes together with the letter reference number, e.g. [UVa019].

Introduction

This book is about a relationship – a forty-year relationship – between an author and a magazine.

For forty years, from 1891 to 1930, Arthur (later Sir Arthur) Conan Doyle contributed regularly to *The Strand Magazine* – one of the most famous authors in the world, and one of the most famous magazines.

How did that relationship come about, and why did it last for so long? More significantly, what did it achieve?

The answers to these questions are what this book explores. Arthur Conan Doyle is still remembered today, over eighty years after his death, first and foremost because of his creation – Sherlock Holmes. There had been two short novels featuring Holmes published before *The Strand* began, but though they created some interest they did not cause a revolution. Yet once a series of short Sherlock Holmes stories began in *The Strand* in 1891, the Earth moved. When Doyle dared to put an end to Holmes two years later there was such an outpouring of grief you would think it had been the end of the world.

There had indeed been a revolution, but who started it? Doyle or *The Strand*? And was that *The Strand*'s publisher, George Newnes, or its editor, Herbert Greenhough Smith? Between all three, they changed the face of popular fiction in Britain and the English-speaking world. They ushered in what has been called the 'Age of the Storytellers'; the success of *The Strand*, which owed much but not everything to Sherlock

Holmes, led to scores of other popular-fiction magazines flourishing from the 1890s to the 1930s. That in turn allowed a new generation of writers to grow and prosper and dominate the literary scene, bringing a vibrant thrill to popular fiction.

More than that, the success of the Sherlock Holmes stories created the genre of detective and mystery fiction, and the new swathe of magazines provided the fertile soil in which this genre could flourish.

There was much more to Doyle that just Sherlock Holmes. It is well known that the reason he chose to put an end to Holmes was because writing those stories diverted his energies from his other literary interests, chiefly historical fiction. It was to Greenhough Smith's credit that he not only allowed but encouraged Doyle to explore all of his interests, literary and otherwise. As a consequence, for forty years the magazine published a huge diversity of material from this one creative individual. There were the light-hearted Napoleonic stories featuring Brigadier Gerard, the more in-depth historical stories such as *Sir Nigel*, such early science-fiction adventure stories as *The Lost World*, and stories of Doyle's favourite sports such as boxing in 'The Croxley Master', or cricket in 'The Story of Spedegue's Dropper'. *The Strand* also allowed Doyle to explore his other passions, notably spiritualism, which dominated his thinking for the last fifteen years of his life, and included his belief in fairies. He also chronicled the major battles of the First World War, cast new light on previously unsolved crimes and mysteries, and led crusades against injustice.

All of this appeared in *The Strand*. Although Doyle contributed to other magazines and newspapers, *The Strand* remained his most significant publisher by far, especially for his fiction. And for all those years, from 1891 to 1930, Greenhough Smith was his editor. It was more than a relationship; it was a literary bond. Soon after Doyle died, Greenhough Smith retired – at the end of a phenomenal era.

Doyle's contributions to *The Strand* included all his major fiction works, and most of the non-fiction which was of importance to him. As a consequence, much of his life is reflected in this body of work. So while this book is not a biography – there are plenty of those, which cover Doyle's life far more impressively than I can here – it is possible to see how his life inspired or influenced what he contributed to the magazine. Effectively he bared his soul in the magazine. *The Strand* acts rather like a prism, splitting Doyle's career into the spectrum of his passions and then re-forming them back into his life.

No other magazine and author had such a close relationship for so long. Few other authors achieved so much during their lifetime, and few other magazines were as popular and influential as *The Strand*. The combination of the two created a phenomenon that has never been bettered and will probably never be repeated.

Cover of the special Royal Edition of the March 1891 issue of *The Strand Magazine* which included Doyle's first appearance with 'The Voice of Science'.

1

Paths to The Strand

THOSE WHO BELIEVE IN FATE may feel that the paths of Arthur Conan Doyle, George Newnes and Herbert Greenhough Smith were destined to cross, even though the journeys they took in their early lives were as likely to take them further apart. In their late twenties each man made a life-changing decision which, like switching the points on a railway, set them on a common path that would result in one of the most momentous events in popular fiction.

★

The path first chosen for Doyle was that of a doctor. I say 'chosen for Doyle' because it may not have been solely his choice. The activities of his family were such that one might have expected him to become an artist. His grandfather John Doyle, of Irish Catholic descent, was a noted painter, particularly of horses. In 1822, he and his wife moved from Dublin to London, where they raised their family. Four of his sons became artists, the most renowned being Richard Doyle, famous as a caricaturist in *Punch* and for his illustrations of fairy tales. The eldest son, James, was noted as a painter in oils and for early colour work in books, including his own *A Chronicle of England* (1864). A third son, Henry, whom Arthur recalled as 'a great judge of old paintings', became Director of the National Gallery in Dublin.

Then there was Arthur's father, Charles Altamont Doyle; another capable artist, often of fanciful, even surreal images, but he was overshadowed by his brothers and was never as successful. Instead, in 1849, aged seventeen (Arthur remembered it as nineteen) he moved to Edinburgh, taking up a post as an architectural draughtsman with Her Majesty's Office of Works. It was there that he met Mary Foley, whom he married in 1855; their son Arthur Conan Doyle was born in Edinburgh on 22 May 1859, and grew up with a hybrid and quite melodic Scottish–Irish burr. He was the third of what would be nine children, although the second, Catherine, had died the previous year when only six months old.

The young Arthur with his father, Charles Altamont Doyle (from *The Strand*, October 1923).

Doyle's mother, Mary, aged 30 in 1867 when young Arthur was eight (from *The Strand*, October 1923).

Doyle spoke about his father's abilities in *The Strand* years later when it serialised his autobiography *Memories and Adventures*:

It is one of my unfulfilled schemes to collect as many [paintings] as possible and to have a Charles Doyle exhibition in London, for the critics would be surprised to find what a great and original artist he was – far the greatest, in my opinion, of the family.[1]

---

[1] Doyle, 'Memories and Adventures', *Strand*, October 1923, p. 325.

One of Charles Doyle's paintings which *The Strand* described as characteristic of his 'weirdly imaginative work' (from *The Strand*, October 1923).

Doyle never did assemble such an exhibition, though there was plenty of material. In addition to working as a draughtsman – his best-known design being that of the fountain at Holyrood Palace – Doyle senior undertook many commissions. But he drank excessively, sometimes trading his art for drink, and with a growing family he lived in one of the poorer parts of Edinburgh, in what Conan Doyle called 'genteel poverty'. It was

Table 1: Arthur Conan Doyle and his brothers and sisters

Ann (called Annette), *born* 22 July 1856, *died* 13 January 1890

Catherine, *born* 22 April 1858, *died* 20 October 1858

Arthur Conan Doyle, *born* 22 May 1859, *died* 7 July 1930

Mary, *born* 4 May 1861, *died* 3 June 1863

Caroline (called Lottie), *born* 22 February 1866, *died* 3 May 1941

Constance (called Connie), *born* 4 March 1868, *died* 8 June 1924

John (called Innes), *born* 31 March 1873, *died*, 19 February 1919

Jane (called Ida), *born* 16 March 1875, *died*, 1 July 1937

Bryan Mary (called Dodo), *born* 2 March 1877, *died* 8 February 1927

only thanks to his rich uncles and his godfather, Michael Conan, that young Arthur was able to receive a good education.

It was from his godfather, the brother of John Doyle's wife Marianna, and thus Arthur's great uncle, that Arthur gained his middle name. Michael Conan had come to join his sister and brother-in-law in London, where he qualified as a barrister. Though he practised for some years, he did not ultimately pursue the bar as a vocation. He was another talented artist, and turned to writing for the *Art Journal* in 1833. He settled in Paris in 1854 and remained there as the *Journal*'s Paris correspondent until his death in 1879. So although the young Arthur corresponded with this distant relative and benefactor, he did not meet him until 1876, when the old man was seventy-three and Arthur seventeen. Arthur remembered him as a 'dear old volcanic Irishman, who spent his day in his shirt-sleeves, with a little dicky-bird of a wife waiting upon him'.[2]

The old Irishman took his role as godfather seriously, and was well aware of young Arthur's nascent literary abilities. Arthur had written what he later referred to as 'my first book' when he was just six years old. He recalled its plot many years later.

> It was written upon foolscap paper, in what might be called a fine bold hand – four words to the line; and was illustrated by marginal pen-and-ink sketches by the author. There was a man in it, and there was a tiger. I forget which was the hero, but it didn't matter much, for they became blended into one about the time when the tiger met the man. I was a realist in the age of the Romanticists. I described at some length, both verbally and pictorially, the untimely end of that wayfarer. But when the tiger had absorbed him, I found myself slightly embarrassed as to how my story was to go on. 'It is very easy to get people into scrapes, and very hard to get them out again,' I remarked, and I have often had cause to repeat the precocious aphorism of my childhood.[3]

His godfather was informed of the story by Arthur's mother and encouraged the boy in his reading, sending him a variety of adventure novels and historical books. Young Doyle became a voracious reader. He declared

---

[2] *Op. cit.*

[3] Originally published in *The Idler*, January 1893, p. 633, and reprinted in 'How I "Broke Into Print"', *Strand*, February 1915, pp. 154–155.

that at this early age his favourite author was Mayne Reid. Also of Irish descent, Reid lived for most of the 1840s in the United States and used this as a setting for a number of frontier adventure stories. Doyle also delighted in the books of fellow Scot R. M. Ballantyne, best known for *The Coral Island* (1858) but who, like Reid, spent his early life in North America and set several novels there. Doyle's predilection for historical fiction was also satisfied by the novels of Sir Walter Scott, notably *Ivanhoe* (1820). These writers sustained Doyle's reading appetite for historical and adventure novels, which would significantly affect his later writing.

Doyle's storytelling skills became evident at school. After a period at a junior school he was sent in 1868 to Hodder, near Preston in Lancashire, a preparatory school for the nearby Jesuit College at Stonyhurst, which he attended from 1870 to 1875. Doyle recalled:

> ...it was discovered by my playmates that I had more than my share of the lore that they hankered after. There was my *début* as a storyteller. On a wet half-holiday I have been elevated on to a desk, and with an audience of little boys all squatting on the floor, with their chins upon their hands, I have talked myself husky over the misfortunes of my heroes. Week in and week out those unhappy men have battled and striven and groaned for the amusement of that little circle. I was bribed with pastry to continue these efforts, and I remember that I always stipulated for tarts down and strict business, which shows that I was born to be a member of the Authors' Society.[4]

While at Stonyhurst, Doyle developed some abilities as a poet, and recalled contributing verse to the college magazine, which he claimed in *Memories and Adventures* that he also edited. But the *Stonyhurst Magazine* did not begin until 1881. He was probably remembering a magazine called *Wasp* that he and his colleagues started in July 1873, and in which he ran some poems and cartoons. No copies are known to survive. He also started, in November 1873, a magazine called the *Stonyhurst Figaro,* which saw just one handwritten edition.[5]

With these literary skills, his artistic heritage and his supportive godfather, it would seem only natural that Doyle should have become a writer, but in his last days at Stonyhurst when discussing careers, Doyle

[4] Doyle, 'How I "Broke Into Print"', *Strand*, February 1915, pp. 155.
[5] Doyle did subsequently contribute to the *Stonyhurst Magazine* as one of the College's 'old boys'.

told one of his masters that he had thought of being a civil engineer. The response came, 'Well, Doyle, you may be an engineer, but I don't think you will ever be a civil one.' Another master told him he 'would never do any good in the world'.

With his father's increasing alcoholism and growing family, it was impractical to consider writing as a career. The home needed a guaranteed income, so it was to his mother's credit that she continued to support his education, despite the financial straits. After leaving Stonyhurst in 1875, Doyle spent a year at the Jesuit College of Feldkirch in Austria to improve his German. He was already mastering French and was reading the works of Jules Verne in their original language.

So with writing too unreliable a career and civil engineering apparently discarded as an option, how did Doyle become a medical student?

One factor may be that his maternal grandfather, William Foley, had been a doctor. A graduate of Trinity College, Dublin, he had died aged only thirty-seven in 1841, so Arthur's mother, Mary, would barely have known him. She was only just four when he died, but his widow, Catherine, who had brought Mary and another daughter (also called Catherine) to Edinburgh in 1847, would doubtless have spoken about him, and Mary may have acquired a romantic image of a father she hardly knew serving as a doctor.[6]

There was another clear factor, and that was Edinburgh University itself. Its medical school was one of the finest in the land, perhaps in the world. It was virtually on the family doorstep, and Mary would have found it relatively convenient to have her son undertake his studies so close to home. It may not have taken much, therefore, to prompt Mary to encourage her son to become a medical student. That prompt soon came.

In the early months of 1875, before Arthur had left Stonyhurst, the Doyles moved to slightly larger premises in Edinburgh, in part to accommodate the growing family. This was, of course, more expensive and to help meet that cost Arthur's mother took in a lodger, Bryan Charles Waller, a recently qualified medical student. Exactly when this happened is uncertain – he was certainly there by March 1876, because he attended to Arthur's sister

---

[6] Mary's mother Catherine died on 7 June 1862 aged 48. Her death left an impression upon the infant Arthur. He recalled in 'Memories and Adventures' that her 'death-bed – or rather the white waxen thing which lay upon that bed – is the very earliest recollection of my life.'

Lottie, who had measles. Waller corresponded with Arthur in Feldkirch and the tone of those letters, which covered a variety of subjects, suggests that Waller was taking an almost fatherly interest in the student.

It was after returning from Feldkirch in June 1876 that Doyle visited his godfather in Paris, and there can be no doubt that the two would have discussed the boy's future. Conan impressed upon Arthur the financial burden on the family to support him through his medical studies[7] but it seems that by then Arthur's mind was made up, as he had considered seeking a bursary to help the finances.

Arthur had also received the news that his father was 'retiring' from the Ministry of Works. In fact his boss had retired, providing an opportunity for reorganisation. Charles Doyle, although aged only forty-four, was probably becoming unreliable because of his alcoholism, and he was pensioned off in June 1876. This reduced the family income, although the eldest daughter, Annette, who was now twenty, took up a governess post in Portugal and sent most of her salary home.

Nevertheless, in preparing for his scholarship in order to obtain the bursary for medical school, Arthur was only too aware of how much his mother was relying upon the income from Dr Waller. The research of Owen Dudley Edwards has shown that from the start of the financial year, April 1877, the rent for the Doyle home in Argyle Terrace was being paid by Waller.[8] Perhaps even more extraordinarily, when the Doyle's youngest child was born in March 1877, she was named after the doctor and his mother, Julia. She was baptised Bryan Mary Julia Josephine Doyle. Waller's father had died in March and he inherited the family estate at Masongill on the Yorkshire–Lancashire border, near Ingleton, but he continued to stay in Edinburgh with the Doyles.

It is possible to read too much into this. Some have speculated that Waller, who was only twenty-three at this time, may have become romantically involved with the eldest daughter, Annette.[9] Perhaps one reason why she left for Portugal was to avoid his advances. It seems less likely that there was a relationship between Waller and Doyle's mother, although she was still only thirty-nine and Doyle may well have felt a rivalry for his mother's affections. What is evident is that at some stage Arthur became

---

[7] See Booth (39).
[8] See Edwards, *Quest* (151).
[9] See Booth (46).

less enamoured of Waller. It probably happened gradually, because Waller was a great support during Arthur's medical studies, and Arthur chose him as his best man at his wedding to Louise Hawkins in August 1885. So for at least ten years Arthur must have been on reasonably good terms with him. The mental state of Arthur's father was rapidly deteriorating and in March 1879 he was admitted to a home for alcoholics at Blairerno, Kincardineshire.[10] With Charles out of the picture, Waller's hold on the Doyle home, for which he continued to pay the rent, became stronger and this must have given Arthur cause for some resentment. Years later, when he came to write *Memories and Adventures*, Doyle made no reference to Waller, other than perhaps in the following veiled comment:

> My mother had adopted the device of sharing a large house, which may have eased her in some ways, but was disastrous in others.[11]

This disaster could refer to the decline in his father's faculties and the insinuation into the family of Dr Waller. Whatever the circumstances, the relationship can only have soured over time, because after his return from Austria, Doyle dedicated his time to earning his place at medical school. He succeeded, even though he was cheated out of his bursary when he learned, too late, that the examination he had passed allowed a stipend for art students only, not medical, and instead of receiving funding of £40 for two years, he received only a meagre compensation of £7. I shall return to his medical studies later, but suffice it to say for now that he qualified in August 1881 as a bachelor of medicine and a master of surgery.

While at university, though, he continued to read voraciously, often spending his lunch money on second-hand books, and found he still had the urge to write. Though this wasn't quite yet the life-changing decision referred to earlier, he was moving in that direction:

> I may say that the general aspiration towards literature was tremendously strong upon me, and that my mind was reaching out in what seemed an aimless way in all sorts of directions.[12]

He was encouraged by friends, who said that his letters were vivid and that surely he ought to be able to sell something. So he tried, and kept on trying. He called his manuscripts 'paper boomerangs' because

---

[10] From there, in May 1885, Charles was moved to the Royal Mental Hospital in Montrose.
[11] Doyle, 'Memories and Adventures', *Strand*, October 1923, p. 332.
[12] Doyle, 'Memories and Adventures', *Strand*, October 1923, p. 336.

much of what he despatched to magazines was returned, but he saw himself entering a kind of literary apprenticeship. He had been driven to write not just because of an inner urge, but out of the necessity of 'Hard Times', as he called them. He had to help pay his way through university, and he wanted to ensure he was playing his part in supporting his mother and siblings rather than relying on Dr Waller. Unfortunately, in these early years he did not generate much income:

> During ten years of hard work I averaged less than fifty pounds a year from my pen.[13]

£50 during the 1880s had roughly the same purchasing power as £4,700 today,[14] which is certainly helpful, but not of the magnitude Doyle required to help his family. The rental alone being paid by Dr Waller on Argyle Terrace was £86 a year.

Doyle's first appearance in print was with 'The Mystery of Sasassa Valley' in the Scottish *Chambers's Journal* for 6 September 1879. It's something of a boys' adventure story, but is full of atmosphere. Set in South Africa, it tells how two young men earn their fortune by braving what many believed was a haunted valley. It was published anonymously, as was so much then in the popular magazines, and Doyle received three guineas for it (about £280).

Over the next decade he would sell just over thirty stories and a dozen or so articles. The latter rarely brought in more than a guinea apiece, and at the outset the stories seldom sold for more than three or four guineas. But there were occasional moments. 'The Captain of the Polestar', a suitably atmospheric Arctic ghost story, which sold to *Temple Bar,* brought in ten guineas (over £900 today) while 'J. Habakuk Jephson's Statement' sold to the prestigious *Cornhill Magazine* for 29 guineas (equal now to over £2,800). These steady sales meant that despite having established a medical practice, his writing was becoming a more steady commitment – but it was still too early to consider it as a profession. What's more, Doyle had married in 1885 and his first child, Mary, named after his mother, came along in 1889. It was all a little too risky for him to become a full-time writer and yet, only two years later in 1891, that's exactly what he did.

---

[13] Doyle, 'How I "Broke Into Print"', *Strand*, February 1915, pp. 155.
[14] Calculations on comparative monetary values are made using the website http://www.measuringworth.com/.

George Newnes (from *The Life of Sir George Newnes*, by Hulda Friederichs, Hodder & Stoughton, 1911).

To understand how, we need to follow the other paths, particularly that of George Newnes.

★

George Newnes, who became the publisher of *The Strand Magazine*, was eight years Doyle's senior. He had been born in Matlock Bath, Derbyshire, on 13 March 1851, the youngest of six children of the Reverend Thomas Mold Newnes. Like Doyle, Newnes was despatched to a boarding school, but not a strict one run by the Jesuits. He went to Silcoates, near Wakefield, a school for the sons of Congregational ministers, which was surprisingly liberal under the wise and kindly headship of the Nonconformist Dr James Bewglass, an Irishman from County Tyrone.

Young George's elder brother Edward (called Ted) was also a pupil at the school and one of the most popular, having led a group of six boys into a victory against six other boys in Halifax. The fight had been over access to a local chapel. Despite Edward's protection, George felt he could look after himself, and unfortunately he came off worse in a scrap with another boy. Some of the boys at Silcoates had decided to hold their own prayer meetings, and attendance was entirely voluntary. George became a devout member and was ridiculed by one of the boys who did not attend. This led to a vicious fight, leaving George unconscious for a whole day. He recovered and seemed none the worse, but it showed he was not one to evade a fight if a principle was at stake. This characteristic would stand him in good stead in the business world.

For it was into the business world that the sixteen-year-old Newnes ventured. He did not follow his father into the Church, but instead entered a five-year apprenticeship with a wholesale haberdasher in the City of London. The terms of the apprenticeship were that while he learned his trade he received no payment other than free board and lodging. One of his initial responsibilities was to record all of the company's sales in a ledger, and it became apparent that the boy had a talent for arithmetic, totting up the figures in the ledger with complete accuracy at a pace faster than any other clerk. In his second year it was decided to make use of Newnes's abilities in the annual stock-take. It came as no surprise to the company that he did this both quickly and accurately. As a result he was promoted, being made head of the Entering Department, but he was still under the terms of his apprenticeship, and was thus without pay. Newnes was, of course, flattered – but also resolute. He told his employer that he was bringing a skill to the business that was of his own making, not something he had learned as an apprentice. He also learned that the man who had held this post at a salary of £100 was moving on, and that Newnes was being asked to fulfil this role for no recompense. He argued that the terms of his apprenticeship were no longer valid and that either he should be paid the proper rate, or he would leave.

The proprietor was taken aback and insisted that the terms were legal, but he could see the determination in the youth and he eventually acceded. Once again Newnes had stood up to fight for a principle, and this time had won. After a year he became a travelling salesman, expanding the firm's business beyond London. At the end of his apprenticeship he was headhunted by a rival company, and by 1874 was managing a shop in Manchester. Although only twenty-three, Newnes was financially secure and courted his childhood sweetheart Priscilla

Hillyard, the daughter of one of his father's friends, the Reverend James Hillyard of Leicester. They were married on 23 December 1875 at the Congregational Church in Darlington, and the officiating minister was none other than Newnes's own father.

The two settled in a house in Stretford in the suburbs of Manchester, where their two sons were born – Frank in September 1876 and Arthur in March 1879. It was a happy and prosperous home during the 1880s. Outside of his work Newnes enjoyed playing cricket – he had earned the nickname 'Not Out Newnes' at school – taking long walks and, above all, playing chess. Both he and his wife were excellent players – Priscilla later became the first President of the British Ladies' Chess Club, founded in October 1895. Newnes also read extensively and, like Doyle, enjoyed haunting bookstalls and newsagents to find anything of interest, particularly in magazines.

The story of how Newnes founded the magazine *Tit-Bits*, which led to *The Strand* and his publishing empire, has become legendary, and is recounted in detail in Hulda Friederichs's biography of Newnes. Each evening, at supper, Newnes would read items of interest to his wife from the local paper, and one evening he saw a piece in the *Manchester Evening News* that caught his attention. It concerned a train of eight carriages that, while being shunted at Halstead Station in Kent, started off on its own down the incline, gathering speed as it passed through three other stations towards south London. Eventually a signalman shifted it on to a siding, where it stopped after crashing into a tannery at the end of the line. The incident was all the more dramatic because the stationmaster's five children were on the train and their father followed in hot pursuit in the steam engine. Thankfully they survived uninjured.

Newnes regarded this item as a 'tit-bit' and said to his wife, 'Why does not somebody bring out a paper containing nothing but tit-bits like this?'[15] It wasn't the first time Newnes had been intrigued by such items, and he had a number of cuttings from papers. He assembled them into a dummy for a prospective magazine but could not find a financial backer. So he used his initiative. There was a strong vegetarian movement in Manchester during the nineteenth century, and Newnes decided to open a vegetarian restaurant. It was soon a success, and Newnes was able to use the profits to launch *Tit-Bits*.

---

[15] Newnes quoted in Friederichs (55).

At least, that's the story. However, the news item about the runaway train appeared in the *Manchester Evening News* for 24 August 1881, and it was in a few other newspapers the day before. The first issue of *Tit-Bits* was dated 22 October 1881, just seven weeks later. Bearing in mind that Newnes still had his full-time job, would seven weeks really have been enough time for him to put together a proposal, seek out two financial backers – both of whom turned him down, find a vacant property for his restaurant and go through all the necessary process to open that up, make a profit and then publish and distribute the first issue of his new magazine?

It seems very unlikely. In her biography of Newnes, Friederichs did not know the date of the news item. She only refers to 'one day'. However, elsewhere she refers to Newnes writing to his parents about the success of his new restaurant. This was on notepaper headed 'The Vegetarian Company's Saloon', dated 13 March 1881. Friederichs must have presumed the news item was earlier than that date, but its date is confirmed by Reginald Pound in his history of *The Strand*.[16]

This allows much more time, and shows that Newnes had opened his restaurant long before he saw the news item, and must have been planning *Tit-Bits* for some time. Clearly when Newnes looked back on this, it was the runaway train that remained in his memory, but it was not the single deciding factor.

Legend aside, there could be no doubt of the success of *Tit-Bits*. On its first day it sold 5,000 copies in Manchester alone. It was a while before Newnes achieved distribution in other major cities, which were reluctant – apparently due to the title. Newnes had not considered the more titillating connotations of *Tit-Bits*, but plenty of newsagents and delivery boys had, and some agents would not stock the title as a result. It required all of Newnes's tenacity and inventiveness to overcome this prejudice, but through various advertising campaigns, notably in London and Newcastle, he demonstrated that it was a family magazine that entertained and informed. Sales passed 100,000 after the first year, rising to 300,000 by 1886 and by 1890 exceeded 500,000. Newnes moved his offices from Manchester to London in 1884, first to Farringdon Street and then, in June 1886, to Burleigh Street, just off the Strand. *Tit-Bits* made Newnes rich. By the end of the 1880s he was drawing a salary of around £30,000 (close to £3 million today).

---

[16] Pound, *Strand* (18).

The offices of George Newnes in Burleigh Street in 1890 boldly displaying the title of *Tit-Bits* (from *The Strand*, January 1891; illustration by George C. Haité).

Newnes's basic technique with *Tit-Bits* was not especially new. The paper was a miscellany of odds and ends culled from other periodicals – pirated, some might say, because Newnes did not pay for these items. This type of miscellany had been around for years. Louis James remarked that as far back as the 1820s the 'most useful apparatus of the editor was generally a pair of scissors', and notes an article in *Sharpe's London Magazine* for August 1829 on how to plunder material from other magazines.[17] Where Newnes differed is that he encouraged the reader to take part and, as a consequence, soon moved away from the culling of items to producing original and therefore more current material, reflecting the public's immediate interests.

Key to the magazine's success were two factors – an insurance scheme, and reader competitions. The first insurance scheme protected anyone travelling by train provided they had a copy of *Tit-Bits* on them. This was later extended so that the relatives of any long-time reader of *Tit-Bits* would receive £100 should the reader die as a result of a railway accident.

In November 1883, Newnes set as a prize the freehold of a £400 seven-room villa for the winner of a contest for the best Christmas story, on the condition they named it 'Tit-Bits Villa'. Doyle entered the contest and was upset when he did not win, as he believed his story was superior. He wrote to Newnes, suggesting that if the magazine would put up £25 he'd match that sum for the two stories to be judged by an impartial adjudicator, with the winner getting the £50. Doyle did not get a response, and one cannot help wondering if he remembered this seven years later when he began to appear in Newnes's new magazine, *The Strand*.[18] By the end of 1891 Doyle would be a shareholder in *Tit-Bits*.

Another competition in 1884 offered a minimum of a year's employment as a clerk to the winner of a contest to answer a total of 130 questions run over thirteen issues that summer. These weren't simple questions. They included 'How much of the surface of England is

---

[17] James (17).
[18] Doubtless Doyle was even more annoyed when he learned that the winning story had been copied from a previously published story. The man who submitted the story, a soldier, had not understood that the story had to be original.

owned by railway companies?' and 'When was Edward IV mistaken for a highwayman?'. The winner was C. Arthur Pearson, then just eighteen years old, who answered eighty-six correctly and scored well on the rest. Pearson entered Newnes's employ in September 1884 and by April 1885 had become the manager of *Tit-Bits*, with Peter Keary who came on board as editor. This allowed Newnes to step back from the day-to-day running of the magazine. Believing he was in touch with the common people, and a strong Liberal at heart, he stood for Parliament in the General Election of 1885 and was elected the MP for the newly created constituency of Newmarket, a position he held for ten years.

Tit-Bits continued to go from strength to strength. There was another major competition in 1890, when the prize for a new and original serial was £1,000 – equivalent to almost £100,000 today. Doyle did not enter it, but the winner was his friend, Grant Allen,[19] with an all-action melodrama, 'What's Bred in the Bone'. After it was serialised in *Tit-Bits*, it was published in book form by Newnes and became a bestseller, soon earning the prize money back for the publisher. *Tit-Bits* was regarded in the publishing world as revolutionary, and part of the growing area of 'new journalism' for the working and lower-middle classes.

The magazine soon generated its rivals from within its own company. One of its popular features was 'Answers to Correspondents', a page where staff and contributors responded to questions purportedly submitted by readers, though many were dreamed up in-house. One of the regular contributors was a young Alfred Harmsworth who, understanding the popularity of the feature, blatantly stole it and issued it as a paper in its own right, including the full title *Answers to Correspondents*, launched on 2 June 1888. After eighteen months the title was abbreviated to simply *Answers*, and so it remained for the next sixty-six years. It was very popular, its circulation almost matching that of *Tit-Bits* through the 1890s.

Its next rival came from Newnes's own manager, C. Arthur Pearson. Pearson worked hard for Newnes and had asked for a raise, but

---

[19] Doyle first met Allen at the *Cornhill* annual dinner in London at the end of December 1884.

Newnes declined. As a consequence Pearson left and set up his own company, launching *Pearson's Weekly* on 26 July 1890. He took with him Peter Keary, so Newnes appointed a new editor to *Tit-Bits*, the redoubtable Galloway Fraser, who remained with the magazine for twenty-eight years. *Pearson's Weekly* also achieved a circulation close to that of *Tit-Bits*. It was clear that they were meeting the demands of a significant market, thirsty for knowledge, information, entertainment and good deals.

It was not all triumph and success for Newnes. A tragic blow was dealt in March 1889 when his ten-year-old son Arthur died of meningitis – known as 'brain-fever' at the time. The illness struck out of the blue and he was dead within a few days. The boy had been playing chess by post with his uncle, and the chessboard remained with its pieces in place for years afterward. Newnes was so overcome by grief that his fair hair turned grey, and his only remedy was to throw himself even deeper into his work.

One outcome was his collaboration with an old school friend from Silcoates, W. T. Stead. Stead suggested to Newnes the idea of another miscellany, commenting upon and abstracting articles of interest from recent magazines. More like a digest than the original *Tit-Bits*, it was called *Review of Reviews* and appeared in January 1890, selling 60,000 copies on the first day. Although once schoolmates, Stead and Newnes were cut from different cloth – Newnes the methodical businessman, Stead the ebullient crusader. It was not long before the two disagreed over the magazine's direction and, after six months, Stead bought Newnes's share for £10,000 and ran the magazine himself, with great success.

Newnes had created a new team to work on *Review of Reviews*, so when Stead bought the magazine, Newnes looked for a new venture to replace it and to keep the staff employed. Even though Pearson and Keary had left, there was still capacity for growth.

Among the new staff was Herbert Greenhough Smith. Here was the third pillar on which the success of *The Strand* would rest, and he was another who had made a significant career change.

Smith was born on 2 January 1855 at Stonehouse in Gloucestershire, where his father was a well-to-do wool-and-cloth dyer. Greenhough had been his mother's maiden name, and it was given to young Herbert as a middle name though, as with Conan Doyle, it took on the form of a double surname. He was educated at St John's College, Cambridge, achieving a BA in 1875, and for the next decade served as a private tutor. He was always interested in literature, though, and secured the publication of a book of verse, *Poems and Sonnets*, in July 1876, which was fairly well received. He was above all fascinated by history and began to contribute articles on famous historical figures to the magazines during the 1880s, which later formed the basis for his book *The Romance of History* (1892). He had married the young Beatrice Harrison in 1885 – she was barely sixteen – and the two lived in Lancaster, their son, Cyril, being born there on New Year's Eve 1888. By now Smith had given up teaching and worked as a journalist for various periodicals.

His work brought him south and the family moved to Wimbledon in 1889. Smith worked in the offices of *Temple Bar*, which had been launched in 1860 as a rival to *The Cornhill Magazine*, at the time the most successful of the mid-Victorian middle-to-highbrow monthlies. *Temple Bar*'s prosperity faded over the years. It had passed through various publishers in its early years and since 1866 had been published by the Bentley family, with George Bentley as its editor. Doyle had sold work to the magazine, notably 'The Captain of the Polestar' published in the January 1883 issue.

Rather curiously, one of Greenhough Smith's stories in *Temple Bar* was later attributed to Doyle. 'The Siege of Sunda Gunge' appeared anonymously in the November 1890 issue, and was reprinted in the United States at the end of P. F. Collier's edition of *The Sign of Four* in 1891. As a consequence the story was considered Doyle's, until its true authorship was identified via the Bentley archives in 1979.

Greenhough Smith left to join Newnes in the summer of 1890, so was not involved with *Temple Bar* when Doyle submitted his story 'Our Midnight Visitor' there in 1890. However Doyle had sent other stories to the magazine, mostly unsuccessfully, and it is likely that Greenhough Smith would have encountered his work directly, besides what he might have read elsewhere.

Smith was not one to show emotion and was renowned for his poker face. Reginald Pound provided the following description:

> Tall, lean, sandy-moustached, with freckles to match on a pallid, expressionless face, he surveyed the world with kindly scrutineering eyes through rimless *pince-nez*. His distrust of emotion gave an impression of a temperament that did not fully warrant the nickname by which he became known to his fellow clubmen, 'Calamity' Smith.[20]

The proposal for *The Strand* is often credited to Smith, but his initial suggestion was just one of many ideas that went into the magazine's conception. Smith had already suggested to George Bentley that there might be scope for a magazine that reprinted translations of stories from various European countries. Bentley turned it down, so Smith proposed it to Newnes. In a sense he was suggesting another miscellany, a sort of translated version of *Review of Reviews*. The idea appealed to Newnes, who added it to his other thoughts.

Newnes was only too aware of the emergence of quality illustrated magazines, particularly in the United States. He later wrote in *The Strand*:

> At the time when *The Strand Magazine* first appeared, I have no hesitation in saying that British magazines were at a low ebb. American magazines were coming here and, because they were smarter and livelier, more interesting, bright and cheerful, they were supplanting those of native birth.[21]

The most recent British edition had been that of *Lippincott's Monthly* in January 1890, but the US invasion dated back a decade to December 1880 when *Harper's New Monthly Magazine* launched a European edition. This was followed by *Century Illustrated Magazine* in November 1881, and *Scribner's Monthly* in January 1887. In Britain the only equivalent was the *English Illustrated Magazine*, published initially by Macmillan, which

---

[20] Pound, *Strand* (56).
[21] George Newnes, 'The One Hundredth Number of "The Strand Magazine"', *Strand*, April 1899, p. 364

appeared in October 1883. This emulated the Arts and Crafts movement with beautiful engravings adorning articles, poetry, stories and studies of major artists. Selling for one shilling, the magazine was aimed at the middle and upper classes.

There were other advances, such as the *Boy's Own Paper*, which had started as a heavily illustrated penny weekly in January 1879. There were also such profusely illustrated papers as the *Illustrated London News*, which had started way back in 1842, and its later rival, *The Graphic*, which began in 1869. These sold for sixpence, and Newnes's innate mathematical and business abilities told him there ought to be a way of issuing a highly illustrated monthly magazine, in the same size and format as *Harper's* and *English Illustrated*, filled with informative articles and entertaining fiction but aimed at the aspiring working class and the ever-growing middle class, and selling for sixpence. And so he brought his team together in the late summer of 1890 to create *The Strand*.

MR. NEWNES'S OFFICE.

George Newnes in his office (from *The Strand*, December 1892).

EDITORIAL OFFICE OF "THE STRAND MAGAZINE."

ART EDITOR'S OFFICE OF "THE STRAND MAGAZINE."

The offices of H. Greenhough Smith (top) and W. H. J. Boot (from *The Strand*, December 1892).

It appeared just before Christmas, its first issue dated January 1891. Greenhough Smith was its Literary Editor and W. H. J. (William Henry James) Boot its Art Editor. Newnes served as Editor-in-Chief at the outset, but this role soon became no more than giving a final editorial approval, leaving Smith and Boot to run the magazine between them – and very successful it was, too. Its first issue had to be reprinted several times and sold around 300,000 copies. Sales would soon rise to half a million.

One reason for that popularity was the appearance of Sherlock Holmes, which brings our three distinct paths together. The business skills of George Newnes, the editorial acumen of Greenhough Smith and the literary genius of Arthur Conan Doyle came together in an explosion of visionary brilliance.

Popular fiction was entering a new realm.

2

Enter Sherlock Holmes

THE FIRST ISSUE OF *The Strand* featured a cover that would remain the same, with only minor changes, for the next twenty-five years. It was an illustration by George Haité of the Strand thoroughfare, looking towards the church of St Mary le Strand, showing the street bustling with crowds of people and horse-drawn cabs. In the foreground is the junction of the Strand with Burleigh Street, and the number 359 with an arrow pointing towards the offices of George Newnes, who is named on the cover as editor. The lead article, 'The Story of the Strand', provided a history of the street and was illustrated throughout by Haité, including a picture of Burleigh Street showing Newnes's offices at that time with the big banner of 'Tit-Bits' on the roof (*see page 27*).

The magazine had 112 pages and measured roughly 9½ by 6½ inches, which had become the new standard size for illustrated periodicals. Newnes had insisted that there be an illustration on every page, which placed a high demand on art editor, William Boot, to find sufficient artists who could illustrate the stories and articles almost on demand. The first issue included work by W. B. Wollen, who would later illustrate Doyle's Brigadier Gerard stories, and Sidney Paget, soon destined to bring the character of Sherlock Holmes to life. In keeping with Greenhough Smith's original idea, the issue ran several stories in translation, including work by Alphonse Daudet, Alexander Pushkin and Voltaire. The latter was the first in a long-running series of stories for children, which would later become the treasured territory of Edith Nesbit. Apart from two other articles – one on the Metropolitan Fire Brigade, and one on the Royal Veterinary College – there was only one new piece of fiction, 'A Deadly Dilemma' by Grant Allen, who remained a regular contributor during the 1890s. The feature that attracted many readers, though, was 'Portraits of Celebrities at Different Times of Their Lives' which reproduced engravings from photographs or paintings of famous people of the day along with a brief annotation. That first issue included Lord Tennyson, Ellen Terry, Henry Irving, Algernon Swinburne and H. Rider Haggard. If it seems that the cult of the celebrity is a modern phenomenon, a look at *The Strand* soon puts this idea into perspective. Doyle would enter those ranks before the year was out.

That issue set a format that remained for the magazine's first volume of six issues. There were plenty of translations amid occasional new stories, plus features on items of popular interest such as Battersea Dogs Home, a night with the Thames Police, Great Ormond Street Children's Hospital, actors' dressing rooms, and a night in an opium den.

Doyle's first appearance was with a short story, 'The Voice of Science' in the third issue, dated March 1891. His name did not appear on the story, which was probably an oversight because he was credited on the contents page and in the index to the first bound volume. On the surface it's a light comedy of manners about how a brother saves his sister from the unwarranted attention of a cad and a coward by the novel use of a phonograph. The phonograph had been around since 1877 so was not a new invention, though it was still not something seen in every household. The story shows Doyle's interest in new technology, which was becoming increasingly apparent in his stories, but it also shows his understanding of the wider advances in scientific understanding, especially with regard to evolution. The story opens with references to noted biologists and evolutionists of the day, now all overshadowed by the giant reputation of Charles Darwin, but at the time key to the debate on evolutionary theory. What's more, the individual focus of this understanding is a woman, whose house is an open salon for scientific discussion. It's a story easily overlooked, but central to Doyle's attitude at the time to the benefits of new technology – which he was already applying in how Sherlock Holmes went about investigating his cases.

Just how this story and Sherlock Holmes found their way into *The Strand* shows how Doyle's alternative career as a writer had developed during the 1880s.

★

The standard narrative is that Doyle sat alone in his practice waiting for clients who never came, and filled his time writing stories. As with so many legends this has a grain of truth, but the real story is far more complicated.

Doyle had been writing regularly since his days at Edinburgh University, selling two or three stories a year but never earning enough to regard it as a career. He had been somewhat footloose, keen to embark on any adventure that came his way. He served as a ship's surgeon on the whaler *Hope* from late February to August 1880, and again as the ship's doctor on the SS *Mayumba* to West Africa from October 1881 to January 1882, on which voyage he almost died of a fever. Thereafter he pursued his career as a general practitioner, working with a rather renegade doctor, George Budd, in Plymouth. This lasted just six weeks before the two fell out, and Doyle moved to Southsea, near Portsmouth, where he set up his own practice in July 1882. His younger brother Innes, who was still at school, came to live with him. It was in a poor area and it took a while before the practice grew, but grow it did – not hugely, but sufficiently. Doyle recorded in *Memories and Adventures* that he made £144 in his first year, £250 in the second, peaking eventually at £300. £300 is roughly equal to £28,000 today, which, though low for a doctor's salary, is about the national average salary as of 2014.

It was through his practice that Doyle met his first wife, Louisa Hawkins. She was the sister of a patient suffering from cerebral meningitis who was under the care of another doctor. Doyle took the patient in and cared for him in his own home. Unfortunately the patient soon died, and this cast some suspicion upon Doyle because of its suddenness. Because there was another doctor involved, Doyle was vindicated, but it was nevertheless a difficult moment. Perhaps this, among other factors, brought Doyle and the poor man's sister close together in what was something of a whirlwind romance. They had only met in March 1885 and were married on 6 August in Yorkshire at Thornton-in-Lonsdale, close to where his mother was living on the estate of Dr Waller.

Doyle believed his marriage gave his mind more focus. 'Both my imagination and my range of expression were greatly improved,' he wrote,

"I polished my own plate every morning,
brushed down my front, and kept the house
reasonably clean."

Doyle sweeping outside his medical practice in Southsea (from *The Strand*,
November 1923).

and he believed that the stories he began to produce represented 'perhaps
as good, [as] honest work as any that I have done'.[22]

While he appreciated the short stories that he sold, he really wanted
his name on a book, and attempted a longer work. He regarded his first,
The Firm of Girdlestone, as too imitative and formulaic and it was only

---

[22] Doyle, 'Memories and Adventures', *Strand*, December 1923, p. 562.

published after the success of other books, though that sale also brought him his first significant advance.[23]

Disappointed with *Girdlestone*, Doyle turned his thoughts to detective fiction. Doyle had long delighted in the stories of Edgar Allan Poe, which it seems he first read while at Feldkirch in 1876 in a volume sent to him by Dr Waller, though he may have read some work earlier. In *Memories and Adventures*, Doyle wrote that 'Poe's masterful detective M. Dupin, had from boyhood been one of my heroes.'[24]

In his early story 'The Fate of the Evangeline', written in the autumn of 1884, Doyle paraphrases Dupin. The story reveals what had happened to a yacht that had vanished. A newspaper, considering the various theories, refers to the 'rules as to the analysis of evidence laid down by Auguste Dupin. "Exclude the impossible," he remarks in one of Poe's immortal stories, "and what is left, however improbable, *must* be the truth."' This dictum is always associated with Sherlock Holmes, but here Doyle used it in a story published in the special Christmas 1885 issue of *The Boy's Own Paper*. In fact, Dupin didn't use those words. In 'The Murders in the Rue Morgue', published in 1841, after considering ways in which a murderer might have escaped from a locked room, Dupin states:

> Now, brought to this conclusion in so unequivocal a manner as we are, it is not our part, as reasoners, to reject it on account of apparent impossibilities. It is only left for us to prove that these apparent 'impossibilities' are, in reality, not such.

Doyle can thus genuinely claim to have coined the more succinct phrase. There is much more to Dupin, of course. At the start of 'The Murders in the Rue Morgue' Dupin breaks into the narrator's silence after fifteen minutes and tells him exactly what he had been thinking during that period. In *A Study in Scarlet* Holmes refers to this trick of Dupin's as 'showy and superficial', but Doyle uses an identical scene in 'The Adventure of the Cardboard Box' (*Strand*, January 1893). Dupin

---

[23] Doyle sold the serial rights in *The Firm of Girdlestone* for newspaper syndication in 1889 for £240, equivalent today to over £23,000. This was the biggest sale he had yet achieved, with further income from the English and American book rights.

[24] *Op. cit.*

undertook the investigation for its own pleasure and was not a private detective – indeed the word detective had not been coined at the time Poe wrote the story. The *Oxford English Dictionary* cites its first usage in 1843 in *Chambers's Journal's* reference to the formation of the plain clothes 'detective police'.[25]

Poe had based Dupin to some degree on the character of Eugène François Vidocq, the world's first real-life private detective. Vidocq was something of a poacher-turned-gamekeeper. After a decade as a criminal and forger he became an informer and, in 1812, established the world's first detective bureau, the Brigade de la Sûreté, followed by the world's first private detective agency, Le Bureau des Renseignements, in 1834. Their success encouraged Britain's Scotland Yard to create the Criminal Investigation Department in 1842. Vidocq enjoyed running rings around the police, who were convinced he was sometimes creating and 'solving' his own crimes, but they could prove nothing and it was years before they eventually trapped him for posing as a policeman.

Vidocq passed into legend and his life became the basis of the literary detective Monsieur Lecoq in the works of Émile Gaboriau. Doyle acknowledged Gaboriau as another influence, remarking that 'he had rather attracted me by the neat dovetailing of his plots.'[26] Doyle must have read Gaboriau in the original French as the first novel, *L'Affaire Lerouge*, published in 1866, was not available in English until 1887 (as *The Widow Lerouge*), by which time Doyle had written the first Holmes novel. In *L'Affaire Lerouge* we are introduced not only to Lecoq, but to the old retired gentleman Monsieur Tabaret, who has become an amateur detective. We learn:

> As soon as he finds himself in the presence of a crime, like this one, for example, he pretends he can explain everything on the instant. [...] He professes, with the help of one single fact, to be able to reconstruct all the details of an assassination, as a savant pictures an antediluvian animal from a single bone.

---

[25] *Chambers's Journal* also published the third of Poe's Dupin stories, 'The Purloined Letter' on 30 November 1844, so if Doyle had access to back issues he might have encountered Dupin long before 1876.

[26] Doyle, *op. cit.*

Gaboriau continues:

The magistrate could not help comparing [Tabaret] to a pointer on the
scent, his turned-up nose even moved about as if to discover some subtle
odour left by the assassin. All the while he talked loudly and with much
gesticulation, apostrophising himself, scolding himself, uttering little cries
of triumph or self-encouragement.

Writing in *The Sign of Four*, Doyle describes Holmes thus:

He whipped out his lens and a tape measure and hurried about the room
on his knees, measuring, comparing, examining, with his long thin nose
only a few inches from the planks and his beady eyes gleaming and deep-
set like those of a bird. So swift, silent, and furtive were his movements,
like those of a trained bloodhound picking out a scent, that I could not
but think what a terrible criminal he would have made had he turned
his energy and sagacity against the law instead of exerting them in its
defence. As he hunted about, he kept muttering to himself, and finally he
broke out into a loud crow of delight.

In both Poe's and Gaboriau's books we see the superiority of the private detective over the official police force and an element of conde-
scension. We also see the detective's methods, which was what made
Holmes so spectacularly noteworthy. Yet no matter how Doyle may have
been inspired by his antecedents, he had a real-life Holmes he could
draw upon: Dr Joseph Bell.

Bell was a surgeon at the Edinburgh Infirmary, where he taught clinical
surgery. Born in 1837 he had graduated from Edinburgh University in 1859
but was never officially part of the faculty. His lectures were always popular
and well attended. He stressed not just medical knowledge but the value
of observation. Doyle served as Bell's outpatient clerk, which allowed him
plenty of opportunity to study his methods. He recalled one occasion when
Bell identified a civilian patient as a former non-commissioned officer in
a Highland regiment, only recently discharged, who had been stationed
in Barbados. Bell's explanation made what seemed remarkable almost
commonplace:

You see, gentlemen, the man was a respectful man, but did not remove
his hat. They do not in the army, but he would have learned civilian
ways had he been long discharged. He has an air of authority and he

Dr Joseph Bell, the inspiration for Sherlock Holmes (from *The Strand*, October 1923).

is obviously Scottish. As to Barbados, his complaint is elephantiasis, which is West Indian and not British.[27]

There was another striking example when Bell immediately identified a new patient as a cobbler. He alerted his students to the wear on the inside of the knee of the man's trousers. 'That was where the man had rested the lapstone – a peculiarity only found in cobblers.'[28]

Dupin, Tabaret and Bell were combined in the character of Sherlock Holmes, though Doyle took some time in developing his name, and that of his amanuensis and colleague Dr John Watson. Doyle's notes reveal that at one stage he was going to be Sherrinford Holmes, while Watson was going to be Ormond Sacker. Sherrinford might have worked, but Sacker

---

[27] Doyle, 'Memories and Adventures', *Strand*, October 1923, p. 335.
[28] 'A Day with Dr Conan Doyle', *Strand*, August 1892, p. 186.

A page from Conan Doyle's notebook showing the alternative names for Sherlock Holmes and Dr Watson, together with other interesting memoranda (from *The Strand,* December 1923).

would have been far from memorable. Part of the success of Sherlock Holmes is that Watson has a straightforward name and is someone with whom the reader can identify. He acts as a more human intermediary between the reader and the ratiocinative machine that is Holmes.

Doyle completed *A Study in Scarlet* in early April 1886 and despatched it with high hopes to *The Cornhill Magazine.* Though its editor James Payn spoke well of the story, he claimed it was overly melodramatic and the wrong length for the magazine. The manuscript started the round of publishers, and it was not until the end of October that Ward, Lock offered Doyle £25 for the full copyright. This means Doyle sold the story entirely and owned no rights at all thereafter. It seems a dismal offer, but by today's purchasing power £25 is equal to around £2,400. Since he had only spent a couple of months writing the story and probably believed he'd earn no more from it, he could view it as a simple sale and move on, despite the disappointment at its poor reception.

The story appeared in *Beeton's Christmas Annual* issued in November 1887, which sold out before Christmas. Ward, Lock issued it in book form in July 1888 and it received good reviews. It was also well received, so Doyle believed, in the United States.

Perhaps as a consequence of this, but certainly as a result of a recommendation by James Payn, Doyle was invited to London in August 1889 to dine with James Stoddart, managing editor of *Lippincott's Monthly Magazine*, who was in Britain finalising plans for a British edition of the magazine. Also at that meeting were Oscar Wilde and the MP Thomas Gill. Doyle was delighted that Wilde had read and was highly complimentary about his recent novel *Micah Clarke*. The outcome of the meeting was that both Wilde and Doyle would write a short novel for *Lippincott's*. In Wilde's case it was 'The Picture of Dorian Gray', while Doyle gave Sherlock Holmes another outing in 'The Sign of Four'. It was his first commission and his fee was £100 (today almost £10,000). The story appeared in the February 1890 issue. Whether some of Wilde's aestheticism subconsciously infected Doyle is a matter of debate, but it is certainly in 'The Sign of Four' that we first see Holmes's reliance on cocaine.

Doyle was at last starting to believe in himself as a writer, but he was not yet ready to plunge into writing as a career. He considered becoming an eye specialist and felt that his writing could support him and his family – his first child, Mary, had been born in January 1889 – while he undertook further studies. He was buoyed by the success of *Micah Clarke*, set at the time of the Monmouth Rebellion in 1685, sales of which had reached 10,000 by the start of 1890, and by selling his next historical novel, *The White Company*, to James Payn at *The Cornhill* for £200 in September 1890.

It is at this stage that we see Doyle becoming a professional writer in all but name. He approached Alexander Pollock Watt to act as his literary agent. Watt was a fellow Scot who is generally recognised as the world's first literary agent. Indeed, he is credited with coining the term when he began operating in earnest in 1881, though he had been undertaking

the work informally since at least 1875. He was another who had made
a life-changing career move. Originally a warehouseman for a drapery
business, he married the sister of Alexander Strahan, publisher of the
monthly magazine *Good Words*, the most popular fiction magazine of the
Victorian period prior to *The Strand*. Watt soon joined the company as
a clerk, and by 1876 had become a partner. Doyle had appeared just once
in *Good Words* with 'Life and Death in the Blood' (March 1883), about
the pioneers of bacteriology.

At the end of 1890 Doyle sold his practice in Southsea with the purpose
of settling in London, but initially he and Louisa travelled to Vienna to
enable him to undertake his eye studies.[29] He continued to write, and it
was in Vienna that he wrote 'The Voice of Science' early in January 1891
– then sent it, with other work, to Watt. It was Watt who placed the story
with *The Strand* and thus made Doyle's first connection with the magazine
and Greenhough Smith. It had been accepted on 24 January, so its inclu-
sion in the March issue, complete with five illustrations by W. S. Stacey,
was rapid.

Doyle returned from Vienna, via Paris, on 24 March 1891 and, after
finding lodgings near the British Museum, he negotiated for premises
for his ophthalmic consulting rooms at 2 Upper Wimpole Street. These
rooms did not officially open until 6 April, but he recorded himself as
an ophthalmic surgeon the day before in the 1891 Census. He recalled
at that point in *Memories and Adventures* that no patient entered his waiting room and that he spent the time writing the Sherlock Holmes stories, but considering he had only just opened the premises that should
come as no surprise. It's possible that either his memory was playing
tricks, or Doyle was embellishing his past for dramatic effect. Only a
year after these events he was interviewed by the *World* newspaper,
which wrote:

> He was compelled to attend to his patients in the morning, and spend
> most of the afternoon at the hospital, so that no time remained for his
> writing but a portion of the night.[30]

It is of course possible that business began slowly in April but increased
during May.

---

[29] Their daughter, Mary, was looked after by her maternal grandmother.
[30] 'Celebrities at Home', *World*, 3 August 1892, p. 10.

He had already written the first Holmes short story, 'A Scandal in Bohemia',[31] before he opened his surgery; it had been received by Watt on 31 March.[32] Since he had been in London only a week by then, and must have spent most of that time securing his lodgings and opening his practice, the assumption must be that he had drafted the story while in Vienna or Paris. It contains a number of German references, not least in its title. Watt submitted the story promptly to *The Strand*. Greenhough Smith recalled the moment nearly forty years later.

> *The Strand Magazine* was in its infancy in those days; good story-writers were scarce and here, to an editor jaded with wading through reams of impossible stuff, came a gift from Heaven, a godsend in the shape of a story that brought a gleam of happiness into the despairing life of this weary editor.[33]

Smith purportedly rushed into George Newnes's office and thrust the manuscript before him, proclaiming that here was the greatest short-story writer since Edgar Allan Poe. He may well have done so, but there may also be some embellishment created by the telescope of time. It is difficult to believe that Smith had grown so jaded after only a few months of editing *The Strand*, especially as he stayed with the magazine for forty years. In those first few months he had read manuscripts by Grant Allen, Walter Besant, E. W. Hornung, J. E. Preston Muddock and Frank R. Stockton, all first-class story writers. And he had, of course, already published one story by Doyle. There can be little doubt that the Holmes story stood out, because it was so original, but it is also likely that Smith's recollection had become exaggerated over the decades.

Before considering the impact of the stories upon both the public and Doyle's career, we need to answer two questions. Why did Doyle suddenly start writing a series of Holmes short stories, and how did they end up in *The Strand* rather than any other magazine?

The reason they were submitted to *The Strand* is, thankfully, clearly recorded in the correspondence between Watt and Doyle. Watt suggested

---

[31] The story was originally called 'A Scandal of Bohemia'.

[32] Doyle's diary notes that he sent it to Watt on 3 April which cannot be reconciled with Watt's letter dated 31 March. The balance of probability would favour Watt's business records as more accurate than Doyle's and that Doyle only began recording details seriously later in the year and went back to complete these earlier details.

[33] H. Greenhough Smith, 'The Passing of Conan Doyle', *Strand*, September 1930, p. 228.

the story be sent to *The Strand* as the only magazine that could use stories of that length (around 8,660 words). Doyle had written in his autobiography that a 'number of monthly magazines were coming out at
that time, notable among which was *The Strand*'. In reality there were
not a 'number'. The only new monthly magazine prior to *The Strand*,
apart from the British editions of American magazines like *Lippincott's*,
had been *Lambert's Monthly*, which ran from January 1890 to May 1891,
before being reborn as *The Ludgate Monthly*. After *The Strand* there was
a profusion of imitations, including *The Ludgate Monthly*, followed by
The Idler in February 1892 and *Pall Mall Magazine* in May 1893. Doyle
may not have seen *The Strand* at this stage. He had been in Vienna when
the first issue appeared, and it had been on Watt's initiative that his stories
were chosen for the magazine, not Doyle's.

As to how Doyle came to consider a series of stories featuring
Holmes, he recalled:

> Considering these journals with their disconnected stories, it had struck
> me that a single character running through a series, if it only engaged the
> attention of the reader, would bind that reader to that particular magazine.
> On the other hand, it had long seemed to me that the ordinary serial might
> be an impediment rather than a help to a magazine since, sooner or later,
> one missed one number and afterwards it had lost all interest. Clearly the
> ideal compromise was a character which carried through and yet instal-
> ments which were each complete in themselves, so that the purchaser was
> always sure that he could read the whole contents of the magazine.[34]

The logic is impeccable and Doyle added that, when casting around
for a likely character for a series, his mind soon settled on Holmes, who
had already featured in two short novels. Yet there was probably another,
unspoken, motive. Doyle had written several novels and novellas in quick
succession – *The Mystery of Cloomber, Micah Clarke, The Sign of Four* and
The White Company, the latter of which was being serialised in *Cornhill*
throughout 1891. He had also just completed a long story for *Answers*,
'The Doings of Raffles Haw', and had started a new novel under
commission to *Harper's* magazine in America, *The Refugees*. These books
took time to write, especially the historical novels, which required much

---

[34] Doyle, 'Memories and Adventures', *Strand*, January 1924, pp. 88–89.

research. Meanwhile a series of connected stories could be completed comparatively quickly and paid for one at a time, which was better for cash flow.

With characteristic immodesty, Doyle claimed, 'I believe that I was the first to realise this and *The Strand Magazine* the first to put it into practice.'

He may well have been the first to think this through in a commercial fashion, but he wasn't the first to write a connected series of stories and neither was *The Strand* the first to publish them. Throughout his memoirs Doyle makes repeated references to *Blackwood's Magazine*, which was the grandfather of all fiction-oriented magazines and had been published monthly in Scotland since April 1817. This carried several numbered series, of which the best known was 'Passages From the Diary of a Late Physician'[35] which began in August 1830 and continued on-and-off for the next seven years.[36] Though published anonymously, it was the work of Samuel Warren. The series covered a range of adventures including ghost stories and murder mysteries. Doyle would almost certainly have been acquainted with Warren's work, if only by reputation, as Warren had trained as a doctor at the medical school in Edinburgh and, in the early Victorian period, was one of the more prolific Scottish writers.

Of more recent vintage were the stories of Dick Donovan, the Glasgow Detective, written by James E. Preston Muddock under the Donovan alias. They were collected in *The Man Hunter* in 1888, but had previously run as a series in the *Dundee Weekly News*. One might excuse Doyle for not knowing the series, but Greenhough Smith certainly knew of them and was close friends with Muddock. Not only was Muddock contributing to *The Strand* from the March 1891 issue (which carried Doyle's 'The Voice of Science') but Greenhough Smith married Muddock's young daughter, Dorothy, as his second wife in 1900.[37]

However, despite these precedents, it is impossible to diminish the genuine delight of the Holmes stories and Doyle's approach to the character. There may have been earlier ratiocinative detectives, and there may have

---

[35] At the start the series was called 'Passages from the Diary of a Physician'.

[36] After *Blackwood's* accepted the first story the editor wrote to Warren saying that he 'was likely to produce a series of papers well suited for [the] Magazine, and calculated to interest the public'.

[37] Dorothy Muddock was only seventeen when she married Smith. She later became a champion figure skater, receiving a bronze medal at the 1908 Olympics.

been earlier story series, but no one brought it all together like Doyle. Sherlock Holmes comes alive in his stories. He stands out from the page because he not only seems real – many readers believed he *was* real – but he also feels wholly original. Doyle invests him with a singularly distinctive character, a history of past cases, a deep knowledge of the criminal under-world and, above all, not just one but several methods of investigation that require both sharp observation and keen deductive powers, with a wide knowledge of minutiae, such as identifying individual tobacco ash, the study of cryptograms, the dating of documents and the study of ropes, all followed up by scientific investigation and analysis. He was a genuine forensic detective of a type not observed before in such detail. Previous fictional detectives would have displayed some of these traits, but Holmes had them all. And he had his weaknesses, such as his cocaine addiction, his petulance and lack of empathy, and being easily bored unless his mind were occupied.

While seeming to be a thinking machine on one level, he was sur-prisingly human on others and this would have struck readers with the very first sentence of 'A Scandal in Bohemia', in the July 1891 *Strand*: 'To Sherlock Holmes she is always *the* woman.' Watson quickly goes on to explain that this is not a sexual appreciation but a cerebral one, but the reader is instantly given the impression that while Holmes always thought himself superior, there was at least one who could rival some of his abilities – and a woman, at that.

Perhaps most attractive of all is how the setting of the stories and Holmes's commitment (once he takes on a case) provide the reader with considerable reassurance. Doyle developed a welcoming formula of Watson recounting an initial exchange in the safe environment of Holmes's con-sulting rooms, followed by the latest client being ushered in, the basics of the mystery outlined … and then the chase is on. Those opening scenes created what became known much later as the 'cosy' mystery, because the reader knows what to expect and can settle down happy in the knowledge that Holmes is on the case and all will be well with the world. In a few later stories Doyle broke that formula, but not enough to upset the general satisfying story profile with which readers were familiar.

That puzzle is also part of the appeal. Very few cases begin with a murder, though a murder may subsequently arise. They almost all start with a mystifying set of circumstances that the client cannot understand

As to my companion neither the country nor the sea presented the slightest attraction to him. He loved to lie in the very centre of five millions of people with his filaments stretching out and running through them, responsive to every little rumour or suspicion of unsolved crime.

Extract from the original manuscript of 'The Adventure of the Cardboard Box' reproduced in *The Strand*, August 1892, in advance of the story's publication in the January 1893 issue. Doyle later transferred this part of the story in the book publication to 'The Adventure of the Resident Patient' and deleted it from 'The Adventure of the Cardboard Box', so the magazine version is the only one featuring this text.

but is convinced must be suspicious or dangerous. A good example in the first series is the second story, 'The Red-Headed League' (August 1891) in which Holmes is presented with the problem of a man who is given a job because of his red hair, but the work involves sitting in a small office for four hours a day copying out the *Encyclopaedia Britannica*. The reader is presented with the facts just as Holmes is, and it becomes an intellectual challenge to solve the puzzle.

An important factor that *The Strand* added to the stories was the artwork. Hitherto few magazines were illustrated in such profusion or with pictures that helped the reader identify with the characters. But 'A Scandal in Bohemia' has ten drawings, starting with an iconic one of Holmes in his study, standing by the fire and talking to a seated Watson. In an instant the reader is there, with them, in the room. The illustrations bring the written word – already conjuring up mystery and suspense – to life.

The illustrations were the work of Sidney Paget, a Londoner just thirty years old who had trained at the Royal Academy of Arts. Ironically, *The Strand*'s art editor, William Boot, and Greenhough Smith had both thought that Paget's younger brother, Walter, might be the right artist for the job, but they commissioned Sidney by mistake. Sidney used his brother as the model for Holmes, and the likeness was so close that people were soon hailing Walter in the street, saying 'There goes Sherlock Holmes.' Walter would later illustrate just one of the Holmes stories after Sidney's early death in 1908.

I

" THEN HE STOOD BEFORE THE FIRE."

2

" HE CURLED HIMSELF UP IN HIS
CHAIR."

A selection of Paget's original illustrations of Holmes and Watson. These show scenes
from (1) 'A Scandal in Bohemia' (July 1891), (2)'The Red-Headed League' (August 1891),
(3) [opposite top] 'The Boscombe Valley Mystery' (October 1891) – the first to depict
Holmes in his deerstalker hat – and (4) [opposite bottom] 'The Man With the Twisted
Lip (December 1891).

3

"WE HAD THE CARRIAGE TO OURSELVES." F F

4

"THE PIPE WAS STILL BETWEEN HIS LIPS."

Sidney Paget (from *The Strand*, December 1895).

Sidney was the better artist, however, and it is his images of Holmes that come instantly to mind. It was Sidney who gave Holmes a deerstalker hat, illustrating it at the start of 'The Boscombe Valley Mystery' (*Strand*, October 1891) when all Doyle had described was a 'close-fitting cloth cap'.[38]

The public reaction to the Holmes stories was instant. Reginald Pound later wrote that 'The circulation response was as immediate and as conclusive as a reflex action.'[39] Newnes's biographer recorded that with the appearance of Holmes, the magazine had to be sent to press a month earlier to allow for the demand. Circulation rose to above half a

---

[38] When *The Sign of Four* was syndicated in British newspapers after it ran in *Lippincott's*, the newspapers provided their own illustrations, and *The Bristol Observer* shows Holmes wearing a form of deerstalker. In the story, though, it is Thaddeus Sholto who wears a 'rabbit-skin cap with hanging lappets which covered the ears'.

[39] Pound, *Strand* (42).

million. Doyle's name on the magazine cover soon meant sales would increase by a hundred thousand. Pound commented:

> The Sherlock Holmes series supplied much of the momentum that carried *The Strand Magazine* forward into the first place in magazine popularity. It meant that Doyle's reputation was as secure in the boardroom as outside it, giving him a status among the business men that was a fairly rare thing in authorship.[40]

The obvious success of *The Strand* led to many imitations, making the 1890s the age of the popular-fiction magazine, including the major rivals *The Windsor, Pearson's Magazine, Harmsworth's Monthly* (later *The London Magazine*) and *The Royal*, while other magazines such as *English Illustrated, The Ludgate, Pall Mall* and *Cassell's Family Magazine* adapted to follow the *Strand* format. Had *The Strand* not been so successful, thanks primarily to Sherlock Holmes, it is questionable how many imitators there would have been and what effect that would have had on popular fiction.

Sherlock Holmes also passed into the public consciousness, and even the English language. The name soon became synonymous with the idea of a private detective. The *Illustrated Police News* for 22 April 1893 reported a case of a private detective, with an office in the Haymarket, London, who described himself as the 'Original Sherlock Holmes'. In July 1894 *The Times* reported an incident where the defendant had stolen a gold watch and made off with it through the streets of London. Although he evaded his pursuer, at one point another man, Joseph Mahoney, accosted the thief and wrestled him to the ground. As they were being escorted away by a police constable the thief thought he recognised Mahoney, to which Mahoney responded, 'I am Sherlock Holmes the second.' There was another case in 1895 where a man was arrested for impersonating a police officer, having had a card printed saying he worked for the CID. When asked why he did this he said that he had been reading *The Adventures of Sherlock Holmes* and he thought he would do a little of the 'Sherlock Holmes' business.[41]

---

[40] Pound, *Strand* (45).
[41] Reports in *The Times* for 9 July 1893 and 10 December 1895 respectively.

The nation took Holmes to its heart, whether for good or ill, and this happened in the space of a few months. Today, with social media, that would come as no surprise; even in the more recent past radio, film and television could lead to such overnight public acceptance ... but in 1891 there was only *The Strand Magazine*. Advertisers usually reckon on three readers per copy, though if word of mouth spreads the reading bug, it could soon become an epidemic. If at the outset sales were the 300,000 as claimed, then at the very minimum, the likelihood is that the stories were being read by about a million people in the UK alone, and that number would rapidly grow with the first book publication of *The Adventures of Sherlock Holmes* in October 1892. Furthermore, those who had not been aware of the two earlier Holmes novels were able to access them because George Newnes acquired the reprint rights to both and ran serialised them in *Tit-Bits*, with 'The Sign of Four' starting at the end of October 1892 and 'A Study in Scarlet' between April and June 1893.

Just as Holmes catapulted *The Strand* to prominence, so *The Strand* gave Doyle his literary freedom. He had long been considering the possibility of writing full time, but it was only now that it seemed a real possibility. During May 1891 Doyle suffered an intense bout of influenza, which might have killed a less robust man. At that point he had completed four of the proposed six Holmes stories for *The Strand*, and one can only wonder about the consequences on the magazine, popular fiction in general and detective fiction in particular, had he not survived. During his fever he gave deep thought to his position, which he recalled in his autobiography:

> I was in great danger, and then found myself as weak as a child, and as emotional, but with a mind as clear as crystal. It was then, as I surveyed my own life, that I saw how foolish I was to waste my literary earnings in keeping up an oculist's room in Wimpole Street, and I determined with a wild rush of joy to cut the painter and to trust forever to my power of writing. I remember in my delight taking the handkerchief which lay upon the coverlet in my enfeebled hand and tossing it up to the ceiling in my exultation. I should at last be my own master. [...] I would be free to live how I liked and where I liked. It was one of the great moments of exultation of my life.[42]

---

[42] Doyle, 'Memories and Adventures', *Strand*, January 1924, pp. 89–90.

It might still have seemed a gamble at that stage, because Doyle had yet to finish the first series of Holmes stories and he did not know for certain that Greenhough Smith would want any more. But he was convinced he could make it work. His earnings over the previous year had risen considerably. In the nine months since selling 'The White Company' to *Cornhill* in August 1890, Doyle's income had just passed the £1,000 mark, equal today to around £100,000.

He was right to have the courage of his conviction, because no sooner had Doyle delivered the sixth story in the series than Greenhough Smith asked for six more. Doyle asked for £50 a story (almost £5,000 today) and Smith agreed without hesitation. Since Doyle could, at that time, complete a Holmes story within a week or two, that income covered only a couple of months' work.

Doyle terminated the agreement on his consulting rooms, and looked for a permanent home, settling in 12 Tennison Road, South Norwood, where he moved with his wife and child on 25 June 1891. At that time South Norwood was part of Surrey; convenient commuter territory with the train station ten minutes walk away, yet surrounded by beautiful countryside where Doyle could go cycling.

At that time the first of the Holmes stories in *The Strand* had yet to appear, so the arrival of Doyle in this new locality did not result in a sudden media storm. In fact for a while Doyle blended in, playing in a local cricket match just five days later.

It was here that Harry How came to interview Doyle for *The Strand* for an article that appeared in the August 1892 issue. Having found the 'prettily built and modest-looking red-brick residence' and met Doyle, who was a 'happy, genial, homely man; tall, broad-shouldered, with a hand that grips you heartily and, in its sincerity of welcome, hurts', How was given a tour of the house. 'The study is a quiet corner, and has on its walls many remarkable pictures by Dr Doyle's father. [...] The dining-room contains some good oil-paintings by Mrs Doyle's brother. On the top of a large bookcase are a number of Arctic trophies ... The drawing-room is a pretty little apartment. The chairs are cosy, the afternoon tea refreshing, and the thin bread-and-butter delicious.' Settling back in the study with their cigars, How

Doyle loved to go cycling often in tandem with his wife who was less enthusiastic (from *The Strand*, August 1892).

learned about Doyle's life and career so far and discovered various facts about the Holmes stories:

Dr Doyle invariably conceives the end of his story first, and writes up to it. He gets the climax and his art lies in the ingenious way in which he conceals it from his readers. A story – similar to those which have appeared in these pages – occupies about a week in writing, and the ideas have come in all manner of times – when out walking, cricketing,

Doyle's new home (top) and study in South Norwood (from *The Strand*, August 1892).

tricycling, or playing tennis. He works between the hours of breakfast and lunch, and again in the evening from five to eight, writing some three thousand words a day. He receives many suggestions from the public. On the morning of my visit the particulars of a poisoning case had been sent to him from New Zealand and the previous day a great packet of documents relating to a disputed will had been received from Bristol. But the suggestions are seldom practicable. [...] His reason for refraining from writing any more stories for a while is a candid one. He is fearful of spoiling a character of which he is particularly fond, but he declares that already he has enough material to carry him through another series, and merrily assures me that he thought the open-ing story of the next series of 'Sherlock Holmes' ... was of such an unsolvable character that he had positively bet his wife a shilling that she would not guess the true solution of it until she got to the end of the chapter![43]

Leaving aside the miserliness of a shilling wager (about £5 today), the story to which Doyle alludes must be 'The Adventure of Silver Blaze', which began the new series in the December 1892 issue. This concerns the disappearance of the racehorse Silver Blaze and the death of its trainer, and is one of the best known Holmes sto-ries, chiefly because of the wonderful observation by Holmes of the 'curious incident of the dog in the night-time'. Doyle does indeed keep the explanation of the horse's whereabouts until the very end of the story, and we can only wonder whether Mrs Doyle won her shilling.

What Doyle did not reveal in the interview (or if he did, How kept quiet about it) were his plans to kill Holmes. He had already considered this when finishing the second series, but his mother talked him out of it and even suggested a plot for that final story, which became 'The Adven-ture of the Copper Beeches' (*Strand*, June 1892). When Smith approached him for a third series, Doyle was reluctant and agreed to do it only if the fee was raised to £1,000 for twelve stories. He expected to be turned down, but Smith agreed.

---

[43] 'A Day With Conan Doyle', *Strand*, August 1892, pp. 187–188.

One might wonder why Doyle would want to kill off Holmes. It was Holmes that had brought him fame and fortune, and it is one thing to retire him or set him aside, but to kill him seems extreme. It is true, as he remarked in the interview, that there was a danger of spoiling him, and it is even more likely that there was a danger the character would become overworked, even a parody of himself, and readers would tire of him. So it made sense to rest him, but Doyle's solution was drastic. It shows that in Doyle's mind there was a clear distinction between the fanciful light entertainment that Holmes provided and the more serious work Doyle wanted to do. He commented to one friend, Henry Lunn, that Holmes had become 'a burden'. Evidently Doyle was sure that unless he took drastic action he would never be rid of Holmes and would be forced to write about him *ad nauseam*.

During a holiday in Switzerland in summer 1893, Doyle was alerted to the Reichenbach Falls near Meiringen,[44] and decided that this would be the spot where Holmes and his arch-enemy Professor Moriarty would plunge to their deaths in 'The Adventure of the Final Problem'. The story was published in the December 1893 *Strand*, and brought to an end a series of twenty-four short stories which had changed the face of popular fiction.

There was, of course, an outcry. 'Everybody I meet is lamenting the tragedy of the last chapter in Mr Conan Doyle's "Adventures of Sherlock Holmes",' wrote H. D. Traill in his 'World of Letters' column in *The Graphic* for 30 December 1893. The London *Daily News* published a fitting obituary in its 13 December edition:

> Sherlock Holmes is no more. He dies with his name ringing in men's ears. The police of the world are left with their inferior resources to deal with crimes as of old. In the new number of *The Strand Magazine* the career of this, the most wonderful detective – amateur or otherwise – known to fiction is brought to an end; how, it would be unfair to say.

---

[44] Several people have laid claim to suggesting the Reichenbach Falls as the place for Holmes's demise, among them Henry Lunn (a former Methodist missionary who was soon to set up the travel agency, Lunn Poly), the Rev. W. J. Dawson (editor of the magazine *The Young Man*) and the author Silas Hocking, all of whom accompanied Doyle at different times on his walks in that area.

Enough that he meets with one who is 'on the same intellectual plane' as himself, and the result is decisive, though there is no place for boasting. This creation of Sherlock Holmes is really great. There seemed no possibility of giving freshness to a favourite character of French fiction, but Dr Conan Doyle has done that, and more. He has touched the imagination anew, and with amazing fertility and daring has made one person famous over the world. Sherlock Holmes will not be forgotten by this generation at least.

Doyle was surprised at the public reaction to Holmes's death. Both he and *The Strand* received hundreds of letters of complaint and abuse. Doyle heard of many people who wept. Greenhough Smith had tried to talk Doyle out of it, as he and Newnes were concerned about the impact on *The Strand*. Newnes referred to the death of Holmes as 'a dreadful event'.[45] Apparently some 20,000 cancelled their subscriptions.

For Doyle, though, it was a relief. It had been a stressful twelve months. His second child, a boy called Arthur Alleyne Kingsley Conan Doyle – usually known as Kingsley – had been born on 15 November 1892, just after Doyle agreed to write the final series of Holmes stories. The stress of the birth may well have had an impact on Doyle's wife as, after they returned from Switzerland in August 1893, Louisa developed a persistent cough and her health deteriorated.

There had been a happier moment, with the marriage on 27 September 1893 of his sister, Connie, to the writer E. W. ('Willie') Hornung, whom Doyle knew through the Idlers, the cricket team of the *Idler* magazine. But the event was tinged with growing apprehension over Louisa's health and the condition of Doyle's father, Charles. He had been kept in various institutions for the preceding decade, always a worry to Doyle and his mother, and he died on 10 October 1893, aged 61. Doyle was unable to travel to Scotland to arrange his father's funeral because of Louisa's health. Her illness was diagnosed as tuberculosis, or consumption as it was more commonly called then. It may be telling that in 'The Adventure of the Final Problem',

---

[45] Pound, *Strand* (45).

Dr Watson is not with Holmes at the moment of his final struggle with Moriarty because he has been called away to deal with a woman with consumption. Doyle believed that the fresh clean air of Switzerland would help, and at the start of November Louisa, along with her sister, left for Davos. Doyle had a lecture tour to complete and so was delayed before he could join Louisa at the end of the year. Although he had other writing commitments and plans, it was a huge relief to be free of Holmes.

3

Idler Interlude

WITH HOLMES DEAD AND DOYLE'S FUTURE contributions to *The Strand* uncertain, *The Strand* had to find ways of sustaining its readership. To continue the appeal of Holmes it needed a regular series featuring a strong, decisive character; preferably a detective or someone involved in strange mysteries.

Originally, between the end of the second Holmes series in the June 1892 issue and the start of the next in December 1892, Greenhough Smith plugged the gap by turning to his friend, J. E. Preston Muddock, who contributed four stories as Dick Donovan in the series 'Romances from a Detective's Case-book', starting with 'The Jewelled Skull' (July 1892). Smith appended the story with a note assuring readers that a new series of Holmes stories was on its way, but that in the meantime 'powerful detective stories by other eminent writers will be published'. However this only emphasised that the Donovan stories were a stop-gap, and though they were adequately written with interesting mysteries, they lacked the flair, personality, intrigue and above all the ingenuity and originality of Doyle's work.

Smith had not been idle, though. In that same July 1892 issue he welcomed a new series, 'Shafts from an Eastern Quiver' by Charles J. Mansford. Mansford was a teacher, hitherto better known as a contributor to the boys' magazines, and there is much about this series, and a later one, 'Gleams from the Dark Continent', that reads like a boys' adventure series, in the style of H. Rider Haggard. The stories were competent but not especially memorable.

Smith even wrote his own sensational mystery, 'The Case of Roger Carboyne' in the September 1892 issue. The story is set at an inquest into the apparently baffling death of Carboyne, who seems to have just vanished from a snow-covered road, with no further footprints. Had Smith incorporated a police investigation the story may have been more memorable, but no sooner is the mystery presented than it is instantly explained by a surprise witness at the inquest. Doyle later wrote to Smith, saying 'I think that we lost a considerable writer when you became editor.'[46]

Considerably better was 'Stories from the Diary of a Doctor', six stories that ran alongside the final set of Holmes stories from July to December 1893. They were by the Irish writer, Mrs L. T. Meade, former editor of the girls' magazine *Atalanta*, who was well known for her stories for adolescent girls. Meade was good at creating characters and plots but was aware of her limitations. For this series she worked in consultation with Dr Edgar Beaumont, who provided the medical details and masqueraded as Dr Clifford Halifax, the fictional narrator of the series. This gave the stories added verisimilitude, which had been part of the appeal of the Holmes series and was missing from the other series Smith had been commissioning.

L. T. Meade, or Elizabeth Thomasina – usually known as Lillie – contributed twenty-two 'Stories from the Diary of a Doctor', plus seven more in the series 'The Adventures of a Man of Science', all with Dr Beaumont, before changing collaborators and contributing three more series with Eustace Barton (writing as Robert Eustace). She also contributed with her colleagues to *The Strand*'s rivals *Cassell's Magazine*, *Pearson's Magazine* and *The Windsor*, so she was a well-known and popular magazine writer of the day.

To keep the pot boiling, Smith commissioned a detective series from another popular writer, Arthur Morrison. 'Martin Hewitt, Investigator' began with 'The Lenton Croft Robberies' in the March 1894 issue. The series is in the style of the Holmes stories, narrated by Hewitt's friend, a journalist, but the crimes themselves are relatively mundane, with little in the way of intellectual challenge to match Doyle's inventiveness. After seven stories in *The Strand* Morrison was lured away by *The Windsor Magazine*.

---

[46] Doyle, undated letter to Greenhough Smith [BL10].

In hindsight it was a mistake to seek a Holmes substitute. Readers wanted Holmes, not some inferior shadow. At least Meade's stories had their own individualism, and her work sustained the demand for such series over several years. When *The Strand* scored again it was not with a detective but a confidence trickster, Colonel Clay, who featured in 'An African Millionaire' and ran from June 1896 to May 1897. The author was Doyle's friend, Grant Allen, whose mind was just as inventive and creative. Clay is the nemesis of millionaire Sir Charles Vandrift, who is well aware of Clay, but the latter's disguises and ingenuity means he keeps fleecing his victim. The fun of the series is in seeing how Clay gets away with it each time. The stories had the audacity of the Holmes stories, and Clay was an endearing figure – the forerunner of the gentleman rogue who would become epitomised by the character of A. J. Raffles, the creation of Doyle's brother-in-law, E. W. Hornung.

Meade and Allen helped sustain reader interest in mysteries and crime stories. Though Doyle would return to *The Strand*, it was not for almost a year.

Doyle's primary concern was for his wife who, thankfully, had responded to the cleaner air of the mountain resort of Davos. She would never be cured of her tuberculosis, but she was remarkably resilient and lived until July 1906, dying at the age of 49. She spent as much time as possible in Switzerland in the years that followed, and Doyle also took her to Egypt. Grant Allen, who also had tuberculosis, believed Louisa might benefit from living further outside London and recommended the area around Hindhead, in Surrey. Doyle bought some land and arranged for a new house to be built, which he called Undershaw. Construction took longer than expected, and the family did not move in until October 1897.

Doyle continued to write, but not for *The Strand*. One of the earliest magazines to appear in the wake of *The Strand* was *The Idler*, published by Robert Barr in association with Jerome K. Jerome, the renowned author of *Three Men in a Boat* (1889), who served as editor. Barr was a fellow Scot, from Glasgow, who had been raised in Canada, where his experiences bred in him an ability to be an amazing if somewhat volatile raconteur. Doyle called him 'volcanic', the same word he had used to describe his godfather, and in Barr's case it was very apt, as he could erupt at any moment. So could Jerome, whose sharp wit and humour would often provoke Barr, and the two were frequently at loggerheads.

Two Idlers – Doyle with Robert Barr at Tennison Road, South Norwood in 1894 (from *The Idler*, October 1894).

The Idler's first issue was dated January 1892 and took its name from Jerome's 1886 book *Idle Thoughts of an Idle Fellow*. Though the magazine had some similarities with *The Strand* in its general content, its attitude was quite different. *The Idler* was there to have fun. It could publish some serious material, but for the most part its contents were for light-hearted amusement and general *bonhomie*. This was evident in its regular bohemian feature 'The Idlers' Club' which was drawn up by assistant editor George Burgin from the banter and discussion at the regular literary tea parties they held at their offices in Arundel Street, near the Strand. Doyle was invited to one of the first, and there he rubbed shoulders with W. L. Alden, J. M. Barrie, Anthony Hope, Eden Phillpotts, Barry Pain, Israel Zangwill and other rising stars of the period. E. W. Hornung was also a member.

In the third issue, one of the Club – probably Jerome – commented that he had recently followed in the footsteps of the hero of Doyle's *The White Company* through the New Forest. He noted:

> Mr Doyle is very ingenious in his treatment of situations. A very good example of his genius in this particular may be found in the grim and ghastly story that appears elsewhere in this number of *The Idler*. You have two methods of explaining the awful and momentary appearance of the dead man at sea. One explanation is natural, the other supernatural. Either fits the story as well as the other.[47]

Doyle's story 'De Profundis' was indeed rather grim, particularly in its final sentences. It was one of a growing number of Doyle's stories exploring the psychic. It was clear that at this stage Doyle did not feel under any obligation to contribute more stories to *The Strand*, especially once he had finished with Sherlock Holmes. Yet he may have felt a tinge of guilt, because in his memoirs he wrote:

> I was not unfaithful to *The Strand*, but there were some contributions which they did not need, and with these I established my connection with *The Idler*.[48]

There is much to unpick in that sentence. First, why would he allude to not being 'unfaithful' if he did not perhaps feel some disloyalty? Of course, he had every right to contribute to other magazines. There was no binding agreement with Greenhough Smith, but Smith had been very fair to Doyle in his working relationship and Doyle may have felt some guilt. Over time, Doyle would remain loyal to *The Strand*, but it was a relationship that developed during these formative years and not one that sprang up in an instant. Doyle justified his work for *The Idler* by saying

[47] 'The Idlers' Club', *The Idler*, February 1892, p. 232.
[48] Doyle, 'Memories and Adventures', *Strand*, February 1924, p. 121.

that his contributions were ones *The Strand* 'did not need'. At the time Doyle probably felt *The Strand* only wanted Holmes, and that he was free to contribute other stories elsewhere. It was a view that later changed, but at this time Doyle was still playing the market, and rightly so.

The May 1892 issue of *The Idler* carried one of the first parodies of Sherlock Holmes, written by Robert Barr under his alias Luke Sharp.[49] He called it 'The Adventures of Sherlaw Kombs' under the general heading of 'Detective Stories Gone Wrong', though he did not develop the series. Kombs is a wonderfully humorous parody, complete with Holmes's contempt for just about everything, his patronising attitude to one and all and his infallible self-belief which, in this instance, goes woefully wrong. The fact that Doyle was aware of the parody and made no objection to it shows he had no problems with the idea, provided it was in the spirit of fun.

Jerome asked Doyle if he could write a series of 'strong' stories for *The Idler* around a central theme that might prove as popular as the Holmes stories. Doyle proposed a set of medical stories, but in the end, the majority of them proved *too* strong. The first, 'The Case of Lady Sannox' (November 1893), which appeared at the same time as the last Holmes story, is a particularly nasty horror story about how a member of the nobility wreaks revenge upon his wayward wife through the unwitting assistance of a doctor. Of special interest is 'The Doctors of Hoyland' (April 1894) because it makes the case for more women doctors and, like Doyle's debut in *The Strand*, 'The Voice of Science', demonstrates the interest some women show in scientific developments. Not part of the series, although it served as a light-hearted prelude, was 'The Los Amigos Fiasco' (December 1892) where a doctor discovers that a criminal who survived being executed by the electric chair has become so infused by the vitality of the electric charge that he is very likely immortal.

Also for *The Idler*, Doyle wrote 'The Glamour of the Arctic' (July 1892) which covered much of the same territory he would incorporate into 'The Life of a Greenland Whaler' for *The Strand* in 1897. There was

---

[49] There was one earlier parody, 'An Evening with Sherlock Holmes' published anonymously in *The Speaker* on 28 November 1891. Soon after, Doyle went to one of the *Idler* dinners and discovered the skit had been written by J. M. Barrie, with whom he became close friends. Barrie wrote another, 'The Adventure of the Two Collaborators', which he sent to Doyle written on the flyleaf of one of his books, and it remained unpublished until Doyle transcribed it in *Memories and Adventures*.

an interview with Doyle conducted by Robert Barr, but in a much less formal fashion. Barr starts by saying that as no two writers ever agree, he needn't interview Doyle, but simply write down the opposite of everything Barr believes. This prompted Doyle to argue that it wouldn't be fair on the readers, and so a discussion begins.

Doyle's major contribution to *The Idler* was his semi-autobiographical novel *The Stark Munro Letters*, which ran for fourteen episodes from October 1894. It's a loosely fictionalised account of his early medical career in the rather renegade practice of George Budd. Its final episode in the November 1895 issue brought to an end Doyle's association with *The Idler*. Jerome and Barr had fallen out by then over how to take the magazine forward, and Jerome continued on his own, but by then Doyle's affair with *The Idler* was over. Though he would occasionally contribute to other British magazines, they became the exception and Doyle now treated *The Strand* as his primary British market for fiction.

While Doyle was in Switzerland with Louisa, he wrote prodigiously and undertook considerable historical research. He told James Payn of *The Cornhill* in a letter written in March 1894 that he had written 100,000 words but was also spending a good amount of his time in the mountains, learning how to use snow-shoes, and skiing. He believed he was the first, apart from a few Swiss, to do any mountain work in snow-shoes. He wrote about his experiences for *The Strand* in 'An Alpine Pass on "Ski"', in the December 1894 issue, which is regarded as the first popular account of skiing. Doyle was one of the pioneer ski tourists and reporters, and his account is all the more interesting because he reports his calamities as much as his achievements:

> Whenever you think yourself absolutely secure, it is all over with you. You come to a hard ice slope at an angle of 75 degrees and you zigzag up it, digging the side of your ski into it, and feeling that if a mosquito settles upon you, you are gone. But nothing ever happens and you reach the top in safety. Then you stop upon the level to congratulate your companion, and you have just time to say, 'What a lovely view is this!' when you find yourself standing on your two shoulder-blades, with your 'ski' tied tightly round your neck. Or again, you may have had a long outing without any misfortune at all, and as you shuffle back along the road, you stop for an instant to tell a group in the hotel veranda

Doyle and his wife on 'ski' in Switzerland in 1894 (from *The Strand*, December 1894).

how well you are getting on. Something happens – and they suddenly find that their congratulations are addressed to the soles of your 'ski'. Then if your mouth is not full of snow, you find yourself muttering the names of a few Swiss villages to relieve your feelings. 'Ragatz!' is a very handy word, and may save a scandal.[50]

Most of the article, though, recounted a remarkable adventure that Doyle undertook. On 23 March 1894, with the help of the brothers Tobias and Johann Branger, he made his way from Davos to Arosa over the Furka Pass, at 9,000 feet. The journey had only been achieved once before, the previous year, by the Brangers. The distance is between twelve and fourteen miles, and it took them seven hours. Doyle seemed to make

[50] Doyle, 'An Alpine Pass on "Ski"', *Strand*, December 1894, p. 657.

it unharmed, apart from one or two falls, whereas one of the brothers sprained his ankle badly. One of Doyle's wry observations en route was that, despite what tailors say about Harris tweed not wearing out, such a theory did not stand a thorough scientific test, as they will find 'samples of his wares on view from the Furka Pass to Arosa'. It was a bold and daring achievement for Doyle, and shows his fitness and adventurous spirit.

Doyle remarked, 'I am convinced that the time will come when hundreds of Englishmen will come to Switzerland for the "ski"-ing season in March and April', and how right he was.

4

Napoleon and The Brigadier

WHEN NOT WRITING OR SKIING, Doyle was reading all he could about the life and times of Napoleon Bonaparte. He had been fascinated with Napoleon ever since he had been at Feldkirch, and had recently written 'The Great Shadow' – the title referring to Napoleon himself – which had been published by Arrowsmith as its Christmas Annual in 1892. He had also written a short story, 'A Straggler of '15 which appeared in *Black and White* on 21 March 1891. Doyle adapted this into the stage play *A Story of Waterloo*, the rights to which were bought by Henry Irving, who first performed it in September 1894.

So Doyle was already well steeped in the life and times of Napoleon, but he continued his research throughout 1894 while in Switzerland and on his tour of the United States. The result would be Doyle's next successful series character, Brigadier Etienne Gerard.

Napoleon seemed to be in the air at that time. Doyle had written the first Gerard story, 'The Medal of Brigadier Gerard', while on the lecture tour and was encouraged in its writing by Sam McClure of *McClure's Magazine*, who was himself a devotee of Napoleonic history. It was Napoleon that saved *McClure's*. The magazine was in financial difficulty and Doyle helped rescue it by investing in 1,000 shares costing $5,000 (or £1,030) in November 1894. It was a sound investment, because that same month *McClure's* published the first of a series of articles by Ida M. Tarbell on Napoleon. Sales of that issue alone more than doubled the circulation to 65,000 copies, and by the end of the series in April 1895 sales topped 100,000 and would continue to rise.

Henry Irving as Corporal Brewster from Doyle's play *A Story of Waterloo* in 1894 (from *The Strand*, February 1924).

With the extra advertising revenue that this realised, *McClure's* became one of the most successful American quality magazines.

Doyle wrote a Napoleonic story for *McClure's*, but not with Brigadier Gerard. 'A Foreign Office Romance', which appeared in the December 1894 issue, features Alphonse Lacour, a French diplomat who is involved in treaty negotiations between the French and the British in 1801. Lacour uses his ingenuity to hide news from the French negotiators that Egypt, which had been in French hands, had fallen to the British. Lacour is more sophisticated than Gerard, but some of the same character traits are there, and the same story frame, with Lacour reminiscing about his past to the British in a café. But Doyle wrote no more about Lacour and may have favoured Gerard because of the sheer zest and gusto of the first story, which had gone down well when narrated to audiences in America.

McClure's did not take 'The Medal of the Brigadier', perhaps because it would have clashed with the Lacour story, and its US debut was in the December 1894 American edition of *The Strand*. However, Doyle made quite a coup when he sold the story to the *San Francisco Examiner*, which was owned by William Randolph Hearst, for 12½ cents a word. Since it was roughly 10,000 words, that sale earned him $1,250 or around £257, which is over £25,000 in today's money.

Before settling down to Gerard, Doyle wrote one other historical story set in France, though in the more recent past of the Franco-Prussian War. As the title suggests, 'The Lord of Château Noir' is a dark story, almost a horror story, showing the influence of the strong material Doyle had written for *The Idler*. Owen Dudley Edwards regarded it as 'one of the very greatest pieces of historical fiction he ever wrote',[51] and Doyle himself called it 'a real clinker'.[52] It's a tale of torture and revenge. Captain Baumgarten is sent to the château to capture the Lord who has been harassing the Prussian troops. When he arrives he can find no one there except a butler and his wife. Baumgarten stations his troops there and, after eating well, falls asleep, but is woken by the Lord who has hidden in wait and has captured the troops. The Lord binds Baumgarten and proceeds to tell him the story of his son, who was captured and tortured by a vicious Prussian officer. As he recounts each of the tortures inflicted upon his son, he repeats them on Baumgarten. It has a neat sudden twist at the end, but as with 'The Case of Lady Sannox', and several later stories, Doyle seemed to enjoy stories of torture. Could it be that the stories allowed Doyle to vent some of his frustration over Louisa's condition? With no one physical to blame, Doyle may have invented scenarios whereby he could seek an outlet. And perhaps it worked, for he then turned to the light-hearted stories featuring Brigadier Etienne Gerard.

As with many of Doyle's best stories these are recounted in the first person, told by a retired brigadier who is approaching sixty and remembering his rousing youth when he made his way through the ranks under the watchful and occasionally critical eye of Napoleon Bonaparte. Most

[51] Edwards, *Quest* (70).
[52] Doyle, letter to his mother, 2 May 1894 in Lellenberg, *Letters* (333).

of the stories bear a precise date, and since the Brigadier sometimes reveals his age at that time then we know he was born in 1783 (or so) and
that most of the events described take place during his twenties and early
thirties, from 1807 to 1815.

Gerard, a Hussar or cavalryman in Napoleon's army, is a very engaging fellow. The beauty of the first-person narrative is that we see
the events personally and understand his thoughts, but we also have to
remember that Gerard is recounting these adventures some thirty years
later, by which time his memory has embellished them, and there are
few around to challenge him. Gerard is free to retell the story as he
wants it to be known and show us the dashing hero he remembers.
And let's be honest – that's what we want. We don't want a whining,
cowardly cur. We want someone who puts his life on the line for the
sake of others (and, of course, himself), and who wins against great
odds using mostly his skills as a horseman and swordsman but, just
occasionally, his brain as a soldier.

At the start of the last story of the first series, 'How the Brigadier
Played for a Kingdom', Gerard wonders whether at times the listener
may think he is conceited. But he defends himself:

> It is true that I have had to depict myself sometimes as brave, sometimes as
> full of resource, always as interesting; but then, it really was so, and I had to
> take the facts as I found them. It would be an unworthy affectation if I were
> to pretend that my career has been anything but a fine one.

So we know that we are in for tales of great valour and heroism
related with tremendous panache and braggadocio, and for that we are
treated to stories that are heart-racingly enjoyable. They are, at one level,
just a cut above a boys' adventure story, which had been Doyle's favourite
reading as a child, but they are written with an older man's experience
of the world, and a delightful twinkle in the eye that means you know
you are entering the realm of the true storyteller. Gerard is Doyle, living
the kind of escapist life that Doyle would have relished.

There was a real historical character called Étienne Gérard (note the ac-
cents) who lived from 1773 to 1852. He had a distinguished career under
Napoleon and survived to serve in successive governments, becoming a
Marshal of France in 1830 and acting briefly as Prime Minister in 1834.
When Doyle's stories appeared, Gérard's granddaughter, Rosemonde, was
24 and living in Paris with her husband, Edmond Rostand, who would

become renowned for his play *Cyrano de Bergerac* in 1897. Perhaps to clarify matters, in the seventh of the stories, 'How the Brigadier was Tempted by the Devil', Doyle has the Brigadier refer briefly to 'my cousin Gerard', but there any family matters rest. Doyle's Gerard is purely fictional.

Doyle's godfather Michael Conan certainly knew of the original Gérard. In 1832, while serving as a war correspondent to the London *Morning Herald*, he was sent to cover the French Siege of Antwerp, where the French troops were commanded by Gérard. There's every chance Conan would have told young Doyle about this when they met in 1876, and the name stayed with Doyle. But the real zest of the stories came from Doyle's reading, in the French edition of 1891, of *Mémoires du general baron de Marbot*, the reminiscences of the Baron de Marbot. Marbot was another great Napoleonic hero, who was with Gérard at the Siege of Antwerp and mentions him briefly in his memoirs. But Marbot, like Doyle's Gerard, loves to exaggerate and embellish his memory of events. They never quite stray into the impossible realms of Baron Münchhausen, for there is always the outside chance that events could have happened as described, but Marbot clearly never let hard facts get in the way of a good story.

Doyle's first Gerard story in *The Strand* was 'The Medal of the Brigadier' in December 1894. It was not part of the later numbered sequence, and its own internal chronology places it later in Gerard's career (March 1814), but it is an admirable introduction to the character and is one of the most enjoyable of the series. It reads at a breathtaking pace, not unlike Robert Browning's famous poem 'How They Brought the Good News from Ghent to Aix' (1845). Gerard is chosen personally by Napoleon, along with Major Charpentier, to take a message from where they are stationed at Rheims to Napoleon's brother in Paris. There are two possible routes to be taken separately by the two soldiers. Needless to say Gerard sets off to prove himself and manages to overcome a variety of obstacles and dangers, including being captured. It is only when he returns to Rheims, feeling triumphant, that his pride is deflated when he discovers he has ruined a ploy that Napoleon had intended. Napoleon nevertheless grants him a special medal of honour while observing that if Gerard 'has the thickest head he also has the stoutest heart in the army'.

And so the stage is set – the readers aware of a new hero, valorous if at times foolhardy, one who acts before he thinks, but always for the greatness of France (and himself). The first series proper began in the April 1895 issue with 'How the Brigadier Held the King'. This and 'How the King Held the Brigadier', set in 1810, are all one episode but too long (close on 20,000 words) to run complete in one issue. Indeed, they work better separately. The first tells how Gerard is captured by guerrillas and then by the English and taken back to England as a prisoner to Dartmoor. In the second, Gerard uses his wits rather more than usual to escape from Dartmoor Prison, though he becomes lost and is recaptured before being released as part of an exchange.

In the magazine sequence, each of the early stories takes the reader further back in time, whereas when the first series was assembled in book form as *The Exploits of Brigadier Gerard*, the stories were revised into chronological sequence. The advantage of the magazine sequence

"AT EVERY CUT I HEARD SHOUTS BEHIND ME."

A scene from 'The Crime of the Brigadier' illustrated by Sidney Paget (from *The Strand*, January 1900).

"I HASTENED TO THE EDGE OF THE WOOD.

"COME OUT, YOU RASCAL!"

Two illustrations by W. B. Wollen depicting Gerard from (top) 'How the Brigadier Took the Field Against the Marshal Millefleurs' (August 1895) and 'The Medal of the Brigadier' (December 1894).

is that you gradually learn more about Gerard's early life, and it helps explain how he rose through the ranks. The fourth story, for instance, 'How the Brigadier Slew the Brothers of Ajaccio', set in September 1807, is the first direct meeting between Gerard and Napoleon, when the Emperor seeks the assistance of someone who is reliable and obedient and will not think too deeply about what is expected of him. By this time the reader knows of Gerard's impetuosity and so wonders whether the Emperor's judgement is misplaced.

It is evident in the first series that Doyle wrote such episodes that appealed to him, regardless of chronology. This resulted in some internal inconsistencies with the later stories meaning that when they are read in chronological order, they can cause some consternation. Consequently it is better to consider all of the stories together, rather than in two sections.

After the first story, 'The Medal of Brigadier Gerard' in the December 1894 issue, the first series of six stories ran from April to September 1895, with a further story in December 1895. These eight were collected as *The Exploits of Brigadier Gerard* and published by Newnes in February 1896. Doyle wrote a one-off episode, 'The Crime of the Brigadier', which appeared in the January 1900 *Strand*. The second series began in August 1902, but then missed two months and the remainder ran from November 1902 to May 1903, the last effectively completing the series. 'I have got my last of the Brigadiers,' Doyle told Greenhough Smith. 'It ends him as it should end him.'[53] These eight stories plus 'The Crime of the Brigadier' were collected as *Adventures of Gerard* in September 1903. There was one final story, 'The Marriage of the Brigadier', in the September 1910 issue.[54]

The internal chronology is set out in Table 2. The first two stories are where most of the inconsistencies appear and are best ignored, as they add little to the series. 'How Brigadier Gerard Lost His Ear' clearly takes place during Napoleon's Italian campaign and occupation of Venice in 1797, but Gerard is cited as a colonel of Hussars, a rank he did not obtain until he was 28, in 1811. Similarly, we discover in 'The Marriage of the

---

[53] Doyle, undated letter to Greenhough Smith written in early 1903 [UVa019].

[54] Doyle did not include it in any of his later Gerard compilations, though it did appear in his volume of historical stories, *The Last Galley*, in April 1911. Owen Dudley Edwards included it in *The Complete Brigadier Gerard* (Edinburgh: Canongate, 1995).

Table 2: The Brigadier Gerard stories in chronological order of events

Year	Magazine title	The Strand issue and original sequence	Plot summary
1797 or 1811?	'How Brigadier Gerard Lost His Ear	August 1902 (#10)	Gerard has an affair with the Doge of Venice's granddaughter but switches places with her lover, only to receive the lover's punishment. The date applied is relevant to the historical events, but Gerard is a Colonel, which he did not become until 1811.
1803	'The Marriage of the Brigadier'	September 1910 (#18)	While trying to avoid marriage an encounter with a bull causes Gerard to change his mind.
1807	'How the Brigadier Came to the Castle of Gloom'	July 1895 (#5)	Gerard helps a new acquaintance take revenge on an old foe.
1807	'How the Brigadier Slew the Brothers of Ajaccio'	June 1895 (#4)	Napoleon seeks Gerard's support in a vendetta.
1809	'How the Brigadier Joined the Hussars of Conflans'	April 1903 (#16)	At the Siege of Saragossa, Gerard enters the town and manages to shorten the siege.
1810	'How the Brigadier Held the King'	April 1895 (#2)	Gerard is captured by Spanish partisans and plays cards for his freedom, but is then captured by the English.
1810	'How the King Held the Brigadier'	May 1895 (#3)	Gerard is held prisoner at Dartmoor, escapes and is recaptured.
1810	'The Brigadier in England'	March 1903 (#15)	While being held in England awaiting an exchange, Gerard becomes invovled in boxing, shooting and cricket, and rescues a kidnapped lady, which leads to a duel.
1810	'The Crime of the Brigadier'	January 1900 (#9)	Venturing behind English lines in Portugal, Gerard becomes involved in a fox hunt.
1811	'How the Brigadier took the Field Against the Marshal Millefleurs'	August 1895 (#6)	Gerard finds himself allied with the English to capture a notorious brigand, while still trying to complete his assignment of capturing the Abbey of Almeixal.
1811	'How the Brigadier Saved the Army'	November 1902 (#11)	Sent to light a beacon of warning Gerard almost ends up becoming the beacon itself.
1812	'How the Brigadier Rode to Minsk'	December 1902 (#12)	Sent to Minsk to find food during the retreat from Moscow, Gerard has to fight for his life.
1813	'How the Brigadier Played for a Kingdom'	December 1895 (#8)	While the French army regathers, Gerard is sent into Germany to test the loyalty of a Prince who supports the French cause.
1814	'The Medal of Brigadier Gerard'	December 1894 (#1)	Gerard makes an amazing ride from Rheims to Paris to get a message to Bonaparte's brother.
1814	'How the Brigadier was Tempted by the Devil'	September 1895 (#7)	Gerard knows the whereabouts of Napoleon's secret papers and is determined to keep them safe.
1815	'The Adventure of the Forest Inn'	January 1903 (#13)	The first of two episodes relating Gerard's exploits at the Battle of Waterloo.
1815	'The Adventure of the Nine Prussian Horsemen'	February 1903 (#14)	With impressive daring and horsemanship, Gerard saves Napoleon's life.
1821	'How the Brigadier Said Goodbye to His Master'	May 1903 (#17)	Gerard becomes involved in an attempt to rescue Napoleon from St Helena.

Brigadier' that Gerard had married when he was twenty, even though there is no reference to a wife (current or former) in any other story. In the Venice story Doyle had written, 'A debonair Hussar has room in his life for love, but none for a wife.' He clearly forgot that eight years later.

While it is not unusual for Doyle to introduce character inconsistencies in his stories (he did so in Sherlock Holmes many times) he was far more cautious over historical facts. He wrote in his memoirs, about Gerard:

> This entailed a good deal of research into Napoleonic days, and my military detail was, I think, very accurate — so much so that I had a warm letter of appreciation from Archibald Forbes, the famous war correspondent, who was himself a great Napoleonic and military student.[55]

Forbes only read the first series as he died in 1900, but Doyle's research was every bit as thorough for the later stories, especially when he came to the Battle of Waterloo.

The first two stories aside, the others, from 'How the Brigadier Came to the Castle of Gloom' to 'How the Brigadier Said Goodbye to His Master', are excellent. Within the context of Gerard's personal narrative and reflection, they run the full range from near farce in 'The Crime of the Brigadier', in which Gerard finds himself involved in a fox hunt, to anguish and hardship in 'How the Brigadier Rode to Minsk', and to pure pathos and heartbreak in 'How the Brigadier Said Goodbye to His Master'. They show, better than the Holmes stories and perhaps better than any of Doyle's other connected stories, his skills as a storyteller. They demand to be narrated, and Doyle would often read one or more on his lecture tours. This worked especially well with 'The Crime of the Brigadier'. Doyle had completed it in July 1899 and read it to various audiences over the next few months, usually resulting in both the audience and the reader being in hysterics. Doyle's friend, Frederic Whyte, who was an editor at Cassell, was present at one such reading in Hampstead and recalled that at the climax of the story 'the entire room was in convulsions and the author himself, catching the infection, could scarcely continue'.[56]

---

[55] Doyle, 'Memories and Adventures', Strand, February 1924, pp. 122–123.
[56] Whyte (72).

Neither was this a one-off, for when Doyle read the story at a lecture in Bristol in October 1899 it 'created much hilarity' according to the local newspaper.[57]

Gerard is in some ways a counter-image of Sherlock Holmes. Both have high opinions of themselves and both believe in their own infallibility. However, at times when Holmes realises he has made a mistake, he will sink into depression from which he will not emerge until he finds a new challenge. Gerard, meanwhile, sees each mistake as a new challenge and will fight on regardless. Gerard is heroic, secure in the knowledge of his own prowess, while Holmes is insecure, and uses his knowledge to constantly bolster his confidence. Gerard would have admired Holmes but would have found it difficult to understand him. Holmes would secretly have admired Gerard, especially as Holmes was himself a good pugilist, but would openly have been dismissive of him. They each have their charm, but if you were in a tight corner and needed help, Gerard would be far more efficient and reliable than Holmes.

The Gerard stories were well received at the time. Reviewing *The Exploits of Brigadier Gerard*, *The Bookman* of April 1896 said:

> Mr Conan Doyle has never done anything better than this – and remembering the good things he has already given us, this is saying a good deal.

Doyle's old friend, Andrew Lang, wrote in *Longman's Magazine* (April 1896):

> He is an absolutely delightful brigadier – brave, vain, not too clever … For humour, excitement, adventure, and manly feeling, Mr Doyle has never excelled this new work, which is a thing of the open air, and much superior to (as I trust it will be even more popular than) *Sherlock Holmes*.

Praise indeed, and one can only presume that many readers of *The Strand* also enjoyed the stories. It is unfortunate that Greenhough Smith remained quiet on the matter. There is no doubt he would have welcomed the return of Doyle with a series character, but it is surprising that when Smith wrote his tribute to Doyle in the September 1930 issue of *The Strand*, he made no mention of the Brigadier at all. Despite the enjoyment

---

[57] 'Sidelights of History', *Bristol Mercury*, 23 October 1899, p. 3.

of the Etienne Gerard stories they have been almost completely overshadowed by Sherlock Holmes and even the Professor Challenger stories, yet they contain some of Doyle's best and most humorous writing.

Gerard appears in one other work. In 1895 Doyle undertook a commission from the society paper *Queen* to write a historical serial, and he turned again to the Napoleonic period. However, the book proved a struggle to write and took the best part of a year. It was eventually serialised as 'Uncle Bernac' in *Queen*, during the first three months of 1897. Doyle was never happy with it and thereafter regarded it as one of his least successful novels. In order to keep some interest in the book, which was set in 1805 and involves a Jacobin plot to assassinate Napoleon, Doyle not only imported into the novel a great chunk of material he had written earlier about Napoleon, which does nothing to further the plot, but he also included the young Lieutenant Etienne Gerard. Here Gerard is observed by a third party, so we only learn about Gerard through what is seen and what he says. He is still the same vainglorious, impulsive young blade, but because we do not get Gerard's innermost thoughts or his wit, the Gerard of *Uncle Bernac* is far less engaging. It was a lesson to Doyle not to play fast and loose with his characters. They should be looked after.

Thanks to Sherlock Holmes Doyle's reputation was so high that he was in demand, and Doyle knew how to use this to his advantage. He treated writing as a business, not simply a vocation, and as his reputation grew, so did his rates. One might think it would be difficult for *The Strand* to keep him, but his loyalty to the magazine and Newnes's knowledge of the earning power of Doyle's name kept the two together. This was evident with his next novel, *Rodney Stone*. Through Watt, he sold the serial rights to *The Strand* for £1,000, and Smith, Elder paid an advance of £4,000 for the UK book rights. A further £875 was received for the American serial and book rights, making a total of £5,875[58] – over £600,000 in today's terms! This was another historical novel set in the Napoleonic period, though in England, and it was about boxing.

---

[58] Doyle told his mother that the total was 'nearly £7,000' in a letter on 10 December 1895, but the monies received, after dollar exchange rates and Watt's commission, was recorded in his diary during 1896.

5

Doyle and The Noble Art

'I HAVE ALWAYS BEEN KEEN upon the noble old English sport of boxing,' Doyle wrote in his reminiscences, where he described himself as 'a fair average amateur'.[59] He had learned to fight as a youth in order to survive in the poorer parts of Edinburgh. He recalled that his comrades were rough boys, and he likewise became rough and 'rejoiced in battle'.

> We lived for some time in a cul de sac street with a very vivid life of its own and a fierce feud between the small boys who dwelt on either side of it. Finally it was fought out between two champions, I representing the poorer boys who lived in flats and my opponent the richer boys who lived in the opposite villas. We fought in the garden of one of the said villas and had an excellent contest of many rounds, not being strong enough to weaken each other. When I got home after the battle, my mother cried, 'Oh, Arthur, what a dreadful eye you have got!' To which I replied, 'You just go across and look at Eddie Tulloch's eye!'[60]

Doyle took some boxing lessons from the former Scottish champion Charlie Ball, and at university found boxing a good way to exercise and keep fit while studying. He describes a scene at university in his

---

[59] Doyle, 'Memories and Adventures', *Strand*, May 1924, p. 448.
[60] Doyle, 'Memories and Adventures', *Strand*, October 1923, p. 326.

Early in his days as a medical practitioner Doyle visited a farmer in Sussex. Discovering that the neighbour was something of a boxer the two made their way into the garden where a crowd soon gathered to watch their match. Doyle recalled, 'We fought several very brisk rounds with no particular advantage either way, but the contest always stands out in my memory for its queer surroundings and the old English picture in which it was set.' (From *The Strand*, May 1924.)

early novel *The Firm of Girdlestone* (1890) where a new student engages in his first boxing lesson, and this may well reflect Doyle's own experiences. He took his boxing gloves with him on the Greenland whaler in 1880. They were spotted by the steward, Jack Lamb, who challenged

Doyle to a fight. It was soon evident that while Lamb was no doubt a good street-fighter, Doyle was well trained and, after giving him an opportunity to square up, Doyle simply let him have it and the steward went down. This earned Doyle respect from the men and helped him become part of the onboard community.

Doyle loved all manner of sports and later reflected on whether he might have enjoyed life more had he become a sportsman rather than a writer. His Idler Club friend, G. B. Burgin, called Doyle, 'the most all-round representative sportsman among modern writers'.[61]

One remarkable moment in his life was when he was asked to referee the world prizefight between the heavyweight champion Jack Johnson and the retired heavyweight champion, James Jeffries. Johnson was renowned as the first black heavyweight champion, and the racial attitudes of the day saw Jeffries as the 'Great White Hope'. When the articles for the fight were signed in December 1909, Doyle was suggested as a possible referee. Irving Jefferson Lewis, the Managing Editor of the *New York Morning Telegraph*, contacted Doyle to see if he would take up the offer, commenting:

> Believe me, among sporting men of the best class in America, you have many strong admirers; your splendid stories of the ring and your avowed admiration for the great sport of boxing have made you thousands of friends.[62]

Doyle declined the offer due to other commitments, but he also considered advice from friends that he might wind up with 'a revolver at one ear and a razor at the other'. The victory of Johnson over Jeffries in July 1910 in Reno, Nevada, set off a wave of racial unrest across the United States. Tex Rickard, the boxing promoter who refereed the fight, sought seclusion in South America because he could see little benefit in promoting further fights until the unrest settled, so Doyle almost certainly made the right decision.

With this background in the sport it should come as no surprise that boxing features in many of Doyle's stories, though it comes as a surprise to many that Sherlock Holmes, depicted so vividly as a thinking machine, should have been good at boxing. When Watson meets Holmes in 'A Study

---

[61] G. B. Burgin, 'Authors at Play, *Pearson's Magazine*, February 1899, p. 159. See chapter 14 for further discussion.
[62] Doyle, 'Memories and Adventures', *Strand*, May 1924, p. 450.

in Scarlet' he noted his skills included being 'an expert singlestick player, boxer and swordsman'. He elaborates further in 'The Adventure of the Yellow Face':

> Few men were capable of greater muscular effort, and he was undoubt-edly one of the finest boxers of his weight that I have ever seen...

Holmes's skills are put to the test in 'The Adventure of the Solitary Cyclist' when Holmes, making enquiries in a local pub, is accosted by Mr Woodley, who gives Holmes a vicious back-hander. Holmes recounts:

> The next few minutes were delicious. It was a straight left against a slog-ging ruffian. I emerged as you see me. Mr Woodley went home in a cart.

However, apart from brief scenes in *The Firm of Girdlestone* and *The Stark Munro Letters*, both of which are autobiographical, and an incident at the end of the third Brigadier Gerard story, 'How the King Held the Brigadier', Doyle did not go into detail about boxing in any of his early works. Doyle was a great fan of the original bare-knuckle fights. 'Better that our sports should be a little too rough than that we should run a risk of effeminacy,' he opined in *Memories and Adventures*. His passion for the sport was explored in loving detail in *Rodney Stone*.

This broke the mould for *The Strand* because it was the first full-length serial the magazine ran, throughout 1896. It was perhaps fitting that since it was Doyle who had introduced and popularised the story series, it would be he who ran the first serial, but this change in policy was sufficient for Greenhough Smith to make an announce-ment in the December 1895 issue at the end of the first Brigadier Gerard series:

> Mr Conan Doyle has written a powerful Story which will succeed 'Brigadier Gerard' in *The Strand Magazine* commencing in the January Number. It will be entitled 'Rodney Stone', and will treat mainly of the period of George III in a manner which has not hitherto been attempted. Though each instalment will, like 'The Adventures of Sherlock Holmes' and 'Brigadier Gerard', have separate incidents of its own, there will be a plot running through them all, and the publication of this important work will continue during the greater part of next year.

It seems strange to have to define and make an excuse for running a serial, which had long been the mainstay of many magazines, but since

"THERE SPUN AN OLD BLACK HAT."

Sidney Paget's illustration to the climax of 'Rodney Stone' (from *The Strand*, September 1896).

The Strand had built its reputation upon the story series, Smith's announcement only emphasises what a radical change this was.

Doyle did not complete the novel until the end of September 1895, so for the first instalment to appear in January, fully illustrated by Sidney Paget, shows remarkable determination by Greenhough Smith and his associates. George Newnes was, it goes without saying, pleased to have new material from Doyle, but he is reported as saying, 'Why that subject of all subjects upon the Earth?'[63] Newnes may, of course, have been reminded of the day he was knocked unconscious at Silcoates school, but bare-knuckle boxing had essentially ceased since the introduction of the Marquess of Queensbury rules in 1867. The last bare-knuckle championship, between John L. Sullivan and Jake Kilrain, had taken place in 1889, while the first under Queensbury rules, between Sullivan and 'Gentleman Jim' Corbett had been played out in 1892. This effectively began the modern boxing era, but its status was not recognised as legal in the United Kingdom until 1901. It had been illegal in the United States since 1859 and only steadily shifted towards legality starting in New York in 1896. Newnes might have seen the novel, and thereby his magazine, as promoting an illegal sport.

As ever, Doyle did considerable research. The previous year, following the success of his stage play *A Story of Waterloo*, with Henry Irving, Doyle had considered a new play, 'In the Days of the Regent', and undertook some provisional work with his brother-in-law Willie Hornung. It came to nothing at that time, but he reworked it as a short story, not intended for publication but as an exploratory sketch.[64]

With the novel Doyle used his tried-and-tested framework of a reminiscence by an old man recalling his youth. At the outset Rodney Stone is nearing his sixty-fifth birthday (in 1851) but we are soon propelled back to his adolescence in the period approaching the Battle of Trafalgar. Rodney notes that the Stone family has for many generations belonged to the Navy, and that the eldest son is given the name of the father's favourite commander.[65] Stone's maternal uncle is Sir Charles Tregellis whom, we are told, 'having inherited the money of a wealthy East Indian merchant, became in time the talk of the town and the very particular friend of the Prince of Wales.' Young Rodney lives in the village of Friar Oaks, just north of

[63] Doyle, 'Memories and Adventures', *Strand*, March 1924, p. 241.

[64] This sketch, 'An Impression of the Regency', later appeared in the UK in *The Universal Magazine* for January 1901. It includes several characters who appear in the novel, notably Sir Charles Tregellis, Rodney Stone's uncle, but Stone himself does not appear.

[65] Captain, later Commander, George Brydges Rodney (1718–1792), was one of the British heroes of the American War of Independence and at the relief of the Siege of Gibraltar.

Brighton, where he is friends with Jim Harrison, the orphaned nephew of the local smith and former prizefighter, Jack Harrison.

One of the back stories, relevant to the book's climax, is the mystery of Lord Avon, a close friend of Sir Charles. Fourteen years earlier (in the 1790s) Lord Avon, along with his cousin, Sir Lothian Hume and brother, Captain Barrington, had played cards with Tregellis for two days. Barrington won everyone's money and the next day was found dead with evidence that Avon had killed him. Avon disappeared, believed in America. Lothian is Lord Avon's heir, but until Avon is proved to be dead or a murderer Lothian cannot inherit.

Tregellis, whom Doyle based on Beau Brummel as one of London's leading dandies, visits Rodney and his mother and wishes to take Rodney to London to witness Society. Tregellis and Sir Lothian have staged a fight for high stakes as both need money to fund their extravagant lifestyles. Tregellis chooses the young Jim Harrison as his champion, but Jim disappears on the eve of the fight and his uncle Jack steps in; the older man against a younger opponent.

The frame plot, somewhat gothic in tone, is almost incidental to the build-up to the main fight, which is described in detail spreading over several pages. It makes a lasting impression. Doyle believed that the book encouraged a revival of interest in boxing[66] and though this is difficult to prove, it doubtless stirred the imagination of young readers and may have encouraged their interest in the sport.

It certainly impressed the young P. G. Wodehouse, who was fifteen when the novel was published. Five years later he called *Rodney Stone* 'an epic of the ring', adding:

> Probably everybody who takes an interest in sport has read 'Rodney Stone,' and has revelled in the fight between Berks and Boy Jim in the coachhouse, and the great battle on Crawley Downs between the smith and the West-countryman. […] However often one may have read the book, and however much one may be prepared for the surprise, that magnificent climax comes as fresh as ever.[67]

---

[66] In 'Memories and Adventures' Doyle wrote, 'At that time boxing had not gained the popular vogue which I have been told that this very book first initiated.' *Strand,* March 1924, p. 241.

[67] P. G. Wodehouse, 'The Pugilist in Fiction', *Sandow's Magazine of Physical Culture*, March 1902, p. 173.

At the time the book edition appeared a reviewer in *The Times* called it 'distinctly the best of Dr Conan Doyle's novels', and remarked:

> ...it must be confessed at once that 'Rodney Stone' gives great and indeed excessive prominence to pugilism. [...] Our author has at least a reasonable apology for resuscitating what most of us are well content to consider a lost art. He has no desire to 'revive the mastodon', but maintains that the ring had its uses in the days he describes.[68]

Its 'uses' were to encourage and discipline the fighting spirit in the youth of the day and so prepare those young men as volunteers in the Army and Navy during the French Wars. At the outset of *Rodney Stone* the eponymous hero reflects upon the olden times:

> It was a time of war, when England with an army and navy composed only of those who volunteered to fight because they had fighting blood in them, had to encounter, as they would now have to encounter, a power which could by despotic law turn every citizen into a soldier. If the people had not been full of this lust for combat, it is certain that England must have been overborne. And it was thought, and is, on the face of it, reasonable, that a struggle between two indomitable men, with thirty thousand to view it and three million to discuss it, did help to set a standard of hardihood and endurance. Brutal it was, no doubt, and its brutality is the end of it; but it is not so brutal as war...

It was a view that Doyle continued to hold and certainly one that the nation recognised. Writing just after the First World War, a columnist in *The Times* began by saying, 'In the days of Rodney Stone – and there is no English schoolboy who does not know his story – boxing was the greatest of English pastimes,' and continued:

> That the popularity of boxing was increased enormously by the war may be accounted as a war benefit. There is no sport in the world which demands cleaner living. There is no more natural sport. Success at boxing depends on the man himself. Low cunning will not help him, but a quick, clear brain, a hard body, and perfect training will carry a man a long way.[69]

---

[68] *The Times*, 13 November 1896, p. 12.
[69] 'In Praise of Boxing', *The Times*, 19 July 1919, p. 15.

The writer of that anonymous feature, 'In Praise of Boxing', could almost have been Doyle himself, as he later expressed the same sentiments in *Memories and Adventures*.

Some commentators were disappointed that the novel ended before the Battle of Trafalgar, as the serial ends with:

> I dare scarce say another word about myself, lest this, which I had meant to be the last word of a chapter, should grow into the first words of a new one. Had I not taken up my pen to tell you a story of the land, I might, perchance, have made a better one of the sea; but the one frame cannot hold two opposite pictures. The day may come when I shall write down all that I remember of the greatest battle ever fought upon salt water, and how my father's gallant life was brought to an end...

Doyle did consider a sequel, writing to his mother in September 1906 and saying that he felt 'drawn' towards a continuation. But this was too soon after the death of his wife, and he soon threw himself into his various campaigns, so the book was never written. He did, however, return to the play, now called *The House of Temperley*. Though based on *Rodney Stone* it featured only a few of the original characters. Doyle built the drama around the big fight on Crawley Downs.

The fight at Crawley Down from the dramatic version of 'Rodney Stone' called *The House of Temperley*, staged in 1909 (from *The Strand*, May 1924).

No theatre manager would take it on, and so Doyle leased the Adelphi Theatre himself for six months with the play opening on 27 December 1909. It seemed initially successful, with people flocking to see the realistic fight scenes, which had been choreographed by a professional boxing instructor. *The Times* reported:

> …when all seems lost it is Captain Jack who throws his hat into the ring, peels to the waist in the classic style, and knocks Hawker's man out with the bare fist in 15 rounds. Of those 15 we only see three – the first and the last two; but those are quite enough to show a pretty display of genuine skill on the parts of Mr Charles Maude and Mr Reginald Davis; and the whole crowded, noisy, brutal vigorous scene is a remarkable piece of vivid reconstruction, for which the 'producer', Mr Herbert Jarman, deserves special praise.[70]

However, it became apparent that women were staying away because it was too bloodthirsty, and the play was soon operating at a loss. Doyle was paying £600 a week for the lease and the Company, and a further £2,000 for the cost of the production,[71] so in order to bolster the proceedings he included a Sherlock Holmes play (adapted from 'The Adventure of the Speckled Band') as a curtain-raiser. In the end Doyle did not suffer as badly as it initially seemed, but it curbed any further desire for the theatre.

It was not the end of *The House of Temperley*, though, as it was adapted into a film in 1913 by the London Film Company with a number of the same actors. This included Reginald Davis, who had played the boxer Gloster Dick and who, during the stage production, had been so caught up in the fighting that he had lost a tooth and broken a finger and a rib. Davis was the kind of fit, strong-spirited man whom Doyle admired. When the First World War broke out Davis volunteered, fought heroically at Gallipoli and was awarded the Military Cross for his bravery at the Battle of Cambrai in November 1917 when he served in the Royal Tank Corps. In the Second World War he served in the Royal Armoured Division and was later awarded an MBE. Here surely was a perfect example of the kind of indomitable fighting spirit that Doyle believed the trained boxer would become.

---

[70] 'Boxing Day Entertainments', *The Times*, 28 December 1909, p. 8.
[71] In today's prices that total cost would be close to £1.4 million.

Doyle had not yet finished with Sir Charles Tregellis. He returned in 'The Fall of Lord Barrymore', published in *The Strand* for December 1912. Tregellis's nephew, Vereker, visits his uncle in need of £1,000 to cover his debts. Sir Charles sees no reason to pay, but Vereker promises to make a fool of Tregellis's rival, Lord Barrymore, who has an ex-prizefighter as his bodyguard. At an evening's revel Barrymore is approached by a girl and her aunt, and the two proceed to humiliate the Lord. When his henchman attempts to rid the Lord of the girls, one of them sets about him showing formidable skills as a pugilist. Tregellis realises that the girl is his nephew in disguise, and he so enjoys the humiliation of both Barrymore and his bully that it is clear Vereker will get his £1,000. The story is played entirely for laughs with the boxing a relatively minor, though critical, episode.

★

Doyle would run three more boxing stories in *The Strand*. The first, and best, was 'The Croxley Master', which at 16,000 words ran from October to December 1899. Doyle used his own experience as the starting point. A medical student, Montgomery, working for a local doctor (Oldacre) in Yorkshire, is desperate for the fee to cover the final session of his course. An incident occurs when Montgomery retaliates against a violent client, knocking him out. The client turns out to be former boxer, Ted Barton, who was lined up to fight Silas Craggs, the Master of Croxley pit, but now feels he can no longer compete. The promoters offer Montgomery £100 if he'll take on the Master. Montgomery had received training from a former middleweight champion at the university, similar to Doyle and, needing the money, agrees to the contest. It is only later that Montgomery discovers how formidable an opponent Silas Craggs is, and finds that Oldacre is against all forms of boxing, especially for money. Montgomery has to keep his involvement in the fight a secret but also find time for training, with the help of Barton.

The outcome of the fight is no real surprise, though Doyle maintains the suspense, and the way Montgomery wins and the unexpected aftermath keeps the story fresh. It is far and away Doyle's best tale of the ring, not as protracted as *Rodney Stone*, more focused and, above all, more relevant. The story is set in 1897, the here-and-now for the readers of *The Strand*, and takes place at a Yorkshire colliery among working men, rather than the dandies of the Regency period. Doyle

Sidney Paget's illustration from 'The Croxley Master' (from *The Strand*, December 1899).

captures the setting and locale perfectly, and the local dialect, which must have confused many American readers, adds both atmosphere and verisimilitude.

The story comes from the heart of Doyle's upbringing. He might at that point have been earning the present-day equivalent of a quarter-of-a-million a year, but his roots were among the poor of Edinburgh and he knew the struggle to put himself through university. He describes those feelings among everyday working men in the story:

> Warped with labour and twisted by toil, bent double by week-long work in the cramped coal galleries or half-blinded with years spent in front of white-hot fluid metal, these men still gilded their harsh and hopeless lives by their devotion to sport. It was their one relief, the only thing which could distract their minds from sordid surroundings, and give them an interest beyond the blackened circle which enclosed them. Literature, art, science, all these things were beyond their horizon; but the race, the football match, the cricket, the fight, these were things which they could understand, which they could speculate upon in advance and comment upon afterwards. Sometimes brutal, sometimes grotesque, the love of sport is still one of the great agencies which make for the happiness of our people. It lies very deeply in the springs of our nature, and when it has been educated out, a higher, more refined nature may be left, but it will not be of that robust British type which has left its mark so deeply on the world.[72]

One can see in passages like this how Doyle related to the working class. Though many of his stories in *The Strand* were written with the middle classes in mind, he had not forgotten his roots and he had not forgotten who it was that had made Britain great. It is no surprise, with stories like 'The Croxley Master', how Doyle endeared himself to the whole spectrum of readers. He was very pleased with the story, telling his mother it was a 'ripper'. It has a pace and rhythm that propels the reader along and it also has a surprise where, once again, Doyle recognises the importance of women in these societies, for it is a strong-minded, powerful woman who delivers the *coup de grâce* at the story's climax.

Although we don't have the views of George Newnes on the story, he must have recognised how this would have appealed to the same readers who enjoyed *Tit-Bits*. Whereas that weekly had been aimed primarily at the working class and *The Strand* at the middle class, Doyle's

---

[72] 'The Croxley Master', *Strand*, November 1899, p. 483.

fiction broadened *The Strand*'s market. Little wonder that whenever his name was on the cover, sales increased by 100,000 copies.

★

The same popular mood pervades a poem Doyle wrote to celebrate the famous bare-knuckle fighter William Thompson, known as Bendy or Bendigo, partly because of his ability to twist and turn in the ring, and partly a play on his middle name, Abednego.[73] Bendigo, who won all but one of his professional fights, was regarded by many as the English Champion of Champions. Born and raised in Nottingham, he and his mother were forced into the workhouse after his father died, but he found work in an iron foundry, which enabled him to develop his strength. He lived from 1811 to 1880, so Doyle would have known of him in his later days, though his last prize fight was in 1850. Since bare-knuckle fighting was illegal, Bendigo was often arrested after a fight and spent further nights in gaol because of his increased drunkenness. After hearing a prison chaplain's sermon he made up his mind to reclaim his life, and became an evangelist in 1872. Although he was not well versed in preaching he nevertheless toured regularly, giving sermons. These events gathered large, often unruly crowds and Bendigo was frequently heckled and taunted, especially by those who believed he used to win his fights unfairly. Legend has it that early in his ministry, Bendigo was not easy to control and at one event he vaulted from the pulpit and prepared to fight his hecklers. It was this event that Doyle commemorated in 'Bendy's Sermon'.[74]

Doyle donated the poem to *The Strand*. 'If you think it any use, accept it as a present,' he told Smith. Smith reproduced it in Doyle's handwriting in the April 1909 issue, accompanied by several illustrations. The poem is a piece of doggerel, rather like Rudyard Kipling's *Barrack-Room Ballads*, and clearly only intended as light fun, but it has a certain charm.

★

---

[73] His brothers were Shadrach and Meshach, named after the three youths in the Book of Daniel.

[74] How much of Bendy's fight is of Doyle's invention and how much actually happened is difficult to determine. I have found no reference to it among the contemporary local newspapers. However, someone signing himself 'May Fair' recalled that he attended a meeting where one of Bendigo's sponsors undertook a discussion with secularists. When Bendigo discovered they did not believe in the Bible he was all for tackling them and had to be restrained. See report under 'Bendigo' in the *Nottinghamshire Guardian*, 9 February 1877, p. 8

BENDIGO IN THE RING.

BENDY'S SERMON.

By

A. CONAN DOYLE.

A STORY IN VERSE.

Reproduced in facsimile from the author's original manuscript.

BENDIGO AS A PREACHER.

Bendy's Sermon

[Bendigo, the well known Nottingham prize fighter, became converted to religion and preached at revival meetings throughout the country]

You didn't know of Bendigo ! Well, that knocks me out !
Who's your board school teacher ? What's he been about ?
Chock-a-block with fairy tales — full of useless cram.
And never heard o' Bendigo, the pride of Nottingham !

Bendy's short for Bendigo. You should see him peel !
Half of him was whalebone, half of him was steel,
Fightin' weight eleven ten, five foot nine in height,
Always ready to oblige if you want a fight.

Facsimile of the start of Doyle's poem, 'Bendy's Sermon' (from *The Strand*, April 1909).

In *Rodney Stone* reference had been made to several of the great professional fighters of the day, including Tom Cribb, Tom Belcher and Joe Berks, all of whom had walk-on parts in *The House of Temperley*. At the time he was re-working that play Doyle wrote a new boxing story, 'The Lord of Falconbridge', also set in Regency times, this time 1818, involving Tom Cribb and Tom Spring. Cribb, having retired as Champion of England in 1811, has become a prosperous publican with open house to any fighter down on his luck. He welcomes Spring and introduces him to a mysterious lady who is prepared to pay a handsome sum if Spring will fight an unnamed opponent. Spring undertakes the task even though he discovers that the fight is not lawful and the woman is seeking revenge.

Doyle thought well of the story, telling his mother that he had never done one better, but the story is not a match for 'The Croxley Master', although it is full of period atmosphere. It appeared four months after 'Bendy's Sermon' in the August 1909 *Strand*.

Doyle's final boxing story did not appear for another twelve years – 'The Bully of Brocas Court' in the November 1921 *Strand*, with three fine illustrations by Steven Spurrier. On one level this is just another boxing story, set in 1878, when bare-knuckle fighting was dying out but modern boxing under the Queensberry Rules had yet to establish itself. An army captain, Milburn, fetches a boxer, Stevens, from London, whom he hopes can best a fighter within the South Midland Yeomanry. As they are returning, Milburn tells Stevens of a local legend about the Bully of Brocas Court, who challenges any who pass by. Inevitably that happens and Stevens faces up against the Bully. It is only at the climax of the story that the reader realises that what Stevens is up against is not flesh and blood. Although a *bona fide* boxing story, it is also one of Doyle's ghost stories. For that reason alone it is distinctive, but it does not otherwise stand out against Doyle's earlier work.

Doyle is not immediately thought of as a writer of boxing stories, and yet *Rodney Stone* had clearly left its mark upon the youth of the 1890s and may even have inspired a recovery of interest in the noble art. But his masterpiece is surely 'The Croxley Master'. Here Doyle does not intellectualise with the deductive qualities of Sherlock Holmes, or boast of his heroics in the shape of Brigadier Gerard. Instead he shows the sport of the common man which he believed was a major factor in making the British soldier and sailor the backbone of Britain's Empire.

6

Doyle and The Sudan

DOYLE'S VIEWS ON BRITAIN and its Empire emerged in his little-known novel, *The Tragedy of the Korosko*. Almost forgotten today, but very popular when it appeared, it arose out of Doyle's trip to Egypt for his wife's health, where he briefly became a war correspondent.

Louisa's health had benefited from her time in Switzerland, and Doyle hoped a winter trip to Egypt, with its dry heat, would provide further relief. They arrived at the Mena Hotel, seven miles south of Cairo, in November 1895 and for a while visited the usual tourist attractions. Louisa responded well, but Doyle soon became bored. He found climbing the Great Pyramid pointless and satisfied himself indulging in various sporting activities. Unfortunately, while he was riding at the local livery stables his mount threw him and he was struck above the right eye, leaving a deep star-shaped wound that needed five stitches. He was grateful he did not lose the sight in that eye.

Looking for more diversions, after the New Year festivities Arthur and Louisa took one of Thomas Cook's tours up the River Nile to Wadi Halfa[75] on the paddle steamer *Nitocris*. En route the steamer passed through the town of Korosko, which was later submerged beneath Lake Nasser when the Aswan Dam was completed in 1971. In Doyle's day, Korosko was often in the news as a key staging post for the shorter

---

[75] In Doyle's day this was spelled as Wady Halfa.

I held on to the bridle, and the horse, pawing about with
his front hoofs, struck me over the eye.

Doyle being thrown by a horse while in Egypt in 1895 (from *The Strand*,
February 1924. Artwork uncredited but probably by Howard K. Elcock).

cross-desert caravan route to Abu Hamed and thence to Khartoum, thus
avoiding the large curve in the Nile with its cataracts. It featured strongly
in the British governments attempt to lift the Siege of Khartoum and
rescue General Gordon – all in vain, as he was killed by the forces of
the Mahdi in January 1885.

The Mahdi was Muhammad Ahmad, who had declared himself the
Mahdi – the messianic redeemer of the Islamic faith – in 1881 and there-
after led a war against the imposition of Turko-Egyptian control in the
Sudan. His death in June 1885 did not bring an end to the hostilities, as

the Mahdi's forces, generally if wrongly referred to at the time as Dervishes (a name the Mahdi had strictly forbidden), continued under other leaders, notably Abdallahi ibn Muhammad, who emerged as the unchallenged leader in 1891, calling himself the Khalifa. The Khalifa was not defeated until the Battle of Omdurman in September 1898, so that at the time Doyle and his wife undertook the Nile cruise, the area to the south of Wadi Halfa was a danger zone.

Doyle reflected on this while at Wadi Halfa, where the party had travelled to the impressive Rock of Abousir from where there was an unrivalled view of the desert and the Nile to the south. 'The banks in the upper reaches were not too safe, as raiders on camels came down at times,' Doyle later wrote, and he realised how helpless the tourists would be at Abousir if a troop of raiders were to come upon them.

These thoughts, which would develop into *The Tragedy of the Korosko*, occupied his mind on the trip back to Cairo and he penned a short article, 'On the Egyptian Frontier', for Cassell's weekly topical affairs paper, *The Speaker*. This made clear how his thoughts were going. He outlined how the Egyptian frontier ended at Assuan (now Aswan) with a 200-mile buffer zone between there and the Sudan, patrolled by a 'highly mobile and efficient camel corps' which could react to and avenge Dervish raids but could not stop them. He continued:

> Such a raid took place some few weeks ago and it is to be feared that its complete success will make it the first of many. I had the opportunity of inspecting the village and of hearing the story from the lips of the Sheikh. It was 4 in the afternoon when the Dervishes came riding over the low sandhills which mark the end of the desert. 'How do you know they were not mere robbers?' I asked. 'No, no: they were Dervishes, said the Sheikh. 'They were in uniform; they all wore red turbans and yellow boots.' Those yellow boots seemed to have made an impression upon the Nubian peasants, for they all corroborated this detail.[76]

It was an image that stayed with Doyle, because when he came to write *The Tragedy of the Korosko*, it is that description which alerts the travellers to the approaching danger.

---

[76] 'On the Egyptian Frontier', *The Speaker*, 8 February 1896, p. 147.

Doyle had little immediate opportunity to develop the novel because events soon overtook him. While in Cairo Doyle decided, with the assistance of Colonel David Lewis of the Egyptian army, to visit an ancient Coptic monastery fifty miles outside the city. The round trip took three days, despite them getting lost, and with Doyle administering some medical assistance to the abbot. Upon their return, Lewis discovered that forces had been mobilised preparing for war, and he was in charge of an advanced brigade.

Lord Cromer, the British Consul-General of Egypt, had long felt there should be no attempt to recover the Sudan, but he now decided it was necessary to send a punitive expedition against the Mahdist forces. This had been prompted by raiding parties of Dervishes at Dongola, south of Wadi Halfa, with the possible threat of those forces massing for an onslaught on Egyptian territory. Moreover, the defeat of the Italians by the Ethiopians at the Battle of Adowa on 2 March 1896 had created further instability south of Sudan, and Cromer believed a show of force was necessary.

Keen to see some of the action Doyle wired *The Times* in London, applying to be its war correspondent, but it already had Edward Knight. Through *The Strand*, Doyle was able to become a temporary war correspondent for the *Westminster Gazette*, an evening paper which George Newnes had started in January 1893 and was now under a new and influential editor, John Alfred Spender.

Suitably kitted out and with an Italian revolver, Doyle set off with several junior officers, including the future general Sir John Maxwell and the young Nevill Maskelyne Smyth, who two years later would be awarded the Victoria Cross for saving the lives of two war correspondents at the Battle of Omdurman. They first went by train to Assiout (Asyut) and from there by river to Aswan, where they were delayed for a week. Doyle was joined by several fellow reporters. From there, mounted on their camels, the party of reporters rode to Korosko. On the way Doyle avoided being bitten by a death adder and a tarantula, but managed to fall off his camel. They reached Wadi Halfa by boat, only two months after Doyle had previously left. While there, Doyle dined with Kitchener, Commander-in-Chief of the Egyptian Army, who openly discussed the coming campaign. Although Doyle progressed further along the Nile to the military outpost at Sarras, where he felt there was a 'whiff of real war', it was clear that nothing was imminent and Kitchener assured him there was little point in hanging around. Doyle was anxious to get back to Louisa, because it was late April and the rising temperature would not help her condition.

So Doyle returned to Cairo, disappointed at not having seen any action, though he filed eight reports with the *Westminster Gazette* and obtained much experience for his novel. He and Louisa were back in London on 1 May before settling in Haslemere in Surrey, at Grayswood, while they waited (and waited) for their house, Undershaw, to be completed.

It was only now that Doyle turned his mind to *The Tragedy of the Korosko*, which he wrote during the latter half of 1896. He felt it was unlike anything else he had written, and although he was not entirely happy with it when he submitted it to Greenhough Smith in January 1897 he was nevertheless delighted with the payment, which he believed to be a record, equal to 10½d (just over 4p) a word. He estimated the story to be around 40,000 words, though by my estimate the printed serial version is closer to 44,000.[77] In fact Doyle received £1,800 (over £182,000 today) with half paid on delivery to help meet some of the building work costs. It meant that Doyle not only wrote the first serial that appeared in *The Strand*, he also wrote the second. It ran in eight parts from May to December 1897, liberally illustrated by Sidney Paget.

The story follows Doyle's original thoughts. The *Korosko*, a stern-wheeler cruising the Nile, carries a party of thirteen plus their guide (or dragoman), Mansoor and six black guards. The party consists of seven Britons (including a nurse and child), three Americans, two Irish and a Frenchman. Seven are men, five women plus the child. Among the men is a retired government official, Colonel Cochrane, a British diplomat, Cecil Brown, a solicitor, James Stephens, and a

---

[77] In the book's preface Doyle noted, 'This book has been materially enlarged and altered since its appearance in serial form.' However the final length of 46,600 words was only marginally more than the magazine version. The differences are minor with some extra detail to clarify certain events and build the atmosphere and climax. There was nothing materially significant missing from the serial.

Sidney Paget's illustration to one of the episodes of 'The Tragedy of the Korosko' in *The Strand* for June 1897.

Nonconformist minister, Reverend John Stuart. The Irish couple are a husband and wife, with Mr Belmont a renowned rifle shot. The Americans are John Headingly, a Harvard graduate completing his education with a world tour, plus an aunt and her niece, both Miss Adams, the younger being distinguished by her first name, Sadie. The Frenchman is Monsieur Fardet, whose profession we never learn but whose views are frequently heard.

The story begins with the party having moored near Wadi Halfa in the evening, ready for their expedition the next day. The reader eavesdrops on various conversations. Fardet is educating Headingly in his belief that there are no Dervishes, as they are an invention by Lord Cromer to imply a much greater danger than actually exists. Fardet has strong views on the way the English seek to take control and make everything neat and tidy, fabricating dangers and situations as a reason for staying in whichever country they've become involved. After Fardet retires for the night, Headingly joins a discussion with Cochrane and Brown. Brown, the diplomat, believes that Britain has 'been the policeman of the world long enough' and that it is about time for Britain to step back and let Europe do more. Cochrane doesn't agree. He believes each country has its strengths: Germany in abstract thought, France in art and literature, and England with its 'moral sense and public duty'. Cochrane explains further:

> 'The world is small and it grows smaller every day. It's a single organic body, and one spot of gangrene is enough to vitiate the whole. There's no room upon it for dishonest, defaulting, tyrannical, irresponsible Governments. But there are many races which appear to be so incapable of improvement that we can never hope to get a good Government out of them. What is to be done, then? The former device of Providence in such a case was extermination by some more virile stock. Now we have a more merciful substitution of rulers, or even of mere advice from a more advanced race. That is the case with the Central Asian Khanates and with the protected States of India. If the work has to be done, and if we are the best fitted for the work, then I think that it would be a crime to shirk it.'[78]

It's not simply a strong imperialist view, but a belief that Britain was morally and culturally superior; the only country with a sufficient sense of justice and duty that it was obliged to exercise that in policing the world. Doyle never really changed that view. Indeed world events, especially the First World War, cemented his belief. It might be viewed as politically incorrect today, but it was an attitude that pervaded most of British government and society at the time. That did not, though, stop Doyle respecting the culture, beliefs and values of others, some of which he expressed in the novel.

The next morning the guide takes the party up the Rock of Abousir. Mrs Belmont stays behind, as does Mrs Shlesinger with her maid and

---

[78] This and previous references are from the first episode of the novel in *The Strand*, May 1897, p. 490.

daughter. The party have with them a small armed guard and a number of donkey boys. It is while they are at the top of the Rock that they see a 'long string of red-turbaned riders' winding their way out of a ravine and heading towards them. Fearing the worst they hide the aunt and niece among the rocks, and sort out what weapons they have between them while facing the approaching Arabs. Gunshots break out and before long there are several deaths. Doyle pulls no punches, starkly portraying the fate of the donkey boys and the guards.

There are other deaths, before the survivors face the Arabs. The Frenchman, hot-headed as ever, cannot understand why the Arabs should want to do them harm, but his attitude and bravado only makes matters worse. The dragoman, fearing for his life, betrays the presence of the women, and the survivors are herded away, initially with the understanding that they will be held to ransom. Things go from bad to worse when the procession meets with another, who have raided the *Korosko* and brought Mrs Belmont with them. Only Mrs Shlesinger and her maid and daughter seem to have escaped.

The party are told that unless they convert to Islam and accept the Koran they will be executed. The various members of the party react differently, but in order to prevaricate they ask to be educated about the Islamic faith. The mullah becomes suspicious of their intent, as does the emir leading the Arabs, and it is decided that only the richest among them will be taken to Khartoum for ransom. The others will be killed.

Throughout this episode Doyle explores the reactions of the individuals regarding accepting or rejecting Islam and in facing their deaths, and he shows that even when up against such adversity people will still argue over a matter of principle or to avoid losing face. Despite this, various plans are put in place that later come to their aid.

It is inevitable that the reader will expect the party to be rescued, but it is never certain who will survive, which keeps the reader enthralled and sustains the atmosphere. In this sense the book is a true thriller and stands up well today. Indeed, its content and arguments are still relevant, and one can only imagine Doyle shaking his head in frustration and desperation were he witnessing the current world situation.

At the time of its publication in book form the novel received generally good reviews. *The Graphic* called it 'as good a narrative as even Dr Conan Doyle has ever written.' The *Pall Mall Gazette* commented that it was not only a good story, but had that rare merit of being told with directness – and that is indeed the novel's strength, as Doyle never flinches from describing events as they would happen. *The Times* reviewer went further:

> It really might have been Mr Conan Doyle's intention to write a story that should serve as an object-lesson to people who doubt the necessity of reconquering the Sudan, and speak of the Baggara as if they were a mild, pastoral tribe, who only seek to pursue their gentle avocations unmolested. No one who knows anything of them will call this story of their cruelty and fanaticism overdrawn.[79]

Doyle's viewpoint though, while common to the Victorian ideal, was not bigoted. He recognised the Moslem dedication and devotion. In one revealing paragraph, as the Arabs pray, he writes:

> The great red sun was down with half its disc slipped behind the violet bank upon the horizon. It was the hour of Arab prayer. An older and more learned civilization would have turned to that magnificent thing upon the skyline and adored *that*. But these wild children of the desert were nobler in essentials than the polished Persian. To them the ideal was higher than the material, and it was with their backs to the sun and their faces to the central shrine of their religion that they prayed. And how they prayed, these fanatical Moslems! Rapt, absorbed, with yearning eyes and shining faces, rising, stooping, grovelling with their foreheads upon their praying carpets. Who could doubt, as he watched their strenuous, heart-whole devotion, that here was a great living power in the world, reactionary but tremendous, countless millions all thinking as one from Cape Juby to the confines of China? Let a common wave pass over them, let a great soldier or organizer arise among them to use the grand material at his hand, and who shall say that this may not be the besom with which Providence may sweep the rotten, decadent, impossible, half-hearted south of Europe, as it did a thousand years ago, until it makes room for a sounder stock?[80]

Doyle provided what was, in his view, an honest and open description of the position in the Sudan. He told Greenhough Smith when submitting the manuscript that 'I hope it will make the man in the bus realise what a Dervish means, as he never did before.'[81]

---

[79] *The Times*, 22 March 1898, p. 2.
[80] Doyle, *Korosko, The Strand*, August 1897, p. 145.
[81] Lellenberg, *Letters*, p. 378

The book remained popular with the public and with Doyle, and in 1906 he adapted it into a stage play, *The Fires of Fate*. It opened in Liverpool on 11 June 1909, moving to London the next week where it ran until 8 October. Unfortunately the power of the original story was diminished by it being presented as a 'morality play', with many of the characters changed and the lead, now named Colonel Egerton, miraculously cured of a rare ailment as a consequence of the drama. The cast were entirely English, regardless of the part they played.

The play ran in smaller theatres as a matinee, and had a brief American run, and it was also made into a film in 1923, still as *The Fires of Fate*, but otherwise the play has generally been forgotten. The book, though, remains a potent example of the attitude to Britain's imperial role at the end of the Victorian era.

A scene from *The Fires of Fate*, the dramatic version of 'The Tragedy of Korosko', staged in London in 1909 (from *The Strand*, February 1924).

7

Round the Fire Stories

THANKS IN NO SMALL PART to the popularity of Arthur Conan Doyle, George Newnes and his publishing company achieved considerable success during the 1890s. Newnes was made a baronet in the New Year's Honours for 1895, 'to commemorate not only your political services, but the good work that you have done in the cause of healthy popular literature'.[82] He took the title Baronet Newnes of Wildcroft, the latter being the name of his house in Putney. The business was refloated in July 1897 with a nominal capital of £1 million. Newnes presented Doyle with 500 of the new Preference Shares, a token of gratitude which Doyle regarded highly. It was another sign of the close relationship between Newnes and Doyle.

Newnes's expansion allowed him to publish more books and magazines. Among the new magazines were *Country Life* from January 1897, *Wide World Magazine* in April 1898 and the boys' magazine *The Captain* in April 1899. It is surprising that nothing new by Doyle appeared in *Wide World Magazine*, considering his travels, though it did reprint his book *The Great Boer War*. Doyle did appear in the first issue of *The Captain*, contributing to a symposium '"What I Wanted to Be", Some Boyish Aspirations of Famous Men', to which he submitted his quip about wanting to be a civil (or 'uncivil') engineer.

---

[82] Letter from the Prime Minister, Lord Rosebery, to George Newnes, 27 December 1894.

Although Doyle did occasionally contribute reportage to the *Westminster Gazette*, so far as Newnes was concerned his one true market was *The Strand*. When the company was refloated in 1897 it reported sales of *The Strand* at 450,000 copies a month with a large circulation in America. *The Strand* had been available in the USA from the start, but these were simply the English edition overstamped with 20¢ and the distributor's name, International News Company. There were problems with these issues appearing a month later and carrying British adverts of no interest to American readers. It was not until July 1895 that Newnes began a separate American edition, edited from the London offices by James Walter Smith, a Harvard graduate, who had come to England in 1894 to work as a journalist and had married and settled there. It now ran American adverts and its contents occasionally varied from the British edition, prompted from the start by Doyle. The American serial rights for *Rodney Stone* had been sold to the McClure Syndicate, which placed it in various newspapers, notably the *New York Sun*. So while the English *Strand* ran the serial from January to December 1896, the *Sun* wrapped it up quickly from 5 April to 26 July 1896. James W. Smith had the problem of finding something to replace the serial in the American *Strand*, which he solved by writing some material himself and reprinting items from earlier issues. This was not the last time Doyle would pose this problem for James W. Smith.

★

Since Doyle was so prolific, *The Strand* could not publish everything by him. Readers of *Pearson's Magazine* were thus delighted when its January 1897 issue featured the first of three stories by Doyle under the heading, 'Tales of the High Seas', featuring the pirate Captain John Sharkey. The stories show considerable research and Sharkey is another of Doyle's well-developed characters, so it is surprising that Doyle killed him off in the third story in the May 1897 issue. Doyle eventually wrote a fourth story, 'The Blighting of Sharkey', which he sent to *The Strand* in May 1910 but which Greenhough Smith rejected. Smith didn't give his reasons, and Doyle wondered if perhaps the language was 'too energetic', but in all likelihood Smith did not want to run a

one-off story featuring a character that had appeared in a series published by a rival magazine.[83] Doyle wrote no more Sharkey stories, and
as a result the character is probably his least known. One might spec-
ulate on whether the stories would have been more successful had they
appeared in *The Strand*.

At the time, though, there was no room for them. Doyle had been
filling *The Strand* with series and serials. The Brigadier Gerard stories
took up most of 1895, *Rodney Stone* filled 1896 and *The Tragedy of the
Korosko* most of 1897. Starting in June 1898 Doyle began a new series,
'Round the Fire', which ran for twelve consecutive issues. These stories
were not connected by any regular character, but by their general concept and atmosphere. They were mystery rather than detective stories,
with the emphasis on the unexpected.

Doyle had excelled at unusual plots and settings in the Sherlock
Holmes stories, and these were his first works since then to have the
same mood. They are fine examples of Doyle the storyteller. Most of
the stories are first-person narratives, and he weaves the reader into a
puzzling mystery from the start. Several of the stories could easily be
reworked as Sherlock Holmes puzzles. Indeed, one of them has been
regarded as a lost Holmes story.

To experience them as *Strand* readers would have done, we need to
explore them one at a time.

'The Story of the Beetle-Hunter' opened the June 1898 issue, allowing for a striking frontispiece by A. S. Hartrick, showing two men
grappling with a third by a bed with what looks like a hammer flying
through the air. The story is narrated by a Dr Hamilton, who is recalling a curious experience he had soon after he had qualified. With
dwindling resources he responded to a newspaper advert seeking a
medical man of a resolute nature, with a strong physique, steady
nerves, and who, bizarrely, had to be an entomologist. The doctor ap-
plies in person, as requested, and meets Lord Linchmere who, having
satisfied himself over the medical qualifications, asks the doctor to talk
about beetles. When Linchmere discovers that Hamilton is not only
an enthusiast but a collector, he employs him on the spot. For £20 a

---

[83] The story appeared in *Pearson's Magazine*, April 1911.

day the doctor must accompany Linchmere and do exactly what he's told. A little light is thrown on the subject when we discover that Linchmere's sister is married to Sir Thomas Rossiter, the world's greatest authority on beetles. Rossiter, who is normally withdrawn and reclusive, warms rapidly to Hamilton when he discovers his interest in beetles.

So the mystery is set. How this puzzle relates to the frontispiece is all part of the allure, and shows Doyle on as fine form as he was with Holmes. It was clear from this opening story that here was going to be a series that would stimulate the reader with the same intellectual challenge as the Holmes stories. However, by now Doyle had his rivals. In the same volume were two other series – 'The Brotherhood of the Seven Kings' by L. T. Meade and Robert Eustace, in which a British biologist tries to outwit the plans of a female criminal mastermind who uses various scientific techniques to destroy her enemies; and Grant Allen's 'Miss Cayley's Adventures', in which the resourceful young adventuress, with hardly any money to her name, sets off to explore Europe and in the process finds herself solving unusual crimes. Allen's stories in particular were always popular and his work rivalled Doyle's at times.[84] Whereas Doyle more or less had the magazine to himself when he started the Holmes stories, he now had to pit his ingenuity against the very rivals he had inspired. The Round the Fire stories were going to have to be as remarkable and as fascinating as possible.

The next tale, 'The Story of the Man with the Watches', in the July issue, moved closer to Holmes territory, though it was somewhat underplayed. It was not the lead story – that was the next episode of 'The Brotherhood of the Seven Kings' – so it did not have a dramatic frontispiece, and Frank Craig's illustrations were rather sketchy. Surprisingly Doyle's name was not on the cover. Yet this was a murder mystery that would have delighted Holmes. It begins on a train bound for Manchester

---

[84] At the time of Grant Allen's death in October 1899, from liver or pancreatic cancer, his series featuring nurse-cum-righter-of-wrongs Hilda Wade was unfinished. A note appended to the final story in the February 1900 *Strand* stated that Allen had drafted a rough outline which Doyle talked through with him, and then Doyle wrote the final version.

from London. At the last minute a couple, believed to be father and daughter, board the first-class carriage. However, as the first compartment contained a man smoking a cigar, they entered the adjoining empty compartment, just as the train began on its journey. The carriage had no corridor, so no one could move between compartments. The train stopped briefly at Willesden Junction, when nobody boarded or left, but upon arrival at Rugby it was discovered that the man smoking the cigar and the elderly man and girl had all vanished. Instead there was a young man on the floor shot dead. When the body of this man was searched it was found he had six valuable gold watches in various pockets.

Here was a crime worthy of Holmes, but the investigators are Inspector Vane of Scotland Yard and a railway detective, Mr Henderson. They find some additional evidence, such as a pocket Bible near the track at Tring at a point where the train had slowed down, but otherwise the railway investigators play no part. Doyle enjoys teasing his readers, though, because he notes that a letter was published in a newspaper 'over the signature of a well-known criminal investigator' which suggests – wrongly as it turns out – a possible solution to the crime. In fact the crime remains unsolved for five years and is only explained when the 'well-known criminal investigator' receives a letter from New York which provides the full facts. As always with such puzzling crimes the solution can seem mundane, but Doyle manages to make quite a story out of it so that although we are robbed of any Holmesian investigation, it is still very satisfying.

Doyle was among the first to develop the idea of the railway mystery. There had been a fascination with railway crimes ever since the first murder on a train, that of Thomas Briggs in 1864, but although trains featured heavily in popular fiction, there had been only a few railway crime stories in the years since the Briggs case. Among these was Mrs Henry Wood's Johnny Ludlow story, 'Going Through the Tunnel', published in February 1869, which involves a theft on a train during the dark passage in a tunnel. There had also been Emile Zola's novel *La Bête humaine* (1890), but no one had yet developed a novel or story series about railway mysteries or detective work. The man who did this, and did it so well that he has ever since been regarded as the pioneer of railway detective stories, was Victor L. Whitechurch, whose stories were appearing at the same time as Doyle's.

Whitechurch was a young Church of England curate when he began writing his railway stories in the 1890s. One of the first appeared in *The Strand* – 'Stopping an Execution' (February 1895), in which a man discovers he can provide an alibi for a friend facing execution, and it's a hectic rush by train to save him. His stories were soon appearing in *Pearson's Magazine, Pearson's Weekly* and *The Railway Magazine* as well as *The Strand*, occasionally in the same issue as Doyle. He began a series, 'Tales of the Rails' in *Pearson's Weekly* in January 1898. Of particular interest had been 'A Narrow Escape' (*Pearson's Weekly*, 2 January 1897) where a wanted man somehow escapes from a moving train.

There was clearly something in the air because between them Whitechurch and Doyle developed a sub-genre of railway mystery stories. Doyle did not just do it the once. In fact his third Round the Fire story[85] is a classic. 'The Story of the Lost Special' (August 1898) doesn't just have a man vanish from a train, it has an entire train disappear. Doyle, as we have seen, was one of the pioneers of that other sub-genre, the impossible-crime story, of which the speciality was the murder in a locked room, a plot which Israel Zangwill had developed with considerable success in his novel *The Big Bow Mystery* (1892), and which Doyle had also used in the Holmes story 'The Adventure of the Speckled Band'. But it is a major step forward to have an entire train vanish, which makes 'The Story of the Lost Special' highly significant. Moreover, it has also been adopted into the Holmes canon because at one point in the story, when everyone is baffled, a letter is published in *The Times* 'over the signature of an amateur reasoner of some celebrity' who attempts to explain the story in a 'semi-scientific manner'. It even quotes the dictum 'that when the impossible has been eliminated the residuum, *however improbable*, most contain the truth'. Holmes does not appear in the story, but as it is set in June and July 1890, which is before Holmes's apparent death at the Reichenbach Falls, it is easy to see it as a case in which he showed interest but had no inclination to become involved.[86]

---

[85] It was the fourth written, completed on 1 May 1898, but Smith chose to publish it third.

[86] If one attempts to reconstruct Holmes's life based on the dates cited within the stories there is a gap in the summer of 1890, making it even more tempting to consider Holmes's involvement with the 'Lost Special'.

The fact that Doyle should tease his readers with a suggestion that Holmes had been aware of the case is clearly an example of his mischievous nature, but it also shows that Doyle had not entirely written off Holmes. He had already resurrected him briefly in a vignette, 'The Field Bazaar', which he wrote for *The Student*, the undergraduate magazine of Edinburgh University. This was a special issue in November 1896 to help raise money for a cricket pavilion, and Doyle obliged with this neat tale of Holmes following Watson's stream of thought. It was not a proper story, merely an incident, but it showed that Doyle still held some affection for Holmes. In fact at the time he was writing the Round the Fire stories, Doyle had already given thought to a theatrical adaptation of Holmes which would in turn lead to Holmes's resurrection. The 'Lost Special' may thus be seen as part of that road to recovery.

The next story to be published, but the third written, 'The Story of the Sealed Room', while not on a par with the two railway puzzles, was nevertheless a compelling read. Once again Doyle had pride of place at the start of the magazine allowing for another startling frontispiece, this time by Claude A. Shepperson. It shows three men standing before an open door, one of whom has fainted. Another is holding a light, staring with shock into the darkened room. It is narrated by solicitor Frank Alder who, on an evening walk in north London, sees a cyclist knocked down by a cab. Alder helps the cyclist, who lives nearby, to his home. As Alder is about to leave, the cyclist, whose name is Felix Stanniford, faints and Alder scurries around the house looking for someone to help. He discovers that, apart from the front room, the house is bare of furniture and fittings and at the end of one corridor is a room sealed shut, its lock covered in wax. Alder learns that Stanniford has no idea what is in that room. Stanniford's father had fled the country seven years before because of a banking scandal and left a note saying that the room he had used for photographic purposes and which was locked must be sealed and remain unopened until Felix reaches twenty-one. That birthday was approaching, and so Alder becomes a witness to the opening of the room. The story retains its shock value; through twenty-first-century eyes the discovery of what is in that room is no longer startling, though it is macabre.

After four such rewarding stories, the fifth story is less remarkable. 'The Story of the Black Doctor' takes us back into the realms of the murder mystery and, like 'The Man With the Watches', requires a detailed back story to explain the apparent murder of a local doctor. It's another that could have been developed as a Holmes mystery, as it has all the relevant ingredients: a puzzling crime involving an individual whom the locals felt had something to hide, followed by a lengthy confession but not, of course, the solution one might expect. Doyle was always able to provide a twist, though in this case it is less of a surprise.

'The Story of the Club-Footed Grocer' led the November 1898 issue and so bore a frontispiece, this time by Sidney Paget, depicting an elderly man, going to fat, manacled to a wall and about to be beaten by a strap while surrounded by sailors, one holding a rifle. We learn that the man, Stephen Maple, is the uncle of the narrator, and had been a grocer in Stepney but was known to be disreputable. Five years before he had been savagely beaten and left for dead. He recovered but his broken leg mended badly and he needed a support fixed to his shoe, so he was not really club-footed in the proper meaning of the term, but had a deformed leg. Maple had retired to the moors in northern England and for five years no one heard of him. Then he writes to his brother's widow and asks if her son will come in haste to his home near Congleton. The nephew has to follow complicated directions so as to avoid being stopped, and though he makes it to the uncle's home the two are suddenly in dire danger as the house is stormed by a group of sailors. The nephew eventually learns how his uncle had wronged these men, though both were up to no good. The story is fairly straightforward but is rescued by another of Doyle's ingenious ideas – one which Holmes would have doubtless detected in an instant, but which will almost certainly come as a surprise to the reader.

Ending the year was 'The Story of the Brazilian Cat', again leading the issue, and again with a striking frontispiece by Sidney Paget. This is more of a terror story than one of horror, and the frontispiece somewhat gives it away. It is essentially the story of a man who finds himself locked in a cage with a black puma, and the suspense lies in whether he will survive or find some way to escape. It is a tense story, but contains no mystery.

The first story of the New Year, 'The Story of the Japanned Box', leads with a frontispiece by Sidney Paget of two men facing each other, one seated and the other clearly angry. This is one of the weakest of the stories

as although it does present a puzzle, and perhaps one that Victorian readers
may not instantly have grasped, it is really only a new working of the use
of a phonograph that Doyle had used in his first *Strand* story, 'The Voice
of Science'. It is a touching story, but with little mystery.

The next story, though, sees Doyle back on top form, as it's another
locked-room mystery, 'The Story of the Jew's Breast-plate', with yet another
Paget frontispiece. Although the illustration is a fairly mundane one of a
woman claiming her loyalty to another, any other attempt at a dramatic
scene would have given away the ending, something that always annoyed
Doyle. Another first-person narrative, it tells of a bizarre event at a museum
which held many ancient Egyptian and other antiquities. Among them
was a breast-plate which would have been owned by the High Priest of
the Jews, resplendent with gemstones known as the *urim* and *thummim*, used
by the High Priest to divine God's wishes. It becomes clear that someone
is trying to steal the stones as each morning there are scratches upon the
breast-plate as if someone had tried to remove them, although they remain
firmly in place. Yet the room in which the object is held is locked and is
regularly patrolled. Doyle scores a double bluff, as not only does he propose
a simple but easily overlooked way in which someone gets into the room,
he also springs a surprise in terms of what is happening to the jewels.

'The Story of B24' leads the March 1899 issue, again with a Paget frontispiece showing an old man slumped in a chair, a younger man being held
by the police, and a woman asking that he should not be hurt, but to let
the law take its course. It beckons you into a story which is told by a prisoner found guilty of murder but still protesting his innocence. The solution
is another clever Doyle twist which would not have fooled Holmes for an
instant, but is nevertheless an ingenious depiction of the perfect murder. It
is also another of Doyle's stories featuring a strong-minded woman.

'The Story of the Latin Tutor'[87] led the April 1899 issue, following
an announcement by George Newnes that this was the one hundredth
number. Paget's frontispiece shows two men grappling and a third
shouting 'Let Him Go.' It's not as compelling a story as the others. It
tells of a particularly nasty teacher at a private school and the hold he
has over the headmaster. The mystery is what that hold is, and though

[87] When collected in *Round the Fire Stories* in 1908 this was retitled 'The Usher of Lea House
School'.

the narrator intends to find out, when he does it is in rather mundane circumstances. The solution is, perhaps, a surprise, but Doyle's ingenuity here is not as commanding as in the other stories.

The final story in the series, 'The Story of the Brown Hand', is one of the best, and the only supernatural one. Paget's frontispiece shows an old man bursting into a room where a younger man is pointing at an amputated hand on the floor. The story is related by the nephew of a retired famed surgeon, Sir Dominick Holden, who had earned a distinguished reputation in India. The nephew visits him and sees that the once unflinching surgeon is reduced to a fragile individual. The uncle shows his nephew his laboratory, which holds several specimen

" MY DOOR FLEW OPEN AND SIR DOMINICK RUSHED IN."

Frontispiece by Sidney Paget for 'The Story of the Brown Hand' (from *The Strand*, May 1899).

jars that had survived a fire in India. The nephew stays the night in the room and witnesses the ghost of an Indian man searching through the exhibits. Apparently he is searching for his hand, which the surgeon had amputated, but as the hand had been lost in the fire, the ghost searches in vain. Doyle follows the nephew's resolve to lay the ghost to rest and relieve his uncle of the nightly stress and this, along with the build-up of atmosphere, makes it a most satisfactory story.

At one point the nephew tells of his experiences with the Psychical Research Society, when he had formed one of a committee of three who had spent the night in a haunted house. Doyle had undertaken just such an investigation. He had joined the Society for Psychical Research in 1893, though prior to this had been involved with the Society because of his interest in telepathy. In June 1894, along with the Society members Frank Podmore and Sydney Scott, Doyle visited the house of Colonel Elmore at Charmouth in Dorset. Elmore, who had served in the Second Afghan War, was concerned over noises that could be heard in the house at night.

Unfortunately Doyle's accounts of the event differ over time. The most contemporary was in a letter to James Payn where he stated that the house was occupied by an Irish family and not the Colonel. Their investigation spread over two nights, at the end of which Podmore concluded it was a hoax set up by the son, and Doyle seemed to agree with this. When he later recounted the episode to Jerome K. Jerome, however, Doyle apparently told him that the house, this time in Somerset, was occupied by Elmore and his family and that they decided it was a hoax perpetrated by the Colonel's middle-aged daughter. Yet when Doyle wrote up the account for *Memories and Adventures* the story had changed again. This time he does not say who lived in the house and although the report of the noises is the same, like a cudgel being rapped heavily on a table, they find no evidence. When Podmore left the house with the 'young master', there were no more sounds.[88]

---

[88] The letter to Payn is discussed in Lycett (215–216). Jerome's account is in *My Life and Times* (174). The later account is in 'Early Psychic Experiences', *Pearson's Magazine*, March 1924, pp. 207–208. Here Doyle also related that some years later the house burned down and the skeleton of a ten-year-old child was exhumed in the garden. Doyle suggested it might have been this child's unsettled spirit that caused the noises. I have not been able to identify a Colonel Elmore living in Dorset or Somerset at that time, nor one who served in the Afghan Wars. His name may have been changed to protect his identity. Neither have I located any newspaper report of a child's body being found in a garden after a house fire in either county between 1894 and 1923.

Doyle's and Jerome's later recollections of the investigation may have become distorted, but it seems likely that this investigation provided some of the inspiration for the story.

Doyle wrote two further stories for *The Strand* which were collected in the *Round the Fire* volume, but were not identified as such in the magazine – 'Playing With Fire' (March 1900) and 'The Leather Funnel' (June 1903). Both are supernatural and reflect Doyle's interest in psychic research. 'Playing with Fire' is really in two parts. It concerns a séance, the first part of which is a discussion between the medium and her spiritual host about what life is like on the other side. Then one of the group, an over-zealous Frenchman, decides to experiment and try a manifestation, based on images already present in the room. The result is a frightened and therefore extremely dangerous unicorn.

'The Leather Funnel' unites Doyle's interest in the supernatural and history. The narrator, an antiquarian, visits an old friend, Lionel Dacre, in Paris, on the same street where Doyle's godfather Michael Conan had lived. Dacre is a student of the occult with a fabulous library and collection of artefacts. The narrator shows an interest in an old leather funnel and the discussion turns to the subject of psychometry. Dacre maintains that if you sleep with an object that has a violent history you will experience that in your dreams. The narrator does so and has a nightmare of a cruel-looking woman who is being tortured for having murdered her husband and two brothers. The torture is to have three pails of water poured down her throat through the leather funnel. Doyle based the story on the actual torture of the Marquise de Brinvilliers in 1676.

Greenhough Smith later ranked this story alongside 'The Lord of Château Noir' – both of which involve torture – as having 'never been excelled by any writer in the world'.[89] Yet at the time he delayed publishing it. The story had already appeared in *McClure's Magazine* for November 1902, but in April 1903 Doyle was enquiring of Smith whether he had decided to publish it, as otherwise he would sell it elsewhere. Smith may have hesitated because of the torture scene, which Doyle told him

[89] H. Greenhough Smith, 'Some Letters of Conan Doyle', *Strand*, October 1930, p. 394.

" THERE WERE TWO STRANGE EYES GLOWING AT US."

Frontispiece by Sidney Paget for 'Playing with Fire' (from *The Strand*, March 1900).

Sam McClure had urged him to include in detail. He told Smith, 'I think myself I have got the happy mean – the horror without the coarseness – but of course the thing must be gruesome – that is what it is for.'[90]

---

[90] Undated, unpublished letter from Doyle to Smith [UVa116].

Smith ran the story in the June 1903 issue, illustrated by Amedée Forestier, but then Doyle complained that the formatting of one of the illustrations had spoiled the story. Having noted that the story was 'literature, or as near literature as I can ever produce', Doyle added, 'It is not right to print such a story two words to the line on each side of an unnecessary illustration.'[91]

One might read into this that Doyle was getting rather too big for his boots – but they were, of course, very large boots. It was only the previous year that Doyle had boosted *The Strand*'s circulation to unprecedented levels with the return of Sherlock Holmes in *The Hound of the Baskervilles*, a story which clearly built on the atmosphere of his Round the Fire stories by combining the frisson of horror with a compelling and fascinating mystery.

---

[91] Undated letter from Doyle, reproduced in Lellenberg, *Letters* (516).

8

The Return of Sherlock Holmes

DOYLE'S ROUND THE FIRE STORIES showed that he had lost none of his flair for creating puzzling situations full of atmosphere and suspense. Despite his preference for historical fiction he could not deny his ability to baffle readers with a challenging situation.

His mind inevitably returned to Sherlock Holmes, but this time for the stage. He revised his earlier opinion that, because his deep thinking and logical abduction was not sufficiently theatrical, Holmes would not work on the stage, and in late 1897 he drafted a script based loosely on 'A Scandal in Bohemia'. It was sent to the theatrical impresario Herbert Beerbohm Tree, who visited Doyle to discuss it, but made so many suggestions that Doyle began to doubt its viability and set it aside.

Nevertheless the theatrical world was now aware of the play and the American actor William Gillette, who was then in London, became interested. According to Harold J. Shepstone, who wrote an article about Gillette for *The Strand* (December 1901), Gillette was alerted by his manager, Charles Frohman, to a newspaper report – which asserted that Doyle had said if anyone should play Holmes, it should be Gillette.[92] Doyle had said no such thing, and had not even met Gillette, although by the 1890s the actor had a formidable reputation. Gillette studied people intensely – he had once pretended to be a doctor in order to observe how different patients presented themselves – and used little emotion himself on stage, preferring to show his mood through the use of props. Gillette's father, a former US

---

[92] Shepstone wrote that this item appeared in an obscure American newspaper, but Richard Lancelyn Green discovered it originated in the London *Daily Mail*. See Green, *Uncollected* (81).

William Gillette as Sherlock Holmes in the play he adapted from Doyle's work, performed at the London Lyceum in 1901 (from *The Strand*, December 1901).

senator and abolitionist, was friends with Mark Twain, and it was through Twain's influence that Gillette gained his introduction to the stage.

When Frohman showed Gillette the journalist's comments he smiled, as he also felt the Holmes stories would be impossible to dramatise. However, they agreed to contact Doyle and see if they could use the name on a royalty basis. Doyle agreed and, at that stage, either he or Tree must have forwarded his version of the play to Frohman.

It was some months before Gillette found time to consider the play. In the autumn of 1898, he cabled Doyle asking what liberties he could take with the character, including 'May I marry Holmes?' Doyle responded, rather heartlessly as he later admitted, 'You may marry or murder or do what you like with him.' Doyle's offhand remark suggests he could not care less about Holmes, though he was increasingly pleased with the prospect of Gillette's adaptation and believed it would bring in substantial revenue. He later recorded, 'I was charmed both with the play, the acting, and the pecuniary result.'[93]

Gillette drafted the play in just four weeks, having acquainted himself with the existing stories and developed a plot of his own, still loosely based on Doyle's script. It also featured Professor Moriarty and, rather than Irene Adler, there is a young lady called Alice Faulkner who has in her possession certain incriminating papers that various factions are after, including an unscrupulous couple, the Larrabees, who have taken Faulkner under their

ACT III. THE TURNING-POINT IN THE PLAY—HERE SHERLOCK HOLMES ACCUSES
From a Photo. by]   LARRABEE OF ROBBERY.   [*Byron, New York.*

Another dramatic scene from Gillette's play *Sherlock Holmes* in 1901 (from *The Strand*, December 1901).

---

[93] Doyle, 'Memories and Adventures', *Strand*, January 1924, p. 93. His diary accounts show that he received substantial royalties from the play over several years.

wing. Having written the play, Gillette took a two-week break in San Francisco at the end of November 1898. Unfortunately the Baldwin Hotel, in which the copy of the play and Doyle's draft were lodged, was destroyed by fire, and Gillette had to completely rewrite it. The play's programme generously co-credited it to Doyle, but it was all Gillette's work.

He showed the final version to Doyle in May 1899 and, for the purposes of copyright, the play received a single performance at London's Duke of York's Theatre on 12 June. Its first formal run began in New York at the Garrick Theatre on 6 November 1899, where it continued for 150 performances until June 1900 before going on tour. Its English run began at London's Lyceum Theatre on 9 September 1901 and ran to the following April. It was a resounding commercial success and earned Doyle a considerable income. The play continued to tour for years, with further revivals in London and New York. Gillette was to play Holmes in over 1,300 performances.[94]

The success must have encouraged Doyle to think again about Holmes, but he did not do anything immediately. There was in any case the problem of the Boer War to contend with. This had erupted on 11 October 1899 when the British refused to withdraw their troops from the borders of the Transvaal and Orange Free State. Doyle believed it was his patriotic duty to volunteer to fight. He wrote to *The Times*:

> There are thousands of men riding after foxes or shooting pheasants who would gladly be useful to their country if it were made possible for them.[95]

Doyle's mother objected to him seeing active service, but a compromise was achieved when Doyle offered to provide medical services for a private field hospital which was supplementing the overworked Royal Army Medical Corps.

Doyle left for South Africa at the start of March 1900 and was back in England at the end of July, so was away for just five months. The only piece he wrote about it for *The Strand* was 'A Glimpse of the Army' in the September 1900 issue, which I shall discuss in Chapter 11. What was of more interest for readers of *The Strand* was what happened on the return voyage.

One of the fellow journalists with whom he struck up a friendship

---

[94] The fourteen-year-old Charlie Chaplin played the role of Billie the Page Boy on tour in 1903, and performed with William Gillette in the 1905 London revival.

[95] A. Conan Doyle, 'Volunteers and the War', *The Times*, 18 December 1899, p. 11.

was Bertram Fletcher Robinson, a correspondent for the *Daily Express*. The two found they had many sporting interests in common, and it was when they subsequently took a short golfing holiday together at Cromer in Norfolk, in late April 1901,[96] that Robinson told Doyle about a Dartmoor legend of a giant hound that terrorised the neighbourhood. Before their holiday was over they had planned to write a creepy horror tale together, which became *The Hound of the Baskervilles*.

At that stage it was not planned as a Holmes novel, and when Doyle sent a letter to Greenhough Smith checking his interest for such a serial, he made no mention of Holmes. He also requested that the payment be his standard £50 per thousand words and that the credit upon publication should be jointly with Fletcher Robinson. However, once Doyle thought about the plot in earnest he realised he needed a strong central character, and Holmes came immediately to mind. Only a few months before, in an interview published in *Tit-Bits* on 15 December 1900, Doyle remarked that while he did not regret killing Holmes, there was 'no limit to the number of papers he left behind …', so the door remained open.

What's more, with the London run of Gillette's *Sherlock Holmes* about to start in September, it provided an ideal opportunity for cross-promotion. So Doyle wrote again to Greenhough Smith in early May, putting to him the option that it either be a non-series novel at £50 per thousand words, or a Sherlock Holmes novel for which he asked £100 per thousand – a quite unprecedented amount. Smith and Newnes had no qualms. Holmes it would be.

This provided an opportunity to curtail a series that Doyle had started but which was not proceeding well, 'Strange Studies from Life', which explored historical crime cases. The first, 'The Holocaust of Manor Place', in the March 1901 *Strand*, recounted the crimes of William Godfrey Youngman who early one morning in 1860 murdered his two brothers, his future wife and his mother. He blamed the first three murders on his mother and claimed he had killed her in self-defence. No one believed him, so it was a simple trial and he was soon hanged. The second, 'The Love Affair of

---

[96] Doyle and Robinson's golfing holiday is usually dated as March 1901, based on his letter to his mother from Cromer [see Lellenberg, *Letters* (477)]. Lellenberg notes, though, that Doyle 'had a tendency to be careless with dates' (13). In the letter Doyle mentions a dinner he is giving at the Athenaeum Club with Winston Churchill as one of the guests. By checking data from Churchill's records Richard Lancelyn Green calculated that the dinner was held on 30 April and that Doyle was therefore in Norfolk on 28 April.

George Vincent Parker' (actually George Vincent Townley, with a name change to save distress to living relatives), was another straightforward case. Townley became engaged to a young girl, though opposition from both families led to a more clandestine affair. The girl met another and asked to be freed from their engagement. Townley pleaded with her, and in his rage he killed her. He openly admitted it, and his fate rested on whether he was considered sane. A first report suggested his sanity was in question, so he was reprieved, even though a second report believed he was sane. His sentence was commuted to penal servitude. The final study, 'The Debatable Case of Mrs Emsley', raised the matter of reasonable doubt. Though Doyle believed the evidence suggested that George Mullins 'probably' killed the wealthy widow Mary Emsley, he was not wholly convinced and suspected that had the Scottish verdict of 'Not Proven' been available in England it would have prevailed in this case. Doyle believed in the oft-quoted dictum that 'it is better that ninety-nine guilty should escape than that one innocent man should suffer'.

While Doyle did his best to make the cases interesting, by analysing the criminal's state of mind, the ones he had chosen were all straightforward and he could not introduce his usual ingenious twist or puzzle; he rapidly tired of the series. When he submitted the first three manuscripts to Greenhough Smith he quite expected them to be rejected and said that he had found it hard to come to an opinion about them. Smith published them because Doyle's name on the cover always improved sales, but complaints were soon received from relatives of those discussed. The series was dropped and Doyle returned to Holmes.

At the end of May 1901, Doyle and Robinson undertook a trip to Dartmoor to develop the plot and locale. Doyle was shown Robinson's family home at Ipplepen on the southern edge of the Moor, where the coachman and general domestic was Henry Baskerville. It is usually believed that Doyle appropriated his name, but as he had already written the first chapter and the title of the book was fixed, the name had clearly already been chosen. It was probably suggested by Robinson, perhaps because of the family retainer, although there were several families called Baskerville in the area as identified on the 1901 Census.

Robinson's other writing commitments meant he was unable to contribute as much as they had originally planned, and the final version is entirely Doyle's. In all likelihood once Doyle decided it would be a detective story rather than a supernatural one, he would have become possessive about Holmes. Nevertheless when the first episode appeared, Doyle added

Sidney Paget's frontispiece for 'The Hound of the Baskervilles' (from *The Strand*, August 1901).

a footnote:'This story owes its inception to my friend, Mr Fletcher Robinson, who has helped me both in the general plot and in the local details.'

Just how much Robinson contributed has always been a contentious subject. Some have argued that Robinson wrote the entire novel, even though such manuscript pages that survive are in Doyle's handwriting. In his reminiscences, Archibald Marshall, who had been friends with Robinson since they were at university, said that he 'wrote most of its first instalment for the *Strand Magazine*'.[97] That doesn't seem likely, as the first episode begins with Holmes ingeniously identifying much of the character of a prospective client from a walking cane left in his study, including the breed of his dog.

[97] Marshall (5).

That is pure Doyle. It is more likely that Robinson contributed the details of the Baskerville legend. Part of Chapter II includes an account of an ancient manuscript, which tells of the Baskerville curse. As this includes some local detail, it's possible that Robinson had either drafted this, or while still in Cromer, that Robinson and Doyle wrote it together.[98]

The story was rushed into print with the first episode, again illustrated by Paget, in the August 1901 issue. So anxious was Smith to publish it that the first episode appeared even before the previous serial, H. G. Wells's 'The First Men in the Moon', had finished. Much has been said about how the re-appearance of Holmes added to *The Strand*'s sales. Reginald Pound claimed it increased by 30,000 copies, or about 10 per cent.[99] Other claims are that the August issue had to go back to press seven times to meet demand, that people were forming long queues at newsagents, and that libraries had to stay open longer so that people could read the current issue. Richard Lancelyn Green discovered that the sales of the American edition of *The Strand* rose by nearly 200,000 copies during the serial.[100]

Whatever the actual sales, it is certain Newnes believed Doyle was worth every penny. Pound recalled he was paid between £480 and £620 per episode, according to length. In total Doyle received £4,795, the equivalent of almost £465,000 in today's terms. And that was only the serial rights.[101]

The Hound of the Baskervilles is the best known of the Holmes canon, partly because it is a novel and almost certainly because it is so sensational, with its almost gothic atmosphere. The first episode, which runs to ten pages, has everything the Holmes enthusiast would want, starting with Holmes's analysis of the walking cane. When the client, Mr Mortimer, returns we have the regular scene of him settling down in Holmes's consulting room, with Watson, to relate the nature of the problem. This includes outlining the Baskerville legend, which allows Doyle to insert a brief historical episode. The family curse seems to have come back to life, as Mortimer reports that Sir Charles Baskerville's body had been found

---

[98] It may be that Chapter II was the first chapter composed, and so may well have been drafted by Robinson, with Doyle adding Chapter I once it became a Holmes story.

[99] Pound, *Strand* (74). Pound also said that Doyle 'was alone in being able to send up the circulation, which responded immediately a new story by him was announced'. *Maypole* (10).

[100] Green, *Bibliography* (130).

[101] Payments for the nine instalments varied from £390 to £620. The advances for the UK and US book editions added a further £3,384 (around £328,000 in today's terms).

with all the appearance that he had died of fright. Nearby were some foot-prints. The episode ends with the immortal words, 'Mr Holmes, they were the footprints of a gigantic hound.'

It is also in the first episode that Holmes says, in response to Watson's deductions about Mortimer's walking cane, 'Interesting, though elemen-tary.' Much has been written about where the phrase 'Elementary, my dear Watson' came from, and it's certainly not a form of words Doyle used. But he did use the single word 'Elementary' several times, starting in 'The Adventure of the Crooked Man' in the August 1893 *Strand*. William Gillette must have seen it there and, in the play, he used 'Ele-mentary, my dear fellow.' Doyle did not use the word again until 'The Disappearance of Lady Frances Carfax' in the December 1911 *Strand*, and even here it is not in that style, but refers to Holmes's 'elementary class of deduction'. So it's use in *The Hound of the Baskervilles*, coming so soon after Doyle would have read Gillette's final script, suggests it may have prompted him to use it. But it was Gillette's version that passed into the public consciousness.[102]

Of particular import in *The Hound of the Baskervilles* is that, despite Doyle's growing spiritualist beliefs, he did not have Holmes explore the supernatural. He told Dr Mortimer:

> I have hitherto confined my investigations to this world. […] In a modest way I have combated evil, but to take on the Father of Evil himself would, perhaps, be too ambitious a task.

Later he made a similar judgement:

> The devil's agents may be of flesh and blood, may they not? There are two questions waiting for us at the outset. The one is whether any crime has been committed at all, the second is, what is the crime and how was it committed? Of course, if Dr Mortimer's surmise should be correct, and we are dealing with forces outside the ordinary laws of Nature, there is an end of our investigation. But we are bound to exhaust all other hypotheses before falling back upon this one.

---

[102] As did Gillette's other initiatives. He popularised the deerstalker hat already illustrated by Paget but not otherwise used by Doyle, and he introduced the curved pipe, which was necessary to allow him to talk audibly on the stage, whereas a straight pipe was inhibiting. P. G. Wodehouse may well have coined the phrase 'Elementary, my dear Watson' as he was a devoted Holmes fan and he used that phrase in his novel *Psmith, Journalist*, first serialised in *The Captain* from October 1909 to March 1910.

In this adventure, the above is the closest Holmes came to quoting his noted dictum about ruling out the impossible, while still allowing Doyle his beliefs. Holmes would not investigate a supernatural mystery, but he did not entirely rule it out.

The phenomenal success of *The Hound of the Baskervilles* further enhanced Doyle's already considerable reputation. Many would argue that he had become the best known and most popular writer of his day, with the possible exception of Rudyard Kipling. Alas, it did little to enhance the career of Fletcher Robinson, a writer virtually unknown today yet clearly the source of Doyle's best-known and most profitable work.

Doyle did pay Robinson for his contribution. The original arrangement, at least as per the recollections of Robinson's friend Archibald Marshall, was that Robinson should receive a quarter of all income. That means of the £4,795 for the publication in *The Strand*, Robinson should have received £1,200, with a further share of book sales. Marshall was, though, recalling events thirty years before, so may have misremembered, or it may be that the share was renegotiated once it was clear Robinson could not contribute as much as first planned, especially as it now featured Sherlock Holmes. Doyle sent Robinson a cheque for just over £500 at the end of 1901, and there were some later, smaller payments.[103] There have been persistent allegations that Doyle and Robinson's relationship soured, even to the extent that Doyle conspired in Robinson's death, but there is no evidence for this at all.[104] Rather the opposite – Doyle and Robinson continued to meet when opportunity allowed. Tragically, Robinson died of typhoid in London, after drinking impure water in Paris, on 21 January 1907, aged only thirty-six.[105]

★

As far as Doyle was concerned *The Hound of the Baskervilles* was a one-off. After a frenetic eleven days, when he churned out a 60,000–word pamphlet, *The War in South Africa*, in which he challenged the defamation

---

[103] Lycett (279).

[104] See in particular Rodger Garrick-Steele, *The House of the Baskervilles*.

[105] Robinson was a prolific contributor to the newspapers and magazines. For devotees of crime fiction his books *The Trail of the Dead* (1904) and *The Chronicles of Addington Peace* (1905) are of special interest.

that had arisen in many countries over how the British had acted in South Africa – a pamphlet that almost certainly contributed to his knighthood in June 1902 – he turned to writing a new series of Brigadier Gerard stories and a Brigadier Gerard play. But the genie was now out of the bottle. The considerable popularity of the serial showed the earning power of Sherlock Holmes.[106] Greenough Smith wanted to secure Doyle's work for *The Strand* and offered him a retainer but Doyle declined, though he assured Smith that *The Strand* would always have first refusal on future work.

However, fortunes were soon to change. The American magazine *Collier's* was on the rise. At the start of 1903 it had appointed a new editor, Norman Hapgood, with responsibility for developing its identity as a crusading magazine on social and political issues. This allowed Robert Collier, who had overall responsibility for the magazine, to concentrate on its fiction content. He was on the lookout for major authors to help boost circulation. He contacted Doyle and offered to pay $25,000 (about £5,140) for six stories, $30,000 for eight or $45,000 (£9,250) for thirteen. These were unheard-of sums, and Doyle responded. 'Very well,' he said, by postcard. Although Collier had wanted all serial rights, Doyle only let him have the US rights, knowing he could get up to another £100 per thousand words for the UK rights in *The Strand*.[107]

What was surprising is that although Doyle had left the way open to write cases before Holmes's apparent death at Reichenbach Falls, he chose to show that Holmes had not died at all, and this opened the floodgates. Despite later attempts to curtail the series, Doyle would continue to write new Holmes stories on and off for the next twenty-five years.

Doyle's mother had reservations about more stories, fearing that her son might not be able to sustain the originality and quality, and that the public may tire of them. Doyle had the same concerns as he struggled to find decent plots. He was fine for the first three or four but then found the going tough, and at one point he was going to stop. But the lure of $45,000 (about £900,000 today) sustained him.

---

[106] In the December 1905 *Strand* a staff writer (possibly Smith himself) acknowledged that the name of Sherlock Holmes had 'passed into a household word in many languages'. See 'The Funniest Picture I Have Ever Published' (p. 623), which reproduced a cartoon by Lyonel Feininger from the German magazine *Lustige Blätter* depicting 'Sherlock Holmes's Latest Problem'.

[107] For the first story Doyle received £675 for the American publication and £787 for the English.

Doyle had help for ideas from others. His close lady-friend, Jean Leckie, who would become his second wife in September 1907, suggested the idea for the first story, 'The Adventure of the Empty House', in which Holmes explains his escape from certain death, entraps an old enemy and, almost incidentally, solves a locked-room murder.

The second story, 'The Adventure of the Norwood Builder', may also owe something to Jean Leckie, as part of the story is set in Blackheath, where her family lived, while Norwood had been Doyle's old hunting ground. But the decisive part of the story – how someone's fingerprint could be left by someone else at the scene of the crime – had been suggested by Fletcher Robinson.[108] Greenhough Smith, though, told Doyle that not all readers felt the story was up to standard, which rattled Doyle. He responded:

> 'The Norwood Builder' I would put in the first rank of the whole series for subtlety and depth. Any feeling of disappointment at the end is due to the fact that no crime has been done, and so the reader feels bluffed, but it is well for other reasons to have some of the stories crimeless. Take the series of points: Holmes's deductions from the will written in the train, the point of the bloody thumb-mark, Holmes's device for frightening the man out of his hiding-place, etc. I know of no Holmes story which has a succession of bright points.[109]

Bright points these may be, but the story actually has a major weakness, namely that the supposed charred ashes of the victim are found in a fire, and yet such bones as are found Holmes conjectures must be those of a dog or a rabbit. If neither the police nor Holmes can distinguish between human bones and those of a rabbit or dog, then it is a poor show.

Smith also remarked that the third submitted story, 'The Adventure of the Solitary Cyclist' seemed weak, perhaps because Holmes has such a small part. Doyle agreed it was 'not up to the mark', and asked for its return. In the meantime he completed the next story, 'The Adventure of the Dancing Men', which became the third published. This involves a series of cryptograms in the form of a set of childlike images of dancing men. Doyle started the story in Norfolk and got the idea of the dancing

---

[108] See Pugh & Spiring (122).
[109] Letter by Doyle quoted in 'Some Letters of Conan Doyle', *Strand*, October 1930, p. 392.

men from the young son of the hotel landlady. Even though Holmes is thwarted from stopping a murder, the way he cracks the code and solves the crime is up to the best of the series.

With 'The Solitary Cyclist' strengthened, Doyle submitted 'The Adventure of the Priory School', which also came in for criticism when readers argued that you cannot tell the direction of travel of a bicycle by the impression of its wheels. Doyle soon put a stop to that objection, writing to Greenhough Smith:

> I don't suppose you take much notice about what cranks write, but with regard to the letters you may be interested to know that I have been out, tried it on my bike, and got the impressions as in the story, the hind wheel cutting across the line of the front one.[110]

Doyle was not too happy with the next story, 'The Adventure of Black Peter', which had taken a month to complete, calling it 'carpenter's work'. At the time he submitted it, he remarked that Sidney Paget's illustrations for the stories had been superb. However, soon after 'Black Peter' was published, Doyle was back on his hobbyhorse about artwork.

> What a pity the pictures are not better chosen. There is none there to induce anyone to read the story. The story would be better without them. Fancy a picture of 'Black Peter' with his beard to the ceiling and a great harpoon driven through him. That's ginger![111]

This bickering between Doyle and Smith seemed out of character, but there was clearly acrimony on both sides. Doyle almost regretted having accepted the offer from *Collier's*. He told Smith that although the Americans had wanted twelve, he was going to stop at eight. He believed it was impossible to avoid a 'sameness' and a 'lack of freshness'. Nevertheless he did say to Smith, who was obviously disturbed that he might have upset Doyle: 'You will never offend me, my dear chap, by saying what you think.'[112]

Doyle continued to write as ideas came to him. After submitting 'Black Peter' he told Smith he had a 'real good No. 7' in his head.' This became 'The Adventure of Charles Augustus Milverton', and is a decidedly

---

[110] *Ibid.*
[111] Unpublished, undated letter from Doyle to Smith [UVa020].
[112] Letter, Doyle to Smith, 14 May 1903, reproduced in Lellenberg, *Letters* (514).

uncharacteristic story in which Holmes not only turns burglar, he effects a disguise so that he can become engaged to a maid, and he witnesses a murder but prefers that the killer goes free. This aside, though, Doyle enjoyed playing with the reader by setting a clue to the murderer's identity but revealing nothing.

Smith had clearly been disgruntled that Doyle had agreed the sale of the Holmes stories with *Collier's* first, rather than with him. It meant the stories could be used only in the British edition of *The Strand* and not the American, where sales had been lucrative. Yet, as the above shows, Doyle submitted his stories to Smith first, valuing his advice, and submitted them to *Collier's* only after Smith had accepted them. Moreover *The Strand* tended to get the stories into print first, or a few days after *Collier's*. 'The Adventure of the Empty House' appeared in *Collier's* on 26 September 1903. At that time *Collier's* went on sale two days before its issue date, so it was available on 24 September. *The Strand* usually appeared three or four days prior to the first of the month, depending on when weekends fell, so the October 1903 issue was probably available on 27 September. There after *The Strand* printing more often than not came out first, especially after the eighth story when there was a gap in *Collier's* running of the stories. 'The Adventure of the Three Students' appeared in the June 1904 *Strand* but not until the 24 September issue of *Collier's*. The final story, 'The Adventure of the Second Stain', was delayed and did not appear until the December 1904 *Strand* and the 28 January 1905 *Collier's*.

Although Smith had the satisfaction of publishing most stories first, this did little to ameliorate the problem of having to find material to replace the stories in the American edition of *The Strand*. Once again James Walter Smith had to use his initiative as he had when denied Doyle's 'Rodney Stone'. There was a big difference though between that serial and the return of Sherlock Holmes. Smith had nothing comparable to incorporate. Because he worked from Newnes's London office he had access to material in the inventory so he could occasionally use a story planned for a future issue of the British *Strand*, or he could reprint something from one of Newnes's other magazines such as *Fry's* or *The Captain*, but there was no headline material, and there's little doubt that sales of the American *Strand* suffered.

Collier's had one other factor in its favour. In Britain, Sidney Paget had become the artist synonymous with Holmes, but *Collier's* needed a new artist. They commissioned Frederic Dorr Steele, who used as his model the well-known image of William Gillette. As a result, Steele's illustrations are full of character. Holmes is almost posing, and always looks pensive – you can almost see his mind working – whereas in Paget's he's often in action. Moreover the cover illustrations were in colour, usually only two tones – blue and brown or grey and sepia – but Steele used that to great effect. Steele's drawings were also closer to how Doyle had imagined Holmes. In 1900, when interviewed for *Tit-Bits*, Doyle had said:

> My own view of Sherlock Holmes – I mean the man as I saw him in my imagination – was quite different from that which Mr Paget pictured in the *Strand Magazine*. I, however, am eminently pleased with his work, and quite understand the aspect which he gave to the character, and am even prepared to accept him now as Mr Paget drew him. In my own mind, however, he was a more beaky-nosed, hawk-faced man, approaching more to the Red Indian type, than the artist represented him…[113]

'The Adventure of the Second Stain' was the last Holmes story Sidney Paget would illustrate. He died of a mediastinal tumour in his chest on 28 January 1908, aged only 47.

★

Once more Doyle maintained that he had finished with Holmes – he told the *Daily Mail* that his retirement was 'absolute and final'.[114] *Collier's Weekly* promoted 'The Adventure of the Second Stain' on its cover as 'The Last Adventure of Sherlock Holmes'.

Yet, as we know, Holmes would return. It's possible that the familiarity of writing about Holmes became therapeutic after a period of emotional turmoil. Doyle's wife, Louisa, finally lost her battle with tuberculosis on 4 July 1906. Doyle was grief-stricken. Despite what some believed, he really did love her, and he did his best to make sure her final years were as comfortable as possible. But Doyle was a very physical, passionate man, and in order to cope with the steady fading of Louisa, he needed the company of Jean Leckie, whom he had first met in 1897. He always

---

[113] 'Conan Doyle Tells the True Story of Sherlock Holmes', *Tit-Bits*, 15 December 1900, p. 287.
[114] See *Daily Mail*, 8 October 1904.

"A LITTLE, WIZENED MAN DARTED OUT."

A comparison of the illustrations by Sidney Paget and Frederic Dorr Steele for 'The Adventure of the Norwood Builder': the frontispiece for *The Strand* November 1903 (above) and the cover of *Collier's Weekly*, 31 October 1903 (opposite).

maintained that their relationship was platonic, but in the years up until Louisa's death there's no doubt that he and Jean bonded – and it was a love that sustained Doyle. To compensate Doyle threw himself into various crusades, most famously the miscarriage of justice in the case of George Edalji (see Chapter 16), which he wrote about extensively in the *Daily Telegraph* but not in *The Strand*. In fact 1907 was the only year from the magazine's birth in 1891 until Doyle's death in 1930 when he failed to make any contributions.

Doyle and Jean Leckie married on 18 September 1907. The service itself was a quiet affair, but there were many guests at the reception, held at the Hotel Métropole. These included Max Pemberton, Coulson Kernahan, George Edalji, Jerome K. Jerome, Bram Stoker and, of course, George Newnes and Herbert Greenhough Smith. After their honeymoon, the Doyles settled in a new home at Windlesham, near Crowborough, as the old house at Undershaw was full of too many memories of Louisa.[115]

---

[115] Doyle kept Undershaw until 1921, and rented it out.

A REVERIE.

Artist H. M. Brock shows Holmes musing over his various cases in 'A Reverie' from *The Strand*, March 1911.

It was from Windlesham that Doyle wrote to Greenhough Smith on 4 March 1908.

> I don't suppose, so far as I see, that I should write a new 'Sherlock Holmes' series but I see no reason why I should not do an occasional scattered story under some such heading as 'Reminiscences of Mr Sherlock Holmes' (extracted from the diaries of his friend, Dr James [sic] Watson). I have one pretty clear in my head and this, I think, really will mature. If you could fix it with Watt, it might do for your Midsummer number and perhaps I could dig out another for your Christmas number.[116]

Leaving aside the error of Watson's first name, an example of Doyle's not infrequent carelessness, this showed that although Doyle did not want the burden imposed by a set series, he liked the idea of an occasional story, and in this more liberated fashion he ended up writing another twenty adventures, including the novel, *The Valley of Fear*.[117]

I will mention some of these stories in later chapters, but for now, Table 3 lists the final twenty stories with both the British and American magazine publication dates and the artists. A look at the Table may surprise some at the variety of artists who illustrated the original Sherlock Holmes stories during Doyle's lifetime, after Paget's death. One of the British artists was Walter Paget, brother of Sidney, who had served as the original model for Holmes.[118] When Doyle was asked whom he thought was the best illustrator of Holmes he answered Frank Wiles, who illustrated the novel *The Valley of Fear* and the last three stories.[119] Doyle also appreciated the work of Arthur Twidle, and would have liked him to have illustrated more of his work, but Twidle had a disagreement with the art editor, William Boot, and did nothing more for *The Strand* after 1909.

---

[116] Unpublished letter, Doyle to Smith, 4 March 1908 [UVa241–3].

[117] Doyle also wrote a non-Holmes crime story, 'One Crowded Hour', in the August 1911 *Strand*. It concerns someone who turns highwayman to take revenge upon a banker whose poor advice had lost him all his money.

[118] Other artists depicted Holmes in cartoons, but not specific stories. In 'Twelve-Object Pictures' in the August 1912 *Strand* nine artists were given a list of twelve objects, all of which had to be included in one picture. The objects included Holmes himself, along with a flying machine, an Egyptian mummy, a shadow, a girl, a dog, a nurse, a cow, a beggar with a wooden leg, a barrel-organ and so on. Each artist briefly explained his picture. Heath Robinson depicted Holmes abducting the girl in an aeroplane. Other artists were H. M. Bateman, Fred Bennett, H. M. Brock, René Bull, A. Leete, George Morrow, Harry Rountree and Starr Wood.

[119] Wiles's depiction of Holmes was also the first to appear on the cover of the British edition of *The Strand* on September 1914, although the American *Strand* had first portrayed Holmes on the cover of its January 1911 issue, drawn by Gilbert Halliday.

Table 3: Doyle's final twenty Sherlock Holmes stories and their artists

Story	UK Publication		US Publication	
	Magazine/Date	Artist	Magazine/Date	Artist
The Singular Experience of Mr John Scott Eccles★	*Strand*, September 1908	Arthur Twidle	*Collier's Weekly*, August 15, 1908	Frederic Dorr Steele
The Tiger of San Pedro★	*Strand*, October 1908	Arthur Twidle		
The Adventure of the Bruce-Partington Plans	*Strand*, December 1908	Arthur Twidle	*Collier's Weekly*, December 12, 1908	Frederic Dorr Steele
The Adventure of the Devil's Foot	*Strand*, December 1910	Gilbert Halliday	*Strand*, January, February 1911	Gilbert Halliday
The Adventure of the Red Circle	*Strand*, March, April 1911	H. M. Brock & Joseph Simpson	*Strand*, April, May 1911	H. M. Brock & Joseph Simpson
The Disappearance of Lady Frances Carfax	*Strand*, December 1911	Alec Ball	*American Magazine*, December 1911	Frederic Dorr Steele
The Adventure of the Dying Detective	*Strand*, December 1913	Walter Paget	*Collier's Weekly*, November 22, 1913	Frederic Dorr Steele
The Valley of Fear	*Strand*, September 1914 to May 1915	Frank Wiles	Associated Sunday Magazines (distributed with *New York Tribune* and twelve other papers), September 20 to November 22, 1914	Arthur I. Keller
His Last Bow	*Strand*, September 1917	Alfred Gilbert	*Collier's Weekly*, September 22, 1917	Frederic Dorr Steele
The Adventure of the Mazarin Stone	*Strand*, October 1921	Alfred Gilbert	*Hearst's International*, November 1921	Frederic Dorr Steele
The Problem of Thor Bridge	*Strand*, February, March 1922	Alfred Gilbert	*Hearst's International*, February, March 1922	G. Patrick Nelson
The Adventure of the Creeping Man	*Strand*, March 1923	Howard K. Elcock	*Hearst's International*, March 1923	Frederic Dorr Steele
The Adventure of the Sussex Vampire	*Strand*, January 1924	Howard K. Elcock	*Hearst's International*, January 1924	W. T. Benda
The Adventure of the Three Garridebs	*Strand*, January 1925	Howard K. Elcock	*Collier's Weekly*, October 25, 1924	John R. Flanagan
The Adventure of the Illustrious Client	*Strand*, February, March 1925	Howard K. Elcock	*Collier's Weekly*, November 8, 1924	John R. Flanagan
The Adventure of the Three Gables	*Strand*, October 1926	Howard K. Elcock	*Liberty*, September 18, 1926	Frederic Dorr Steele
The Adventure of the Blanched Soldier	*Strand*, November 1926	Howard K. Elcock	*Liberty*, October 16, 1926	Frederic Dorr Steele
The Adventure of the Lion's Mane	*Strand*, December 1926	Howard K. Elcock	*Liberty*, November 27, 1926	Frederic Dorr Steele
The Adventure of the Retired Colourman	*Strand*, January 1927	Frank Wiles	*Liberty*, December 18, 1927	Frederic Dorr Steele
The Adventure of the Veiled Lodger	*Strand*, February 1927	Frank Wiles	*Liberty*, January 22, 1927	Frederic Dorr Steele
The Adventure of Shoscombe Old Place	*Strand*, April 1927	Frank Wiles	*Liberty*, March 5, 1927	Frederic Dorr Steele

★ Retitled 'The Adventure of Wisteria Lodge' for book publication.

The ideas for these twenty stories came from a wide range of sources, one of which was suggested by Greenhough Smith – 'The Problem of Thor Bridge'. Smith drew Doyle's attention to a case recorded in Germany in which a man wanted to commit suicide but planned it to look like murder so that his wife would still benefit from his life assurance. The suicide tied a stone around the handle of a revolver and shot himself; the stone fell into the river over a bridge parapet, taking the revolver with it. One of the detectives investigating the death noticed a chip in the bridge railing and, on having the stream dredged, found the revolver. When he learned of the case Doyle believed it was the most remarkable example on record of the application of Holmes's methods.[120]

Doyle was always being sent suggestions for stories, one of which was to pit Holmes against the gentleman-thief A. J. Raffles. Raffles was the creation of Doyle's brother-in-law Willie Hornung, and had first appeared in a series of stories in *Cassell's Magazine* in 1898. Hornung dedicated the first volume, *The Amateur Cracksman*, to Doyle, saying 'This Form of Flattery'. Doyle commented in his autobiography, written after Hornung's early death from pneumonia in 1921, that he told Willie he should never make a criminal the hero, as it was dangerous. Even so, it did not stop the success of the stories, and for a while Raffles was second only to Holmes in popularity.

Smith passed on an idea sent to *The Strand* about Holmes confronting Raffles, but Doyle was not interested:

> The Holmes-Raffles idea is a kind of recurrent thing which turns up every six months or so. One man in Yukon was so struck by it that he came all the way from there to Crowboro' to discuss it – at least, so he said. Personally I could not write such a thing. Inspiration would fail me.[121]

Words seldom failed Hornung, though, and Doyle believed he had a fine wit and a quick mind. He enjoyed quoting Willie's pun about Holmes, 'Though he might be more humble, there is no police like Holmes.'[122]

---

[120] The September 1922 *Strand* ran an article 'Sherlock Holmes in Real Life' by a barrister and former official of New Scotland Yard, which looked at remarkable feats of detective work conducted by various police forces and experts.

[121] Unpublished letter, Doyle to Smith, 14 April 1911 [UVa249]. It is worth noting that the American humourist John Kendrick Bangs managed to combine Raffles and Holmes by creating the character of Raffles Holmes in *R. Holmes & Co.* (1906). Raffles Holmes is the son of Sherlock Holmes and Raffles's daughter. There was an article about Raffles, 'Does "Raffles" Exist? or, the Myth of the Gentleman Burglar' by Alphonse Bertillon in the October 1913 *Strand*.

[122] Doyle, 'Memories and Adventures', *Strand*, April 1924, p. 344.

9

Back to the Past

HAVING FINISHED THE THIRTEEN STORIES for 'The Return of Sherlock Holmes', Arthur Conan Doyle determined to get back to historical fiction. He had long wanted to write a prequel to his early novel *The White Company*, the book that heralded his early success in 1891, but there never seemed to be the time. It was little wonder that he found having to work on the Sherlock Holmes stories an irritating diversion. At last during the summer of 1905 he settled down, dug out his old research papers, read further primary works and put pen to paper.

This book was to record the early life of the hero of *The White Company*, Sir Nigel Loring. Although based upon the historical character of Sir Nele Loring, one of the original knights honoured by Edward III with the Order of the Garter in 1348, it is best to forget the historical original because the book and its characters have a life of their own, set amid events related to the Hundred Years' War.

It is interesting that the concept of the numbered story series that Doyle introduced to *The Strand* in 1891, and which had made the magazine so distinctive and popular, was now the exception rather than the rule. Serials had returned. When 'Sir Nigel' began in the enlarged Christmas 1905 issue, *The Strand* was already running Edith Nesbit's serial for children, 'The Amulet' and, with the next issue, began Rudyard Kipling's 'Puck of Pook's Hill'. Both of these are regarded as children's books and that may explain why they are better known today than Doyle's novel, but it shows that the content and presentation of *The Strand* had been changing over the years, and Doyle's non-Holmes works had strong competition.

'Sir Nigel' should be better remembered because it is, in short, Doyle's masterpiece. In an era in which the popularity of the historical novel was waning, it stands head-and-shoulders above many rivals for its remarkable historical detail, its depth of knowledge, its stirring characters, its vivid adventures and its powerful evocation of a long-lost age. Throughout the story we marvel at Doyle's understanding of day-to-day life, from the care and maintenance of fishponds, to obscure medieval law, to falconry, to armoury and the sheer struggle of existence in the years following the Black Death.

Doyle wrote about his research in a symposium in 1924:

> My system, before writing such as book as 'Sir Nigel', was to read every-thing I could get about the age and to copy out into notebooks all that seemed distinctive. I would then cross-index this material by dividing it under the heads of the various types of character. Thus under Archer I would put all archery lore, and also what oaths an archer might use, where he might have been, what wars, etc., so as to make atmosphere in his talk. Under Monk I would have all about stained glass, illumination of missals, discipline, ritual, and so on. In this way if I had, for example, a conversation between a falconer and an armourer, I could make each draw similes from his own craft. All this seems wasted so far as the ephemeral criticism of the day goes, but it is the salt, nonetheless, which keeps the book from decay.[123]

The opening episode, which was longer because of the extra space of the Christmas issue, is as exciting as any could hope. Its opening scene, describing the countryside after the Black Death, is apocalyptic and seems to have remained with him when he later wrote 'The Poison Belt'. We see the last survivors of the Loring family who had once been knights and lords of renown, but now there is only a widowed grandmother and her grandson, Nigel, living in their old manor-house of Tilford and in debt to the nearby Abbey of Waverley. Nigel is a headstrong youth, though he's 22 when the novel starts, and is always in trouble with the Abbey, but he saves some monks who are set upon by an uncontrollable horse. Nigel is given the horse, chiefly because the monks hope it will endanger him,

---

[123] Doyle, 'How Our Novelists Write Their Books', *Strand*, December 1924, p. 644.

"WITH NEITHER SADDLE NOR STIRRUPS TO HELP HIM, AND THE BEAST RAMPING
AND REARING LIKE A MAD THING BENEATH HIM, HE WAS HARD
PRESSED TO HOLD HIS OWN."

Arthur Twidle's depiction of the young Nigel breaking the horse in 'Sir Nigel'
from *The Strand*, December 1905.

and in a thrilling chapter we see him mastering the beast, but only after a
magnificent, wild gallop across the Surrey Hills.

Doyle had commented to an interviewer that one problem with writing a novel you know is going to be serialised is that you tend to write

Back to the Past

it in instalments, ensuring that each episode ends with an exciting incident. That may be so, but the result is a book that drives the reader along
at a relentless and exhilarating pace. No sooner has Nigel tamed the
horse than he is hauled up before the Abbey Courts, only to be rescued
in a bizarre sequence of events by one of the great knights of history,
Sir John Chandos. Soon after he is battling with one of the wild men of
the woods (in an episode that suggests Doyle could have written a fine
Robin Hood novel had he chosen) and then finds himself made squire
to Sir John Chandos by the king himself, and is soon heading for France
to help in the defence of Calais. Doyle's description of the Battle of
Winchelsea is a superb example of how his depth of research is inter-
woven seamlessly into a stirring narrative.

One could argue that it is more in line with contemporary boys'
adventure serials than adult work, and certainly one can see compar-
isons with such as Robert Louis Stevenson's *The Black Arrow*, but this
is chiefly because of its stirring, heroic action, its sense of chivalry and
fair play, and its clean-cut characters. It may lack the psychological
insight and complex political motivations we have come to expect
from current historical works, but it makes up for it in its period
atmosphere and portrayal of another age. Like so much of Doyle's
writing, it works best if read aloud, emphasising again Doyle's skills
as a master storyteller.

When Doyle submitted the serial, he told Smith:

> I have put into it every ounce of research, fancy, fire and skill I possess. It
> rises to the very highest I have ever done or could do at the last.[124]

Doyle was never short of self-puffery, but here he was right. 'Sir Nigel'
is a first-class historical novel. When Doyle submitted it to the McClure
Syndicate in the United States – for this was another serial that did not
appear in the American *Strand* – the response was: 'We think Sir Nigel
the greatest of all historical romances.'[125]

The serial ran in *The Strand* from December 1905 to December 1906,
illustrated liberally by Arthur Twidle. In America the serial was syndicated
through the Associated Sunday Magazines network, in such newspapers
as the *New York Tribune* and *Baltimore Sunday Herald*, from 3 December

---

[124] Letter by Doyle to Smith, quoted in Lellenberg, *Letters* (529).
[125] Unpublished letter by Doyle to Smith, about December 1905 [UVa033]

1905 to 15 April 1906, illustrated by Joseph Clement Coll. It was thus completed in America long before it finished in Britain, and the American book edition from McClure, Phillips appeared first, on 1 October, while the British edition from Smith, Elder, was published on 15 November.

Doyle did very well financially from the novel. He received £5,776 (after Watt's commission) from *The Strand*. The US serial rights went for $25,000, or roughly £5,200, so for the magazine publication alone Doyle received £10,976, or close to £1 million today. The book sales were in addition, and both the British and American editions sold well, earning him at least another £1,900 (almost £200,000 today).

The critics recognised its strength as an adventure novel, but Doyle was disappointed that they did not also recommend it for the historical detail and encouragement of chivalric virtue. Once again Doyle felt that his qualities as a historical novelist were overshadowed by what he considered his lesser work, namely Sherlock Holmes and, to a degree, the light-hearted Brigadier Gerard.

Nevertheless, while 'Sir Nigel' was being serialised, *The Strand* ran a feature on what symbol or badge ought best represent an author and his work. It called them 'totems'. Each badge presented the author's initials alongside an image instantly related to their work. Jerome K. Jerome, not surprisingly, had three men rowing a boat. H. G. Wells had a Saturn-like planet. As for Doyle, the author of the piece, Stephen Hallett, said that initially one might think a pair of handcuffs would be the most fitting totem, but he continued:

> Sir Arthur has hoped of being best remembered in another and more classic vein, of which 'The White Company' and 'Sir Nigel' are examples. Certainly the 'Song of the Bow' is a fine performance.'[126]

'Song of the Bow' was a poem included in *The White Company*, which praised the glory of the bowmen and yeomen of old England, whose strength and abilities had made the country great. So whereas today we might imagine a totem for Doyle being a deerstalker hat or a magnifying glass, the badge reproduced in *The Strand* showed the 'A' or Arthur adapted into a bow and arrow.

---

[126] Stephen Hallett, 'Totems for Famous Authors', *The Strand*, July 1906, p. 113.

In light of this, it is surprising that 'Sir Nigel' was his last historical
novel. Perhaps he felt that having achieved his best, that was an end of
it. But it wasn't the end of his historical fiction, because he soon turned
to a series of historical short stories, later collected in the book *The Last
Galley* in 1911. These showed he had a profundity of ideas even if none
lent themselves to full development as a novel. The novels he would later
write, apart from *The Valley of Fear*, would in fact revolve around science
fiction, fantastic adventure and his spiritual beliefs. Yet his passion for
historical fiction and research had not left him. Years later, when the omnibus edition of his works was assembled, most of the historical stories
were grouped as *Tales of Long Ago* (as *The Last of the Legions* in the US).
He commented:

> ...if all my work were to be destroyed save only that one single section
> which I might elect to preserve, my choice would certainly be those short
> historical pictures which come under the heading of 'Tales of Long Ago'.[127]

Most of these stories were written during 1909 and 1910, and Watt
sent them to various magazines with the purpose of having them published in a short time so they could be issued in book form in April 1911.
As a consequence most of them appeared in either *The London Magazine*
or *Scribner's Magazine*. Doyle had already sold two to *The Strand* – 'The
Pot of Caviare' and 'The Silver Mirror' – and *The Strand* would acquire
one more, 'The Home-Coming', which it ran in December 1909. The
last two, plus the boxing story, 'The Lord of Falconbridge', in the August
1909 *Strand*, were illustrated by Arthur Twidle.

'The Pot of Caviare' (March 1908) really belongs to this group, but was
squeezed into the Round the Fire stories. But it's out of place there, even
though it is a near contemporary story. It's set during the Boxer Rebellion
of 1900, when there was an uprising against foreign powers in China, many
of whom found themselves besieged in a quarter of Peking. The story is
essentially a discussion between those who are besieged but are planning
a meal drawn from a hamper of goods which had arrived just before the
siege began. Unfortunately the climax of the story, depicting the fate of
the individuals, is somewhat deflated by the frontispiece by R. Caton
Woodville, which entirely gives away the denouement.

---

[127] Doyle, 'Preface' to *The Conan Doyle Stories*, London: John Murray, 1929.

"HE SCREAMED AND PRAYED, WHILE EVERY TUG OF THE STRAINING SLAVES
BROUGHT HIM ONE STEP NEARER TO THE BRINK."

Arthur Twidle's dramatic frontispiece showing the climax of 'The Home-coming' in *The Strand*, December 1909.

'The Silver Mirror' (August 1908) is not strictly a historical tale. It is an occult tale, very like 'The Leather Funnel'. Both stories consider an object which provides an experience of the past. In this case an accountant, under stress due to work, believes he is losing his sanity when he begins to see events playing out in an old silver-framed mirror he had been given by a friend. The events show a beautiful young lady with rich chestnut hair dressed in an ancient fashion, perhaps Elizabethan, and a young, thin, haunted-looking man who, in the final scene, is attacked and murdered by a group of men. The accountant recounts the events to his doctor, who believes he had witnessed the murder of David Rizzio, private secretary to Mary, Queen of Scots. The mirror had once belonged to Mary, and the accountant had reached the right stage of psychic awareness to respond to the vibrations in the mirror. This story would have fitted better into the Round the Fire stories, but that volume was already assembled and was published the following month.

So the only remaining historical story that *The Strand* published was 'The Home-Coming'. Set in AD 528 it follows the return of the ten-year-old illegitimate son of Theodora, now the Empress and co-regent of the Byzantine Empire with her husband Justinian. Knowledge of his existence would compromise her position, and the Empress faces the dilemma of how to deal with the child and the abbot who brought him. Although it is not as extreme as some of Doyle's earlier horror fiction, it is still a powerful story of maternal love versus political responsibility.

It is unfortunate that this story appeared on its own in *The Strand*, because chronologically and thematically it relates to at least eight of the other stories in *The Last Galley*, which follow the rise and fall of the Roman Empire and the start of Islam. They run from 'The Last Galley', set in 146 BC, which shows the final Roman conquest of Carthage, through various episodes in the Roman Empire to the end of Roman rule in Britain in 'The Last of the Legions', the arrival of the Saxons in 'The First Cargo' and the awareness of the power of Mohammed in 'The Red Star', set in AD 630. These make a powerful nine-story sequence, which allows Doyle to explore parallels between the Roman and British Empires and the latter's possible fate. 'The Last Galley', for instance, compared the weakness of Carthage's naval power to that of Britain's, while 'The Last of the Legions' raised questions about Britain's role in India compared to how Rome abandoned Britain. That cohesion between the stories and their clear imperialist message was lost when the stories were split over magazines, and they were not even placed in sequence when collected as *The Last Galley*. Had he written them a decade earlier they would have made an excellent story sequence in *The Strand*, and their message would have been more potent.

So it is all the more surprising that Doyle did not try and have them published together. It was not as if *The Strand* was overwhelmed with material by Doyle. There would have been room to publish all nine in sequence during 1909 and 1910. Doyle did alert Smith to the fact that Watt had all of the stories in a letter of 4 June 1909, but it does not seem that Smith pursued them. Almost a year later, on 14 May 1910, Doyle asked Smith if he had seen 'The Last Galley' and 'The Passing of the Legions' [*sic*], but Smith had not.

The fact that Smith did not pursue these as part of a series raises several points. It was clear that by now the numbered story sequence had had its day in *The Strand*. The magazine, along with its competitors, was moving not just into a new century but, with the death of Edward VII in May 1910 and of George Newnes himself in June 1910, a new era. But it was also as if Doyle no longer had an interest in pursuing story sequences. As he had learned with Holmes, these committed him in ways that restricted his creative freedom. The fact that he wrote this sequence of stories and was so satisfied with them owes much to the fact that he could do it as he pleased without feeling duty bound and committed to *The Strand*.

It was part of a freedom he needed and treasured. Since the death of Louisa and his marriage to Jean, Doyle had found he could breathe afresh. His love for Louisa had been stifled to some degree by her incapacity but now, as he reached the age of fifty, Doyle had a full life again. And he had a new family. Denis was born in March 1909, and Adrian in November 1910. A daughter, Jean, would follow in December 1912.

Doyle no longer looked to the past. His eyes were set on the future.

10

Doyle and the Dawn of Science Fiction

OYLE'S NAME IS SO CLOSELY associated with the early days of detective fiction that few associate him with the early days of science fiction, yet he wrote two novels in the genre and enough stories and novellas to fill another book.

It is unlikely that Arthur Conan Doyle ever heard the phrase 'science fiction', though he came close to it himself when he referred to Grant Allen's story 'John Creedy' as combining 'science and fiction'.[128] The term was formally coined in America by the entrepreneur Hugo Gernsback, who promoted it in his new magazine *Science Wonder Stories*, which appeared on the American newsstands on 3 May 1929. It would have filtered into Great Britain soon after as copies of the magazine were imported, but Doyle is unlikely to have seen them. None of his work was reprinted in the science-fiction magazines during his lifetime.

Doyle's best-known work of science fiction is undoubtedly *The Lost World*, in which dinosaurs are discovered living in the present day on a remote plateau in South America. This novel introduced us to the larger-than-life character of Professor Challenger, whose exploits would run through five adventures. But Doyle had been dabbling with ideas on the borderline between science and the strange for over twenty years, and was always interested in new technology. He had invested in one particular project, which could have revolutionised the production of replica works

---

[128] Doyle, 'Memories and Adventures', *Strand*, May 1924, p. 444.

Yours truly (to use the conventional lie)
George Edward Challenger.

"THE LOST WORLD."

The Leader of the Explorers, with some of their Adventures.

Harry Rountree's frontispiece with a portfolio of images from 'The Lost World' plus the mock photograph of Doyle as Professor Challenger from the April 1912 issue of *The Strand*.

of art. He had seen a machine, the 'Meccaneglofo', demonstrated in Naples by its inventor, Augusto Bontempi – and as a result Doyle, with others, established the Automatic Sculpture Company in London. The process was featured in the November 1903 *Strand*, and Doyle told Greenhough Smith he was paying 'a large sum to secure the rights of it in this country'.[129] Unfortunately the process had too many teething troubles and the company closed down, but not for lack of support from Doyle.[130]

Doyle's earliest story to qualify as science fiction had been 'The American's Tale' in the special Christmas issue of *London Society* in 1880. It's really a tall tale, with Doyle's tongue firmly in his cheek. Set in the 'wild west', a rowdy local, laying in wait for his victim, becomes a victim himself to a previously unknown form of carnivorous plant. Doyle's technological interest surfaced in 'The Great Brown-Pericord Motor', published in the extremely rare *Ludgate Weekly* on 5 March 1892. The eponymous Brown and Pericord invent a form of motor which enables a craft, like a helicopter, to fly. This was written before any heavier-than-air manned flight. Doyle, with a typical twist, uses it as an ingenious way of disposing of a body.

These two strands of early science fiction – previously unknown flora and fauna and new technological advances – would be the inspiration for Doyle's more robust science fiction, which began in *The Strand* in 1910.

The new popular fiction magazines were a fertile market in which the infant science fiction genre rapidly matured. Doyle's friend Grant Allen had been a regular contributor. 'The Thames Valley Catastrophe', in which London is destroyed by volcanic action, appeared in the December 1897 *Strand*, which also ran the last episode of Doyle's 'The Tragedy of the Korosko'.

Its best-known author at the time was, of course, H. G. Wells, and though most of his science fiction had been in the rival *Pearson's Magazine*, notably 'The War of the Worlds', Wells also made a mark in *The Strand*. The magazine serialised his novel, 'The First Men in the Moon' (December 1900 to August 1901) and several short stories including 'The Land Ironclads' (December 1903), 'The Country of the Blind' (April 1904) and 'The Empire of the Ants' (December 1905). Doyle was friends with Wells. They had first met in Rome in April 1898[131] when Doyle was visiting his brother-in-law,

[129] Doyle, undated letter to H. Greenhough Smith [UVa066].

[130] See 'The New Sculpturing Machine' by M. Dinorben Griffiths, *Strand*, November 1903, pp. 569–574. Bontempi persevered with the process and achieved a US patent in 1927.

[131] Doyle believed that he must have met Wells when they both lived in Southsea. Wells worked at a draper's shop where the proprietor was one of Doyle's patients.

Willie Hornung, and Wells came over for dinner. Doyle had read *The War of the Worlds* and the two hit it off immediately. They continued to correspond and meet occasionally, both exploring each other's interests in psychic research, science and technology.

Whereas Doyle was a pioneer in his development of detective fiction, with science fiction he was contributing towards an existing trend and most of his works are imitative. For instance, 'The Terror of Blue John Gap' in the August 1910 *Strand*, which features another doctor-narrator, concerns the famous cave in the Derbyshire Dales. Sheep have gone missing, and the doctor explores deep inside the cave where he encounters a monstrous creature from which he narrowly escapes. He speculates that far underground there may be life-forms that followed a different evolutionary thread. Doyle's treatment of the idea is powerful and effective, but far from original. Twelve years earlier, the February 1898 *Strand* had published 'The Lizard' by C. J. Cutcliffe Hyne, best known for his stories featuring Captain Kettle who was second only to Sherlock Holmes in popularity in the magazines. In 'The Lizard' a caver exploring a newly discovered cave near Kettlewell, in the Yorkshire Dales, encounters a giant lizard and barely escapes with his life.

Doyle may not have read the story, but the idea of other forms of life underground was in any case far from original and can be traced back to Jules Verne's *A Journey to the Centre of the Earth*, which Doyle had certainly read. Regardless, though, of any literary inspiration, Doyle's interest in pre-historic creatures had been rekindled in May 1909 when he found giant footprints and related fossils at a quarry near Windlesham. He notified the British Museum, who sent a geologist to investigate. Doyle retained a keen interest in fossil hunting, and discovered a near full-size fossil of an iguanodon in February 1911.

Doyle's interest in exploration was also rekindled. As a lad he had been fascinated by the remote corners of the world, and though the world was effectively shrinking, he was still interested in events in central Africa and South America. It is pertinent that at this time his Sherlock Holmes story, 'The Adventure of the Devil's Foot', in the December 1910 *Strand*, includes a big-game hunter and explorer Dr Leon Sterndale. The devil's foot of the title is a hitherto unknown poison, which Sterndale had discovered in West Africa, and its use makes this story borderline science fiction.

At the same time Doyle had been championing another of his causes. He was incensed by the atrocities being committed in the so-called Congo

Free State, a private possession of King Leopold of the Belgians. The natives working on the rubber plantations and elsewhere were subject to brutality and murder. The situation had been investigated by the British colonial officer Roger Casement, who reported on the abuse and indignities in 1904. With journalist Edmund Dene Morel, and others, Casement set up the Congo Reform Association that same year. Doyle was only remotely aware of the situation, but he encountered it full on when he read Henry De Vere Stacpoole's novel, *The Pools of Silence* (1909), which vividly described the situation. Doyle promptly contacted Morel and the two met in London in June 1909. Doyle agreed to write a pamphlet detailing the atrocities based on material provided by Morel. This emerged as the 45,000-word *The Crime of the Congo*, published by Hutchinson's in October 1909. It rapidly sold over 60,000 copies and was translated into French and German. Morel was convinced that Doyle's involvement proved a considerable influence. A few years later he commented that people took notice because 'he was Conan Doyle, and that he was with us. I do not think any other man but Conan Doyle could have done for the cause just what Conan Doyle did at that time.'[132]

Doyle joined Morel on a lecture tour and worked on a testimonial for Morel. This brought him into contact with Roger Casement, whom he met in London in May 1910. Casement was now the British Consul in Brazil, investigating a new atrocity – the treatment of employees of the Peruvian Amazon Rubber Company. Doyle outlined his idea for a story set in a remote part of the Amazon, where dinosaurs survived on a plateau cut off from the rest of the world. Casement promised to notify Doyle if he heard of any unusual discoveries. The following February Doyle attended a lecture given by Colonel Percy Fawcett, who was mapping the Amazon basin at that time. Doyle showed interest in Fawcett's description of the flat-topped plateau of the Ricardo Franco Hills in the Mato Grosso, now known as the Huanchaca Plateau, near Bolivia's north-eastern border with Brazil.

Doyle now had all the background data he needed. He settled down in October 1911 and, in his usual way, barnstormed through *The Lost World*, completing it by Christmas. He created a team of four memorable characters who venture into the Amazon basin to discover

---

[132] E. D. Morel, *The Bookman*, November 1912, pp. 96–97.

"CHALLENGER FELL, AND AS I STOOPED TO PICK HIM UP I WAS AGAIN STRUCK FROM BEHIND
AND DROPPED ON THE TOP OF HIM."

Illustration by Harry Rountree from the July 1912 *Strand*.

THE PLATEAU AND THE PINNACLE.
From a Sketch by Maple White.

llustration by Patrick Forbes depicting the Lost World plateau (from *The Strand*, April 1912).

this Lost World. Leading the team was the man who had first encountered the remote mountain, Professor George Challenger, a considerably larger-than-life character with total belief in his profound knowledge and scant time for the ideas of others. Doyle had based him partly on his old anatomy professor at Edinburgh University, William Rutherford, whom he described as 'squat', with an Assyrian beard, a prodigious voice, an enormous chest and a 'singular manner'. He would sometimes begin his lecture before reaching the classroom, his voice booming down the corridor.

Although Challenger may resemble Rutherford, his personality reflects much of Doyle. A certain headstrong arrogance, a bombastic determination and a strong self-belief all meld together in a character that dominates the book. The name Challenger came from the HMS *Challenger*, which from 1872 to 1876 undertook the first complete oceanographic survey of the globe. The chief scientist on board was Sir Charles Wyville Thomson, whom Doyle had known at Edinburgh University where he held the Chair in Natural History.

Professor Challenger is vehemently against journalists but young Edward Malone wins the Professor's confidence, albeit after a fight! Malone is based on Edmund Morel, as both an investigative journalist and someone with a mission. In the story, Malone believes he needs to undertake something heroic in order to impress his girlfriend, though this backfires at the end of the novel.

Also in Challenger's team was Lord John Roxton, explorer and big-game hunter. For his character Doyle drew partly upon Roger Casement, particularly in his fearlessness and knowledge of the world, notably South America. The final member of the team, Professor Sumerlee, is not based on any one individual but is the token sceptic in the group, always arguing with Challenger about the latest theory. Challenger is, of course, always right.

The novel is a straightforward adventure tale. Doyle regarded it as the closest he had come to writing a boys' story, which he wrote for the sheer joy of it. The four adventurers, along with their native porters and guide, retrace Challenger's footsteps to find the plateau where he was convinced there was an isolated world of prehistoric creatures. He had found evidence of an earlier attempt to reach the plateau, by an American called Maple White, but a recent rockfall had cut off the identified route. Instead they have to climb an adjacent pillar of rock and fell a tree to cover the chasm between them and the plateau. Unfortunately, once on the plateau two of the native bearers dislodge the tree, removing the party's only escape route. On the plateau they must find a way to survive. They witness a variety of dinosaurs, are captured by ape-men, rescued by cavemen and eventually find another way off the plateau.

Boys' adventure or not, it proved immensely popular. Greenhough Smith was delighted when he learned of the novel, and regarded it as the very best serial Doyle had done, outside of Sherlock Holmes. Smith also enjoyed Doyle's mischievous idea of disguising himself as Professor Challenger and posing for a photograph to be used as the frontispiece for *The Strand* when the serial began in the April 1912 issue.

Although the majority of the illustrations were by Harry Rountree, there were others identified as being by Maple White, the explorer whose few papers Challenger had found. Doyle had called on the help of Patrick Forbes, the husband of Jean's sister Sara Mildred (Milly), and Forbes's friend William Ransford. Forbes produced some drawings of the plants and creatures of the Lost World derived from the book *Extinct Animals* by E. Ray Lankester, which had been published in London in 1905. Lankester was Director of Natural History at the British Museum and had become a close friend of Doyle's. He was delighted with how his own speculative drawings were used.

Ransford took photographs of Doyle disguised as Challenger, with himself as Malone and Forbes as both Roxton and Summerlee. These appeared both in *The Strand* and the American serialisation syndicated through the Sunday supplements. Doyle also provided two maps, one showing the route to the plateau, and the other of the plateau itself. There was an opening statement to say that Professor Challenger has withdrawn both the injunction for restraint and the libel action and would place no further impediment upon publication. All of this gave a feeling of authenticity to the account that may have convinced some, even though Doyle was simply having fun.

In the end Smith did not use all of Doyle's mock pictures and instead used illustrations by Rountree, much to Doyle's annoyance. 'How anyone could prefer Rowntree's Central Lake aquarium to the mystery and suggestion of Forbes' picture fair beats me,' he wrote in a long complaining letter to Smith.[133]

---

[133] Letter Doyle to Smith, 8 August 1912 [UVa041]. Note Doyle's misspelling of Rountree's name.

E. D. Malone, "Daily Gazette."   Prof. Summerlee, F.R.S.   Prof. G. E. Challenger, F.R.S., F.R.G.S.   Lord John Roxton.
THE MEMBERS OF THE EXPLORING PARTY.
Copyright.   From a Photograph by William Ransford.

The mock photograph of Doyle and his colleagues as Challenger and his fellow explorers in 'The Lost World' from the May 1912 *Strand*.

An example of Doyle's humour comes when they encounter the ape-men, and Malone realises how much they resemble Professor Challenger.

> Beside him stood his master, the king of the ape-men. In all things he was, as Lord John had said, the very image of our Professor, save that his colouring was red instead of black. The same short, broad figure, the same heavy shoulders, the same forward hang of the arms, the same bristling beard merging itself in the hair chest. Only above the eyebrows, where the sloping forehead and low, curved skull of the ape-man were in sharp contrast to the broad brow and magnificent cranium of the European, could one see any marked difference. At every other point the king was an absurd parody of the Professor.[134]

Further evidence of Doyle's humour came in a response he gave to Greenhough Smith. Towards the end of the novel Challenger discovers

---

[134] 'The Lost World', *Strand*, September 1912, p. 250.

"THE APE-MAN STOOD BY CHALLENGER AND PUT HIS PAW ON HIS SHOULDER."

Illustration by Harry Rountree comparing Professor Challenger with the leader of the Ape-Men (from *The Strand*, September 1912).

that a gas bubbling through a pool of mud was 'markedly lighter than the atmosphere'. Challenger plans to fill a pouch full of this gas so that it would lift them off the plateau – a plan which, thankfully, they don't have to pursue. Smith queried this with Doyle, and Doyle responded with a postcard:

> My dear Smith – The Gas was Levogen, a volcanic product peculiar to plateau conditions, which has been calculated by Prof. T.E.S. Tube, F.R.S. to be 35.371 times lighter than hydrogen.[135]

In the final episode, in the November 1912 issue, we discover that the party has smuggled back to England a pterodactyl's egg, which has hatched. When Challenger gives a lecture about their adventures to a highly sceptical audience he releases the pterodactyl, which causes much havoc before it flies away across the London rooftops, heading back to South America.

For *The Strand*, Rountree provided over forty illustrations in addition to Doyle's mocked-up pictures and photographs, but few of these were reprinted in the book edition. *The Strand* printing is thus the only source for Rountree's complete set of striking pictures, which includes several images of dinosaurs such as pterodactyls, an iguanodon, a stegosaurus and an allosaurus.[136] It would have been an innovative introduction for many readers to the monsters of the prehistoric world.

There is a darker element in the serial. With the help of the explorers, who are armed with guns, the cavemen defeat and destroy the entire race of ape-men. This reflects Doyle's view of the authority of superior races over inferior ones, which he had expressed as far back as *The Tragedy of the Korosko*. Doyle concludes the extermination of a race with the following chilling summary:

> All the feuds of countless generations, all the hatreds and cruelties of their narrow history, all the memories of ill-usage and persecution were to be purged that day. At last man was to be supreme and the man-beast to find for ever his allotted place.[137]

---

[135] Doyle to Smith, 2 August 1912 [BL07].

[136] The American serialisation in the Sunday newspaper supplements was illustrated by Joseph Clement Coll, and only a few of his illustrations were included in the first American book edition.

[137] 'The Lost World', *Strand*, October 1912, p. 367.

Challenger's attitude towards this is unforgiveable, especially for a scientist. With his eyes shining 'with the lust of slaughter', he says:

> We have been privileged to be present at one of the typical decisive battles of history – the battles which have determined the fate of the world. What, my friends, is the conquest of one nation by another? It is meaningless. Each produces the same result. But those fierce fights, when in the dawn of ages the cave-dwellers held their own against the tiger-folk, or the elephants first found that they had a master, those were the real conquests – the victories that count. By this strange turn of Fate we have seen and helped to decide even such a contest. Now upon this plateau the future must ever be for man.[138]

The world was itself edging closer to a global war where the fate of millions was decided. Challenger's soliloquy is a reminder of Doyle's belief in Britain's imperialist superiority.

Doyle was soon envisaging another form of devastation. *The Lost World* proved so popular, and Doyle so delighted in the character of Professor Challenger, that he promptly threw himself into a new adventure, 'The Poison Belt', which ran from March to July 1913 in *The Strand*.[139] Again illustrated by Harry Rountree, his frontispiece for the first episode makes it very clear what the serial is about. It depicts the four adventurers from *The Lost World* gathered together again, with Challenger announcing to the others, 'It is, in my opinion, the end of the world.'

Challenger had announced, via a letter to *The Times*, his belief that the Earth was about to pass through a toxic cloud in the ether of space that will have a detrimental effect upon all life on the planet. He highlights that the reported outbreak of illness in Sumatra is but the start, and that it will soon extend to 'the more complex people of Europe'.

Malone, Sumerlee and Roxton are summoned to Challenger's home in Surrey, and each is asked to take a tank of oxygen. They travel by train and witness each other betraying signs of hysteria, later explained by Challenger as the early effects of the poison. Although Challenger believes the gas will exterminate all life, if they are able to reduce the effects by breathing pure oxygen in a sealed room, they

---

[138] *Op. cit.* pp. 367–368.
[139] Also in the US edition, issues April to August 1913.

may at least survive long enough to witness the end of humankind. In fact they survive long enough for the Earth to pass through the poison cloud and for them to be able to breathe fresh air again. This allows them to drive into London to witness the devastation caused as people collapsed while still driving cars, cabs, trains or boats. They discover one woman still alive who had needed oxygen because of her medical condition, and they wonder whether there may be others. It transpires, however, that the poison cloud had only put people into a deep sleep, like catatonia, and as its effects wear off everyone awakes and go about their duties as if nothing had happened.

Doyle may have had the basic idea for 'The Poison Belt' in his mind for some years, perhaps since he wrote 'Sir Nigel', with its image of Britain after the Black Death. The depiction of a desolate London, however, had appeared in H. G. Wells's *The War of the Worlds*, which Doyle had read when it was first published in 1897. Doyle's friend James Ryan, whom he had known since his days at Stonyhurst, reminded Doyle of Wells's work and suggested he might want to check it over to avoid any duplication.

It is all the more ironic, therefore, that after publication of 'The Poison Belt' Doyle was accused of plagiarism by the French writer J.-H. Rosny *aîné*, who suggested Doyle may have been overly influenced by his serial, 'La Force mystérieuse'. This had run in the French magazine, *Je sais tout*[140] from 15 January to 15 May 1913 and, as the first two instalments appeared before Doyle's serial began, Rosny raised the inevitable question. His challenge did not appear in print though until his novel was published in book form in early 1914. Doyle, through his agent A. P. Watt, refuted it at the end of April, their response being published in both *The Times* and the French *Le Temps*:

> Sir Arthur Conan Doyle, against whom a charge of plagiarism has been brought in connexion with his last work, 'The Poison Belt' by M. J. H. Rosny, *aîné*, author of 'La Force mystérieuse', has written to the French

---

[140] *Je sais tout* was a popular monthly magazine inspired to some degree by *The Strand*, though with even more illustrations. It ran from February 1905 to January 1922, with each issue dated the fifteenth of the month.

"THE STILLNESS AND THE SILENCE OF UNIVERSAL DEATH."

Part of the devastation witnessed in 'The Poison Belt', illustrated by Harry Rountree (from *The Strand*, May 1913).

translator of his works pointing out that the first chapters of 'The Poison Belt' were written nearly a year before the book was finished and began to appear in the *Strand Magazine*. M. Rosny replies that at that time two sections of his work had already been published, to which Sir A. Conan Doyle rejoins that, if he had wished to imitate M. Rosny, it would have been impossible for him to do so and to prepare illustrations in time for publication two months after the appearance of M. Rosny's work.[141]

The two serials are in fact very different, but just happen to have two striking similarities in the first episode. In Doyle's story Challenger is first aware of something odd in the ether because of a blurring of lines in the spectrum, and the concept of a reducing spectrum is at the heart of Rosny's work. In both cases the impending doom has advance effects on humans in the form of eccentric behaviour, hysteria and even homicidal and suicidal outbreaks. There is more than enough evidence in Doyle's letters that he had already written the bulk of 'The Poison Belt' long before Rosny's serial appeared. His correspondence with Ryan over the scenes of devastation in London was in September 1912, while a letter to his mother dated 23 November 1912 notes that he had already written 20,000 words of the novel and was only delayed in completing it because he had a cold.

Rosny's attempt to discredit Doyle may have been a sign of frustration. He was France's leading writer of science fiction and the natural successor to Jules Verne, and had written several novels covering areas in which Doyle was now trespassing. The most recent was *La Guerre du feu*, which had run in *Je sais tout* during 1909 and appeared in book form in 1911. Set in prehistory, it follows the discovery of fire and the evolution of humanity. Rosny was planning another novel set in prehistory, which finally emerged as *Le Félin géant* in 1918. He must have been

---

[141] *The Times*, 'A Charge of Plagiarism', 1 May 1914, p. 8.

[142] In the March 1914 issue of *Je sais tout* that serialised *The Lost World*, Doyle noticed the story 'Le Tunnel de Gibraltar' by Jean Jaubert. He recommended it to Greenhough Smith who had it translated and published in the September 1914 American edition of *The Strand* and the October 1914 English edition. Doyle's comment that this story 'should be about your mark' [UVa045] shows Smith's continued interest in science fiction.

annoyed when Doyle's *The Lost World* began serialisation in *Je sais tout* in November 1913, as it was soon after that Rosny raised his objections to 'The Poison Belt'.[142] However, Rosny was prepared to accept that the similarities were a coincidence and the matter ended.[143]

In fact H. G. Wells would have had a better claim against Doyle. His novel, *In the Days of the Comet*, published in 1906, has much more in common with *The Poison Belt*. An approaching comet, which is detected by its effect on the spectrum, threatens all life on Earth and the main character prepares to die along with his friends. In fact the nitrogen and other elements in the comet's atmosphere have a beneficial effect upon humanity and Earth enters a New Age. Doyle might be excused if he was not aware of this novel, since it appeared when Louisa was in the final stages of her illness and just before Doyle began his Edalji campaign, but it is surprising that no one else highlighted the similarity when the later charge of plagiarism was raised.

What is also surprising is that throughout 'The Poison Belt', Challenger refers to the 'ether' in space. This concept, usually called luminiferous ether, was one Doyle would have grown up with, as it was presumed there had to be some medium in space through which light could travel. However, a famous experiment conducted by Michelson and Morley in 1887 disproved the need for any such medium, and thereafter the idea was dismissed. Doyle's reference to ether rather dents Challenger's constant claims of superior knowledge.

The subject matter of 'The Poison Belt' does not make for as stirring an adventure as *The Lost World*; in fact rather the opposite. Much of the novel takes place in one room, where Challenger and his colleagues, including his wife, reflect upon death, whether the Earth may ever be repopulated and what form that new evolution might take. There is an interesting exchange between Challenger and Sumerlee over Challenger's hypothesis that mankind is 'the highest thing in Nature' and that all of Earth's history has led to that development.

---

[143] It may be pertinent to note that *Je sais tout* chose not to run a translation of 'The Poison Belt' until near the end of the war, when it appeared as 'Le ciel empoisonné' from March to July 1918.

Challenger, the ultimate atheist, even concedes to turning to prayer as he believes their end is imminent. Both these are signs of Doyle's increased involvement in spiritualism.

Challenger otherwise has a rather cavalier attitude towards the fate of others. Although he believes they will all succumb to the poison, he nevertheless chooses to prolong the lives of only himself, his wife and his three colleagues. He does not attempt to include among the number his servant, Austin, because that would scatter the gas throughout the house and deplete it for themselves. There is an exchange in which Challenger thanks Austin for his faithful service:

> 'I've done my duty, sir.'
> 'I'm expecting the end of the world to-day, Austin.'
> 'Yes, sir. What time, sir?'
> 'I can't say, Austin. Before evening.'
> 'Very good, sir.'
> The taciturn Austin saluted and withdrew.[144]

More than one critic has commented upon the possibility that Austin may have been the origin of P. G. Wodehouse's Jeeves, manservant to Bertie Wooster.[145] Wodehouse recalled that the primary inspiration for Jeeves was the novel *Ruggles of Red Gap* by American humorist Harry Leon Wilson, in which an American couple win a gentleman's gentleman. There are certainly similarities between Ruggles and his employer and Jeeves and Wooster, although as *Ruggles* is narrated by the butler it lacks the detached aloofness of *Jeeves*. The first story featuring Jeeves, 'Extricating Young Gussie', appeared in the *Saturday Evening Post* seven months after the serialisation of *Ruggles*, so the timing is appropriate.[146] But we cannot overlook the fact that Wodehouse practically worshipped Doyle's work. He will certainly have read 'The Poison Belt' – Wodehouse regarded Doyle as the perfect example of how to write commercial magazine fiction – so there is a possibility that Austin was another forebear of Jeeves.

---

[144] 'The Poison Belt', *Strand*, April 1913, p. 367.

[145] See Usborne (205) and Dirda (41).

[146] *Ruggles* was serialised in the *Saturday Evening Post* from 26 December 1914 to 27 February 1915. 'Extricating Young Gussie' appeared in the *Post* on 18 September 1915, and in *The Strand* in January 1916.

While not as exciting as 'The Lost World', 'The Poison Belt' is a more sobering novel in the context of a world headed towards the First World War. Doyle wrote just one more piece of science fiction before war broke out, 'The Horror of the Heights' (November 1913), which took him back to his interest in aeroplanes. He had taken his first (and only) flight in a bi-plane on 25 May 1911 at Hendon aerodrome, a not altogether enjoyable experience. The development of aeroplanes and pushing the limits of flight were all the rage at this time. Louis Blériot had flown across the English Channel in July 1909. By 1913, dubbed 'the glorious year of flying', pilots were performing a variety of stunts and setting new records. Although balloons had set several altitude records as far back as 1862, the highest achieved by a heavier-than-air machine was 16,240 feet by French aviator Roland Garros, in September 1912. A year later he would become the first to fly solo across the Mediterranean from France to Tunisia.

Doyle's story consists mostly of a fragment of a blood-soaked notebook which was found with a few other items and identified as belonging to the missing aviator Joyce-Armstrong, who had been attempting a new altitude record. Not long before there had been a disaster in which Lieutenant Myrtle had reached over 30,000 feet before falling from his plane. His body was found lacking its head. Joyce-Armstrong's notebook provides a partial account of his ascent to over 41,000 feet, when the plane could go no higher as the air was too attenuated. At this point, the aviator becomes aware of jellyfish-like creatures floating through the thin atmosphere, and he discovers to his peril that they are hostile.

The story is highly effective, even though you have to suspend your disbelief that someone in such peril would still be writing in his note-book. At the time it did not feel so strange because only a few issues earlier, in July 1913, *The Strand* had published Captain Scott's account of his expedition's journey to the South Pole including his own last message. It thus seemed quite possible, and Doyle's usual first-person narrative adds to the story's impact. Moreover the story was beautifully illustrated in full colour by W. R. S. Stott, whose four pages of artwork show the strange beings of the upper atmosphere.

It was perhaps fortunate that the French writer Maurice Renaud was not as litigious as J.-H. Rosny. Renaud's 1911 novel *Le Péril bleu* dealt with a race of invisible sky-folk who inhabit the far upper reaches of our atmosphere and have an interest in human beings, whom they fish

"I FOUND MYSELF AMIDST A PERFECT FLEET OF THEM."

One of W. R. Stott's beautiful illustrations for 'The Horror of the Heights'
depicting the alien life-forms (from *The Strand*, November 1913).

for and dissect. Part of the story includes an extract from the diary of one of those who was snatched skywards. Even if Doyle had not read Renaud's original novel he could well have read its English adaptation by John N. Raphael called 'Up Above', which was published in the December 1912 issue of *Pearson's Magazine*.

All of which shows that, despite Doyle's remarkable originality with detective fiction, when it came to science fiction others were usually one step ahead of him. Towards the end of his life, Doyle returned to science fiction, as I shall explore later, but at this time he wrote one other story, just before the outbreak of war, which proved highly prophetic. In fact, Doyle managed to write a story that gave an advantage to the enemy.

11

Doyle at War

A S A TRUE-BLOODED VICTORIAN Irish-Scots-Englishman, full of imperialist fervour, Doyle's interest in war had long been evident. We
have already seen how desperate he was to become a war correspondent
when he was in Egypt in 1896. He was keen to fight in the Boer War but,
heeding his mother, volunteered instead for the private field hospital.

He did get close to one of the front lines in the Boer War and wrote
about it in a piece for *The Strand* – 'A Glimpse of the Army', published
in September 1900. That April he had followed in the wake of Lord
Roberts's force as it advanced towards Pretoria. Before leaving for South
Africa, Doyle had despaired of the progress. In a letter to Greenhough
Smith, he had written:

> This War! Our commanders seem to have all gone demented. It's no use
> wishing anyone a Merry Xmas in the circumstances.[147]

By the time Doyle was in South Africa, though, the situation had
changed with Lord Roberts in charge, and Doyle noted this in his article:

> Walk among the fierce brown infantry, see the splendid Colonials, mark
> the keenness of the cavalry, note the lines of the guns and the hard, savage
> faces of the men who will handle them. Who can stop this army on the
> open veldt, now that it has weeded out some of its incompetence and

---

[147] Undated letter (probably December 1899), Doyle to Greenhough Smith [UVa194].

had time to learn in war a few of those lessons which should have been taught in peace? It makes one's heart bleed to think of the deaths and the mutilations and (worse than either) the humiliations which have come from our rotten military system, which has devoted years to teaching men to walk in step, and hours to teaching them to use their weapons.[148]

Doyle was full of the glory of war. Even when he was called out to a wounded soldier who, alas, died before Doyle could reach him, Doyle would still write, 'So he met his end – somebody's boy. Fair fight, open air, and a great cause – I know no better death.'

Doyle believed in the gallantry and heroics of the British soldier, provided he was properly trained and supported by the military machine. For over thirty years there had been writers seeking to alert the British establishment to how unready British forces were to the possibility of an invasion – especially from Germany, whose military and naval power was growing. The story 'The Battle of Dorking', published anonymously in *Blackwood's Magazine* in 1871, set off a national scare and ushered in a new genre of what became known as Future-War fiction.[149] Doyle believed that Britain needed a fully trained militia that could supplement the regular army in the event of an invasion. To this end he established his own Rifle Club at Undershaw in the autumn of 1900.

> The general of the future will hesitate, be his army never so numerous, ere he attempts to overrun a country whose civilian inhabitants (apart from the military forces who assist them) are prepared to defend it field by field. And he will hesitate the more when he reflects that those inhabitants, besides being minutely acquainted with the geography of their own homes, are expert in the use of the rifle.[150]

Keen to promote his initiative Doyle invited Greenhough Smith to Undershaw at the end of 1900 to see the Rifle Club for himself. Doyle's friend Captain Trevor Philip interviewed him for *The Strand* and this was published in the June 1901 issue as 'A British Commando'.

---

[148] 'A Glimpse of the Army', *Strand*, September 1900, pp. 345–346.

[149] 'The Battle of Dorking' was by Lieut.-Col. George Tomkyns Chesney. For a detailed study of Future-War fiction see *Voices Prophesying War, 1763–1984* by I. F. Clarke (London: Oxford University Press, 1992).

[150] Doyle interviewed by Captain Philip Trevor in 'A British Commando', *Strand*, June 1901, p. 640.

From a Photo. by]   CONAN DOYLE AS FIELD CORNET.   [Captain Trevor.

Conan Doyle training at his Rifle Club (from *The Strand*, June 1901).

Doyle was frequently at odds with the military and political establishment over his concern for Britain's defences. He was, for instance, in
favour of a Channel Tunnel, which he saw as being a great potential
source of profit to the country by stimulating trade and providing a safe
line of communication for troops and food in the event of war. Against
the charge that it would leave the country open to invasion in wartime,
Doyle wrote:

> This can, of course, only mean invasion by France, which cannot surely
> be regarded as a serious danger, although I admit that every defensive
> precaution should be taken. As to invasion by any other country, it means
> that they have first to win and to hold both ends of the tunnel. Such a
> contingency is, I hold, beyond all bounds of common sense.[151]

He was also concerned about the possible threat of submarines in warfare. His friend the retired Admiral Sir Percy Scott had contended for some

---

[151] Doyle, letter to *The Times*, 11 March 1913, p. 4.

Illustration by Edward S. Hodgson to Doyle's story of submarine warfare, 'Danger!' (from *The Strand*, July 1914).

while that no matter how many battleships Britain had, they would be under constant threat from aeroplanes and submarines. Scott was accused by the new naval establishment of scaremongering. Doyle came to his defence. The July 1914 *Strand* published Doyle's story 'Danger!'. It was really an essay in fictionalised form, and is legitimately classified as science fiction because it is set a few years in the future and describes a new form of submarine which would surely soon be developed. The story tells of the small country of Norland, which comes into conflict with Great Britain over a boundary dispute. Britain demands an apology but Captain John Sirius, who is in command of Norland's small submarine fleet, convinces the King and his Ministers not to acquiesce but to hold out against Britain. Sirius's plan is to use his submarines, just eight of them, to blockade Britain's ports and so stop supplies. This he achieves so effectively that Britain surrenders within weeks.

Doyle started the story by expressing Norland's surprise that the 'English' had not been aware of the danger to which they were exposed by submarines. He ended with two recommendations by which

such a threat could be avoided in the future. First, by ensuring sufficient food was grown within the island to reduce its reliance on imports, and second, the immediate construction of a Channel Tunnel
complete with a two-way railway.

Greenhough Smith sent story proofs to several leading naval experts, and their responses were published in the same issue. A few supported Doyle's argument, although mostly with regard to the
establishment of granaries and supporting farmers. Most ignored or
dismissed the suggestion of a Channel Tunnel. One, Admiral Sir
William Kennedy, identified the weakness in the story, namely that
our own submarines were not engaged in the defence. Doyle's view
was that he could not see how one submarine could fight another.
Leaving aside the pompous response of Admiral Sir Compton
Domvile – who was 'compelled to say that I think it most improbable,
and more like one of Jules Verne's stories than any other author
I know …' – most did at least recognise that Doyle had raised some
important issues, and the author Arnold White commented that he
believed it was a 'national service'.[152]

The British naval powers may have dismissed Doyle's story as fantastic,
but the Germans didn't. Captain Magnus von Levetzow, who became
the German High Sea Fleet's Chief of Operations in 1916, noted Doyle's
story and passed it to Fleet Commander Admiral Reinhard Scheer.[153]
Doyle was horrified to read the following in *The Times* in February 1915
regarding Germany's planned blockade of British ports:

> 'We had the idea ready-made for us in England. [...] Conan Doyle sug-
> gested the outlines of a plan which every German has hoped would be
> used. His story, 'Danger', will tell you far better than I can what we intend
> to do, for we have the submarines now, and as England is attempting to
> starve us, we must show her that two can play at that game.' This was said
> to me with all seriousness, and I heard Conan Doyle's story referred to
> repeatedly in defence of the blockade.[154]

---

[152] Quotes are from 'What Naval Experts Think', *Strand*, July 1914, pp. 20–22.
[153] See Holger H. Herwig, 'Total Rhetoric, Limited War: Germany's U-boat campaign, 1917–18',
Journal of Military and Strategic Studies, Volume 1 (1998).
[154] 'Six Weeks with the Enemy' by a Neutral Observer, *The Times*, 18 February 1915, p.9.

Doyle's story had appeared in *The Strand* almost on the same day that Archduke Franz Ferdinand was assassinated in Sarajevo, and the dominoes began to fall that led to the United Kingdom declaring war on Germany on 4 August 1914. Doyle immediately wrote to *The Times* reminding them of the need for there to be local reservists and that he had already held drill practice in his own local butts. He distributed a one-page leaflet titled *Civilian National Reserve* on 6 August.

Thankfully readers of *The Strand* could seek refuge in a new Sherlock Holmes serial, 'The Valley of Fear', which ran from the September 1914 issue through to the following May.[155] Articles and stories about the war were few and far between at the start, though F. Britten Austin, a renowned writer of military fiction, was the first off the mark with 'The Air-Scout' in the November 1914 issue.

By the start of 1915, however, *The Strand*, like every other publication, was doing its best to raise the nation's morale. The January 1915 issue featured 'The Nation's Heroes' by Frederick Dolman, showing where 'our great sailors and soldiers were born'. Richard Marsh began a series about an everyday volunteer with 'Sam Briggs Becomes a Soldier'. Sir Ray Lankester contributed an article about German culture, while in the February 1915 issue F. Cunliffe-Owen looked at the various medals for heroism in 'For Valour'.

Apart from the Sherlock Holmes serial, and a contribution to a symposium titled 'How I Broke Into Print' in that February 1915 issue, Doyle was relatively quiet in *The Strand*. That was because he was extremely busy writing propaganda and encouraging volunteers. Another pamphlet, *To Arms!*, published at the end of September 1914, was issued to encourage recruitment by stating clearly the British case for the war. This was also included in the American edition of *The Strand*, the only time it ran a piece by Doyle not included in the English edition. Doyle asked Greenhough Smith if it could be arranged and Smith obliged, including it in the December 1914 edition as 'The War. A Statement of the British Case'.[156]

---

[155] Although this was not included in the American edition of *The Strand*, the researches of Phillip G. Bergem have shown that a special edition of the English *Strand* was released in the USA with a modified cover and the notation 'British edition' sometimes added.

[156] The American edition of *The Strand* ceased in February 1916 because of wartime restrictions.

"THREE MUSKETEERS."

THE CROWBOROUGH VOLUNTEER CORPS IS THE FIRST IN DATE IN GREAT BRITAIN, HAVING BEEN ENROLLED UPON AUGUST 4TH, 1914. THESE ARE THREE ORIGINAL MEMBERS—FROM THE LEFT, SIR ARTHUR CONAN DOYLE, HON. REGINALD BROUGHAM, H. E. SHEPPARD, J.P.

Doyle in uniform with two of his colleagues in the Crowborough Volunteers Corps at the outbreak of War (from *The Strand*, October 1915).

Other leaflets, some reprinted from newspaper articles, included *Great Britain and the Next War, The World-War Conspiracy* and *The German War*, all produced within the first few months. He also began a lecture circuit talking about 'Great Battles of the War', which was the start of what would become his six-volume history, *The British Campaign in France and Flanders*. It was a work that would dominate his writing throughout the rest of the war, and the contents of the first four volumes were published first in *The Strand*.

However, Doyle had considerable problems with the censors over the content and timing of his articles, and months passed without anything being approved. Greenhough Smith suggested that maybe Doyle should turn his hand to fiction while he was waiting, but Doyle responded that he could not attune his mind to fiction. In the end, though, he did produce two pieces for *The Strand* – one article and one story.

The first, 'An Outing in War-Time' (October 1915), is Doyle's account of how he spent one day in July 1915 at home in Crowborough, followed by a drive through the countryside to the coast. He recounts how, with the change in the wind direction, you could hear the booming of the guns across the Channel in Flanders. He mentions the local gossip about Zeppelins being seen and recalls the death of a British aviator when for some unknown reason his plane plummeted to the ground. He spends a morning with other local volunteers learning semaphore and sending messages before, at noon, he and his wife and children are driven to Hayling, where he witnesses the shoreline defences. Taking the long drive home, via Brighton, it is dark before they reach Crowborough and Doyle recounts a surprising number of incidents as they are stopped in the dark to check identity. At one point, they help a military policeman take a drunken prisoner to a nearby village.

The day was 10 July 1915, a Saturday. Doyle had yet to hear that his nephew, Oscar, the twenty-year-old son of his sister Connie and Willie Hornung, had been killed in action at Ypres on 6 July. Doyle's extended family suffered several wartime casualties. His brother-in-law, Malcolm Leckie, had died within a month of the outbreak of war at Mons on 28 August 1914, but there was no confirmation of this until just before Christmas. Malcolm had been a surgeon working at a field hospital and was posthumously awarded a DSO. Major Leslie Oldham, husband of Doyle's sister Lottie, was shot by a sniper while inspecting trenches at Festubert on 28 July 1915.[157]

Doyle's other contribution, while waiting for the censors, was 'The Prisoner's Defence', a short story in the January 1916 issue. It concerns an Army Captain who had fallen in love with a French woman while billeted with his regiment in Essex. The Captain is on trial for the murder of this woman and has hitherto given no defence. The story is his account of what led to her death, and the discovery that she had been a German spy.

Doyle's story may have been inspired by the trial of two spies at the Old Bailey in September 1915 – George Breeckow and Lizzie Wertheim.

---

[157] Jean's nephew, Alex Forbes, the son of Doyle's artist friend, also died as a result of wounds received in August 1916, aged only 22.

Breeckow was sentenced to death and was shot by firing squad in October, but it was considered that Mrs Wertheim had been heavily influenced by Breeckow, and she received a ten-year prison sentence. At this same time the British were furious over the execution of Nurse Edith Cavell by a German firing squad in Belgium on 12 October 1915. She had been found guilty of helping injured French and British soldiers escape from Belgium, and charged with treason. Her execution was the subject of international condemnation. This action, alongside Britain's relatively mild treatment of Mrs Wertheim, would have been fresh in the minds of those reading Doyle's story. They would have had no qualms about how Doyle deals with the female spy's death.

All this time, through papers, diaries, letters and interviews, Doyle had continued to gather data for his history of the British Campaign in France. The first of these articles, covering the Battle of Mons, finally appeared in the April 1916 *Strand*. The series received considerable advance publicity. *The Strand* announcing:

> Without doubt this history forms the most important and engrossing record of actual happenings at the Front, and of the battles that have been fought. Written in Sir Arthur Conan Doyle's graphic, inimitable style, this narrative brings home to us as no other account has done the wondrous heroism of British soldiers. It will be read with intense interest.[158]

The Times had a large two-column advert in its number for 28 March 1916 declaring, 'The Facts at Last. The Inside Story of the War.' Doyle's ability to present 'the facts' was, though, limited by wartime censorship, which had been introduced by the Defence of the Realm Act within days of the declaration of war. Every one of his articles had to be submitted to the censors, who frequently caused him despair and frustration. When he had first started talking about the war in his lecture tour, which he began in March 1915, he had told his mother:

> It will amaze people for I am the only man who knows the facts & I know them down to the small details.[159]

---

[158] Announcement, *Strand*, March 1916, p. 327.
[159] Doyle, letter to his mother, March 1915, in Lellenberg, *Letters* (611).

After the war, when he looked back on writing his history, he regarded it as one of the books that gave him the most satisfaction. He wrote:

> I had devised my own system of intelligence, quite apart from (in fact, in opposition to) that of the War Office. I knew that my facts were true, and I knew that I had got them by my own wits, and that no one else had got them, and that was naturally a source of satisfaction. I have had little to change save to fill up names and places which the Censor deleted.[160]

Whether he did know all the facts or only thought he did, is another matter, but his talks, which covered the progress of the war from the Battle of Mons to the first Battle of Ypres at the end of October 1914, were appreciated. When he delivered his lecture at the Queen's Hall, London on 20 March 1915, Lord Haldane acknowledged the indebtedness of the audience for Doyle's vivid description of events matched only by 'the amount of detail he had packed into a short space of time'.[161] Doyle's script was vetted, which he regarded as 'hindrance from the War Office', but it was far harder to get approval to the series for *The Strand*.

Although the first two chapters, dealing with the battles of Mons and Le Cateau, were approved, chapters three and four, covering the battles of the Marne and of the Aisne, were not. Doyle was told on 14 May 1915 that the War Office had objected because, 'the General Staff think they should not be published yet'. There was no point in *The Strand* starting publication until a sufficient number were completed and approved. An exasperated Doyle was soon letting off steam to Greenhough Smith, saying 'I wish those fools would let me begin my History in your Xmas number. It is a year old now.'[162]

There were, of course, good reasons why the General Staff were not approving Doyle's history. The war had certainly not gone the way anybody had expected, and there had been frequent disagreements between the higher echelons of both the military and the government over strategy. Field-Marshal Sir John French, the Commander-in-Chief of the

---

[160] Doyle, 'The Book I Most Enjoyed Writing', *Strand*, March 1922, p. 240.
[161] See report, 'Battles of the War', *The Times*, 22 March 1915.
[162] Doyle, letter to H. Greenhough Smith, undated, in Lellenberg, *Letters* (616).

British Expeditionary Force, had believed that the war would be short provided he was allowed sufficient men and weaponry. He had neither, and there was soon a calamitous shortage of shells as well as the horrendous loss of men. The significant casualties and losses at the start of the war were later blamed on French, although it was unfair to single out one individual when the circumstances and the lack of a clear strategy were so chaotic. French had endeavoured to employ tactics that minimised the loss of troops, but this was tantamount to a retreat. Eventually, French stood down in December 1915, due as much to a personality clash as a matter of warfare. Doyle had himself detected this from responses he had received during 1915. He told Greenhough Smith:

> It seems that French is beginning to be a very difficult man to handle, *vide* Kitchener, Smith-Dorrien, Rawlinson – and now my own experience. I imagine he thinks I have not praised him enough. Something in it has quite upset him.[163]

In fact Doyle had been tied from the start. One of his earliest responses to Smith, on 12 May 1915, based on advice from the War Office, had been, 'No, we must on no account mention Sir J. F. That would make it semi-official.'[164] Doyle also had problems with many of those he contacted for information, as some were considering writing their own accounts, but Doyle was helped considerably by the two generals who had been operating under French, Haig and Smith-Dorrien, both of whom provided direct and personal data.

Once French had moved on, part of the blockage was removed and *The Strand* could finally run the articles. Every essay still had to be approved, but sufficient were agreed that they were able to appear monthly over the next fifteen issues to June 1917. Conscription had been introduced with the Military Services Act in January 1916, and Doyle's stirring accounts may well have given hope to those now forced to serve.

This was also indicative of another of Doyle's problems. The first year of the war had been a disaster, and though Doyle wanted to present the facts as much as he was able, he wanted to post at least some positive gloss so as to sustain public morale. The way to do this was to highlight

---

[163] Letter, Doyle to Greenhough Smith, undated [BL12].
[164] Postcard, Doyle to Greenhough Smith, 12 May 1915 [UVa138].

the heroism of the British soldiers against such insurmountable odds. Typical of his hyperbole was this, from his opening chapter as the soldiers embarked from Southampton:

> No finer force for technical efficiency, and no body of men more hot-hearted in their keen desire to serve their country, have ever left the shores of Britain. It is a conservative estimate to say that within four months a half of their number were either dead or in the hospitals. They were destined for great glory, and for that great loss which is the measure of their glory.[165]

Again, in describing the first moments of the Battle of Mons as the German Taube aircraft provided details for the range of the guns aimed at the British trenches, Doyle writes:

> A rain of shells roared and crashed along the lines of the shallow trenches. The injuries were not yet numerous but they were inexpressibly ghastly. Men who had hardly seen worse than a cut finger in their lives gazed with horror at the gross mutilations around them. 'One dared not look sideways,' said one of them. Stretcher-bearers bent and heaved while wet, limp forms were hoisted upwards by their comrades. Officers gave short, sharp words of encouragement or advice. The minutes seemed very long, and still the shells came raining down.[166]

It was this direct, personal detail that made Doyle's account stand out. In all probability every single reader of *The Strand* would have known someone who was killed or injured in the War and they would have read heavily censored newspaper accounts or heard stories from those re-turning from the Front. What Doyle gave them was as true an account as he could, flavoured heavily with his view that every single man who was facing the enemy was a hero and gave his all for the British cause. Doyle also recognised the bravery and skill of the German army. His text is full of phrases such as 'with fine courage' or 'staggered on bravely' about the German troops. He recognised there was heroism and deter-mination on both sides, which emphasised the gallantry of all soldiers.

His text was accompanied by an array of detailed, often graphic il-lustrations by a range of talented artists, sometimes reproducing official

---

[165] Doyle, 'The Battle of Mons', *Strand*, April 1916, p. 340.
[166] Doyle, 'The Battle of Mons', *Strand*, April 1916, p. 346.

war photographs with such skill that the printed image looked vividly realistic. Not all artists were credited but they included Frank Dadd, Joseph Ratcliffe Skelton, Dudley Tennant, W. B. Wollen and R. Caton Woodville. They did not skimp on detail or effect, their illustrations depicting the full brutality, horror and carnage of war. There was no point in sugar-coating the account. Between them Doyle, Smith and the artists showed the British public what their relatives and friends were witnessing, enduring and achieving, recognising that this took true courage.

This was particularly true as Doyle's history reached the first Battle of Ypres, at the end of October 1914. The cover of *The Strand* announced this as his account of 'the glorious Battle of Ypres', while in his essay Doyle called it 'the great epic'. His vivid account of the first stage of the battle showed the dreadful odds of the Allies against the German troops, and the stoic resolve of the British, French and Belgians to hold the territory around Ypres. Doyle reckoned the climax came on 31 October when he reported that Sir John French believed he was at the end of his resources but his words of hope and encouragement 'stiffened the breaking lines.' Doyle believed that 'the Empire owed more that day than has ever been generally realized' to both French and Douglas Haig. Doyle's summary of that day's events would have stirred the hearts of all readers of *The Strand*:

> The struggle was not over. For a fortnight still to come it was close and desperate. But never again would it be quite so perilous as on that immortal last day of October when, over the green Flemish meadows, beside the sluggish watercourses, on the fringes of the old-world villages, and in the heart of the autumn tinted woods, two great Empires fought for the mastery. Such was the British epic.[167]

Doyle's accounts continued through the encounters at Neuve Chapelle and Hill 60, the second Battle of Ypres, the battles of Richebourg and Festubert and the Battle of Loos. All along Doyle was hampered by the heavy-handed editing of the censors, which interfered with the style of his writing, and he was frequently having to redraft sections to keep the narrative flow, and to redraw diagrams. Nevertheless in May 1916 Doyle took up an offer to visit the Front just ahead of the

---

[167] Doyle, 'The First Battle of Ypres', *Strand*, October 1916, p. 449.

Somme offensive, where he came close to the action and witnessed the appalling conditions. While in France one of the French generals asked Doyle what Sherlock Holmes would have been doing during the war. It gave Doyle pause for thought.

His composition of the war history had a natural break after Loos, which had happened in September/October 1915 and about which Doyle wrote in the April to June 1917 issues of *The Strand*. Doyle felt that the censor was now so restrictive that he would have to stop after Loos.[168] While considering his options, Doyle's mind returned to the question of what Sherlock Holmes would have been doing. His initial response to the general had been that Holmes was too old, but was he? Doyle had always been vague about Holmes's age, noting only that he was 'middle-aged' in 'The Boscombe Valley Mystery', which was set in June 1889. But in 'His Last Bow', which is subtitled 'The War Service of Sherlock Holmes' and takes place on the eve of the outbreak of war in August 1914, Doyle decided to make Holmes sixty. In the chronology of events in the Holmes stories, this is the Great Detective's final case. He had, to all intents and purposes, retired to a small farm on the South Downs to keep bees and write about apiculture, but he was also keeping an eye on events, and came out of retirement to penetrate a German spy ring. Doyle would later write more Sherlock Holmes stories, but they are all set earlier. This one sees us at the end of Holmes's career.

The story was written in the third person, so is not a Watson narrative, and indeed there was no way it could have been because the opening events take place before Watson's reunion with Holmes. But in the third-person it allows for Holmes's final comment, which is as stirring as any that Doyle had been writing in his accounts of the war:

> 'There's an east wind coming, Watson.'
> 'I think not, Holmes. It is very warm.'
> 'Good old Watson! You are the one fixed point in a changing age. There's an east wind coming all the same, such a wind as never blew on England yet. It will be cold and bitter, Watson, and a good many of us may wither before its blast. But it's God's own wind none the less, and a cleaner, better, stronger land will lie in the sunshine when the storm has cleared.'[169]

---

[168] See unpublished and undated letters from Doyle to Smith [UVa184, UVa225].
[169] Doyle, 'His Last Bow', *Strand*, September 1917, p. 236.

The Strand's September 1917 cover boldly declaring the return of Sherlock Holmes to serve his country.

At the time Doyle wrote this, the outcome of the war was not certain, as there was still over a year of fighting to come, but there was a sense that the tide was turning. The censors at last agreed to Doyle's account of the first day of the Battle of the Somme (on 1 July 1916), which ran in the May and June 1918 issues. Despite censorship Doyle was able to report that some 50,000 'of our gallant infantry had fallen' and that the combined British, French and German losses must have exceeded 100,000. In fact the combined total killed on that first day was in the region of 32,000, but including those injured the total was closer to 70,000, so Doyle was certainly not minimising the casualties.

Doyle reported three more encounters for *The Strand*: the Battle of Arras, in October 1918, labelled 'The Greatest British Victory in Three Years'; the Battle of Messines in November 1918; and a two-parter on the Battle of Cambrai, in January and February 1919. Cambrai was in November/December 1917, so Doyle's accounts were still over a year later. By 1919, of course, the war was over and censorship was slowly being relaxed. Doyle continued to write his history, filling two further volumes, but no more appeared in *The Strand*, as by then they would have been neither topical nor historical. Magazine readers wanted escapism and entertainment, not a reminder of the horrors of those four years.

There was, though, one further revelation in *The Strand*. As Head of the Mechanical Warfare Supply Department Sir Albert Stern had been a key figure in the development of the armoured tank. In 'Tanks. Revelations of the Secret History of Their Construction' (September 1919), he revealed that in early 1916 he had taken Doyle into his confidence because Doyle had been writing to the press about the scale of casualties at the Front and seeking better protection for troops. Doyle expressed his doubts that the tank could achieve the scale of success that Stern claimed, but their effect during the Battle of Cambrai caused him to change his mind. Doyle wrote to Stern on 22 November 1917, saying:

> I think your tactical ideas have been brilliantly vindicated by this battle, and that you should have warm congratulations from all who know the facts.[170]

Doyle wrote one last tribute to the gallantry of the British soldiers in the First World War. His poem, '"Now Then, Smith!"', in the July 1922 *Strand*, looks at how in moments of crisis it is the everyday man, 'just a

---

[170] Doyle, *Strand*, December 1919, p. 226.

chap among the chaps', who rises to the occasion. Doyle looks at how this everyman saves the day, concluding:

> And when War raised its fearsome shape
> And Europe shrank before its form,
> Our England stood with no escape,
> Unarmed before the rising storm,
> 'Twas Smith to whom at once we turned.
> Five million Smiths obeyed the call.
> To Smith the praise that he has earned,
> For by his blood he saved us all.

THE 1st WEST YORKSHIRES TAKING PART IN A COUNTER-ATTACK
AT THE BATTLE OF THE AISNE.

"THE ADVANCE WAS OVER HALF A MILE OF GROUND, MOST OF WHICH WAS
CLEAR OF ANY SORT OF COVER, BUT IT WAS MAGNIFICENTLY CARRIED OUT
AND IRRESISTIBLE IN ITS IMPETUS."

Depiction (almost certainly by Reginald Cleaver) of the Battle of the Aisne, drawn from Doyle's series, 'British Campaign in France' (from *The Strand*, August 1916).

12

Family Lives

THE END OF THE WAR WAS CRUEL to Doyle's family. At its start his
son, Kingsley, had been undertaking medical studies. Wounded
on the first day of the Somme in July 1916, he was sent home to con-
valesce. Although he briefly returned to his medical studies he was
posted again in October and returned to the Front. He was never
quite the same again, though, and was retired from the British Expeditionary Force in December 1917 to resume his medical studies in
England. Tragically he succumbed to the Spanish influenza epidemic
that spread through Europe towards the end of the war and died on
28 October 1918, just short of his twenty-sixth birthday and only two
weeks before the Armistice.[171] Only four months later Doyle's brother
Innes also died of the Spanish flu. As we shall see, Doyle consoled
himself through his growing commitment to spiritualism, and at a
séance just a few weeks later Doyle believed he made contact with
Kingsley.

During and after the war Doyle sought some comfort by fictionalising
his family life, though this was his new family, his children with Jean,
not his older children with Louisa. He wrote an occasional series of tales
under the general heading of 'Three of Them', five of which ran in *The
Strand* during 1918. The three were his eldest son Denis, 'whom we shall

---

[171] The cause of death was formally recorded as septic pneumonia.

The Three of Them, Laddie, Dimples and Baby with Lady in *The Strand*, December 1918. The photos are of Doyle's children Denis, Adrian and Jean with Lady Jean Doyle.

call "Laddie"', aged eight, Adrian ('Dimples'), who is nearly seven, and his little daughter Jean ('Baby'), 'a dainty elfin Dresden-china little creature of five, as fair as an angel and as deep as a well'. Their father, Daddy, who is known as 'The Great Chief of the Leatherskin Tribe' is 'a lumpish person with some gift for playing Indian games', while their mother is 'Lady Sunshine', a nickname that Jean had acquired when they were in New York.

The children are, not surprisingly, described in glowing terms. Laddie's soul is 'the most gallant, unselfish, innocent thing that God sent out to get an extra polish upon earth'. Dimples 'has the making of a big man in him. He has depth and reserves in his tiny soul. But on the surface he is a boy of boys, always in innocent mischief.' As for Baby, 'something

Table 4: Arthur Conan Doyle's children

First wife: Louisa Hawkins, *born* 10 April 1857; *died* 4 July 1906

(1) Mary Louise, *born* 28 January 1889; *died* 12 June 1976

(2) Arthur Alleyne Kingsley, *born* 15 November 1892; *died* 28 October 1918

Second wife: Jean Elizabeth Leckie, *born* 14 March 1874; *died* 27 June 1940

(3) Denis Percy Stewart, *born* 17 March 1909; *died*, 9 March 1955

(4) Adrian Malcolm, *born* 19 November 1910; *died* 3 June 1970

(5) Lena Jean Annette, *born* 21 December 1912; *died* 18 November 1997

very strong and forceful seems to be at the back of that wee body. Her will is tremendous. Nothing can break or even bend it. Only kind guidance and friendly reasoning can mould it.'

Each little story is a charming account of some episode sparked by the children. The first, 'A Chat About Children, Snakes, and Zebus' begins when Dimples asks Daddy whether roses know us, a question he raises because one of the roses in the garden had nodded at him. The conversation takes a surreal course through the nature of roses when they rustle, on to jaguars, snakes, crocodiles and zebus. Daddy recalls moments when he awoke in the Sudan to find a death-adder close by and when he went swimming off the coast in Africa and only later realised a shark was circling nearby. In the next episode, 'About Cricket', Daddy investigates a noise at night which turns out to be Laddie trying to bowl a cricket ball, and becomes a discussion about Daddy's various cricket memories.

Perhaps the most wonder-filled of the 'chats with children', as the series called itself, was the third, 'Speculations', which begins with the children wondering if there are toys in heaven, and then suddenly shifts to the story of the Ark, and puzzling over what, if there were only two of every animal, the carnivorous ones ate. It then shifts to trying to understand the nature of Jesus, God and Father Christmas, and especially how his reindeer keep presents dry.

In the fourth episode, 'The Leatherskin Tribe', the children play at being North American Indians, only their game becomes a little too realistic when they find themselves locked in a hut. The fifth episode, 'About Naughtiness and Frogs and Historical Pictures', is the longest and shows Doyle probing the children's imagination and thought processes. 'If you want to study the strange, quick workings of the child-mind, get a book with interesting pictures which excite the imagination, and then ask the young students what they are,' is one of Doyle's observations, along with 'It is surprising what a lot of information the eager little brains can pick up, if you make the thing a game instead of a task.'

It was clear that Doyle enjoyed writing these accounts, but his war writings, growing spiritualist interests and other commitments interrupted this simple pleasure and he was not able to return to them for four years, when he produced two more.

In 'Billy Bones' (December 1922) the children are three to four years older, and Baby will no longer answer to that name. She has become Billie and is in love with the boy next door, John, who is also eight but, as Daddy tells us, that's another story. This story is a treasure hunt, looking for the plunder hidden by pirate Billy Bones. The children follow a set of clues which Daddy had laid earlier. At the story end Daddy talks to all other daddies who are reading the story, and gives them the present of the game so that they can play it with their children – this was, after all, in the Christmas issue.

The story does have a dark element. Daddy, for some reason, has a revolver, which he draws in order to add some grim reality to the possible danger should they come across Billy Bones or his partner Jack Gilmore. Today this certainly seems out of character with the general fun of the story and the game, and even in 1922 it must have seemed overly dramatic, but it reflects the world of Arthur Conan Doyle, which always had been full of action and possible danger. Today the game would come with a health-and-safety warning, as at one point the children tumble down a twenty-foot incline among brambles, but in Doyle's world, that was all part of growing up.

The final story was 'The Forbidden Subject' in the August 1923 issue. It was really an excuse for Doyle to reminisce about his favourite boxers – as boxing was clearly a forbidden subject so far as Mumby (as Lady Sunshine had become) was concerned. It's a charming trip down memory lane, and the magazine also ran a photograph of Doyle's two boys sparring in their newly acquired boxing gloves.

It is interesting that two issues after this final story, with the children now entering their teenage years, *The Strand* began serialisation of Doyle's autobiography, 'Memories and Adventures'. It was as if recording his own games and adventures with his children had enlivened in Doyle thoughts of his own youth and, as he was now sixty-four, it was time to recapture those memories.

★

'Three of Them' shows Doyle's closeness to and pleasure in his three young children with Jean, but it may seem strange that there was no reference to Doyle's eldest daughter, Mary. She was approaching thirty when the first of the stories appeared, but there had been a distance between her and her father since his marriage to Jean. Soon after that Mary, then eighteen, had been despatched to Dresden to study music and her pleas to come home were ignored. She missed her younger brother, Kingsley, dreadfully and wrote to him in November 1907, saying:

> I can't think why my father is so hard – I have not had one gentle word, or sign of love from him during the whole two years since Mother died.[172]

It was many years before their relationship grew closer. The death of Kingsley affected Mary deeply and she found her father's interest in spiritualism embarrassing. When he accused her of prejudice, she went to the United States in November 1919. She returned after nine months to pursue her musical career, but now accepted her father's beliefs and from 1925 helped run his Psychic Bookshop in London. This reconciliation may account for the appearance of Professor Challenger's daughter in the third Challenger novel *The Land of Mist* in 1925, even though there had been no mention of her in the previous two novels.

Yet, despite Mary being his eldest child, Doyle barely remembered her in his will, passing the copyrights in his work on to Jean and their three children.

---

[172] Letter from Mary Doyle to her brother Kingsley, 24 November 1907, quoted in Doyle (154).

The early 1920s saw Doyle's wider family shrinking. His mother, Mary, died on 30 December 1920 while Doyle and Jean were on tour in Australia. His brother-in-law Willie Hornung died on 22 March 1921 aged only 55. Hornung's widow, Connie, who had lost her son in the war and now her mother and husband, died of cancer on 8 June 1924, aged 56.

Doyle, though, was able to accept these losses because he firmly believed they had passed into the spirit world where he could continue to commune with them. Of all the causes Doyle championed, that of spiritualism was his most ardent and most passionate.

13

Spirits and Fairies

ARTHUR CONAN DOYLE HAD LONG been interested in the paranormal. It may have been his Irish heritage, or the stories his mother told, or the vivid and surreal images painted by his father. His mother certainly instilled into the young Doyle an enquiring mind. She had joined the Philosophical Institution in Edinburgh, a literary and scientific debating society, and continued to extend her knowledge through voracious reading. Doyle followed her example and when at Southsea, he joined the Portsmouth Literary and Scientific Society in 1883. Its President, the retired Major-General Alfred Drayson, was a confirmed spiritualist.

Doyle's discussions with Drayson began to open a door in Doyle's mind that had never really been closed. He had kept an open mind about most things and around this time had decided he would rather be agnostic than slavishly follow his Catholic background. Doyle did not instantly embrace spiritualism, but was prepared to experiment and learn.

His earliest writings had been related to the supernatural. In 1877 or so he had submitted 'The Haunted Grange of Goresthorpe' to *Blackwood's Magazine*, which was neither accepted nor rejected. It simply stayed in its archives, passing eventually to the National Library of Scotland, from where it was resurrected and published in 2000. While amateur in its execution it nevertheless turned on the clever idea of a ghost being haunted by another ghost. He produced a variety of ghost stories during his literary apprenticeship in the 1880s, of which by far the best was 'The Captain of the Polestar' (*Temple Bar*, January 1883), but also of interest were those that explored the supernatural in a scientific manner.

Doyle was especially interested to learn of the Society for Psychical Research (SPR), founded in February 1882 under its first president, Henry Sidgwick.[173] Doyle was not yet prepared to join the Society but he was keen to know of any research it conducted. He had two areas of special interest – thought transference (or telepathy, a word coined by one of the founders of the SPR, Frederic Myers, in 1882) and hypnotism (or mesmerism as it was still known). Mesmerism formed the basis for several stories such as 'John Barrington Cowles' (*Cassell's Saturday Journal*, 12 and 19 April 1884), in which a beautiful woman has Svengali-like powers that can drive men to their deaths, and 'The Great Keinplatz Experiment' (*Belgravia*, July 1885), where, through hypnotism, two individuals exchange personalities.

At Southsea, Doyle befriended local architect Joseph Henry Ball, whom he later commissioned to design his house, Undershaw. In 1887 Ball and Doyle attended several séances, which were not especially illuminating, apart from one. After one session in late June, the medium passed a handwritten note to Doyle. It read, 'Do not read Leigh Hunt's book.' Doyle was startled. He had wondered about reading Hunt's *Comic Dramatists of the Restoration*, but delayed because he thought it might be too lewd. He had not mentioned it to anyone. He was sufficiently impressed to write a letter to *Light*, the journal of the London Spiritualist Alliance, where it was published in the issue of 2 July 1887, under the heading 'A Test Message'. This was Doyle's first recorded writing about spiritualism. He later wrote,

> This, then, was a very final and excellent test so far as telepathy went, but I would not fully grant that it was more.[174]

Doyle persevered in his studies of the paranormal, reading the works of Professor William Crookes, Dr Richard Hodgson and A. P. Sinnett among many others. He was, for a while, interested in theosophy, the teachings of Madame Blavatsky, which intrudes into his early novel *The Mystery of Cloomber* (1889), but later accepted the findings of Richard Hodgson that Blavatsky was a charlatan.

---

[173] One of Sidgwick's nephews was the writer E. F. Benson, who was with Doyle in Switzerland when Doyle chose the Reichenbach Falls as the spot to kill Sherlock Holmes.

[174] Doyle, 'Early Psychic Experiences', *Pearson's Magazine*, March 1924, p. 205.

Until his conversion Doyle wrote little on the subject, but he did incorporate his growing beliefs into a few stories. We have already encountered the Round the Fire story set during a séance, 'Playing with Fire' (March 1900). At one point there is a rapid exchange between the medium and the host spirit, which covers a range of matters in the spirit world. The spirit informs the medium that they are happy, have no pain or wish to return to earthly life, are kept busy working on their own improvement and the advancement of others, and that those spirits who have truly loved do meet again. These would all be exchanges that Doyle had heard at séances and which gave him hope, but he still delayed in committing himself.

Doyle was evidently marshalling his thoughts when he wrote 'Stranger Than Fiction' for *The Strand* (December 1915), in which he still refers to himself as a 'student' rather than a 'dogmatist'. He noted that he is 'always conscious of the latent powers of the human spirit, and of the direct intervention into human life of outside forces which mould and modify our actions.'[175] As an example he recalled that when in Switzerland in 1892 he passed an isolated inn which gave him the idea for a story that he plotted further in his head. A few days later, before writing it down, he chanced upon a collection of stories by Guy de Maupassant wherein was 'L'Auberge', which described the story exactly as Doyle had imagined it. Coincidence or fate? He provided other examples of psychic experiences, including the time when he was subjected to an occult examination in which it was suggested that he might be initiated into the Hermetic Order of the Golden Dawn – which he chose not to pursue.

Doyle's conversion to spiritualism was clearly not an overnight decision. It was something he had investigated for thirty years before declaring his beliefs in 'A New Revelation' in *Light* on 4 November 1916. This formed the basis for his first public speech on spiritualism, given in October 1917, and his first book on the subject, *The New Revelation*, in 1918.

His conversion coincided with a rise in public interest in spiritualism following the horrendous scale of death during the First World War. People looked for some consolation in the idea that their lost ones had not died in vain and were happy in an afterlife. Inevitably this interest

---

[175] Doyle, 'Stranger Than Fiction', *Strand*, December 1915, p. 613.

brought with it those who took advantage, and the police regularly prosecuted fraudulent mediums. It became a challenge for the courts to decide whether spiritualism constituted a religion with its concomitant benefits under the law. Doyle saw it as a personal crusade to help those mediums he believed were genuine and to promote the wider awareness of scientific investigations into spiritualism.

Two factors determined Doyle's final commitment. One of Jean's friends, Lily Loder-Symonds, was a spiritualist with a talent for automatic writing, meaning she recorded messages dictated by the spirits. Lily, who suffered from poor health, moved in with the Doyles at Windlesham at the start of the War and was a good companion for Jean. Lily was almost certainly the inspiration behind a very short story in the *Strand*, 'How It Happened' (September 1913), in which Doyle's well-tried technique of the first-person narrative was this time a message written by a medium about a fatal car crash. It is a very minor story, perhaps one of Doyle's slightest, but it gets his message across with a quick punch. It was probably also inspired by an accident experienced by Doyle, who loved motoring. On one occasion his car ran up on a bank and turned over, falling on top of Doyle. The steering column held for a while but then broke so the full weight of the car, over a ton, came down on Doyle's back. Thankfully a crowd had gathered and the men were able to lift the car and pull Doyle out, with no lasting injury.

In one of her writing sessions, Lily produced a message from Jean's brother, Malcolm, who had died at Mons in August 1914. The message related to a conversation between Malcolm and Doyle some years before, and Doyle was convinced there was no way Lily could have known of it. It also convinced Jean, who hitherto had been sceptical, and she discovered she also had a talent for automatic writing:

> From that instant she threw herself with all the wholehearted energy of her generous nature into the work which lay before us.[176]

The second factor in Doyle's conversion came from an experience of his friend Sir Oliver Lodge, a highly respected physicist who, like Doyle, had conducted experiments in psychic research. Doyle had first met him via the SPR, and Lodge later served as its president. Lodge's

---

[176] Doyle, 'What Comes After Death', *Pearson's Magazine*, April 1924, p. 311.

son Raymond was killed at Ypres on 14 September 1915, and soon after Lodge received a message from Raymond, during a séance, containing information Lodge was convinced the medium could not have known. After further research, Lodge presented the facts in *Raymond, or Life and Death*, published in November 1916. This became a bestseller and is reckoned one of the key milestones in the rise of spiritualism.

Lodge wrote two essays about his experiences for *The Strand*, 'Is It Possible to Communicate with the Dead?' in the December 1916 issue, and 'How I Became Convinced of the Survival of the Dead' in June 1917. Greenhough Smith set up a response, 'Is Sir Oliver Lodge Right?', which ran in the July issue. On the 'Yes' side was Sir Arthur Conan Doyle, whose response showed how much his growing appreciation of spiritualism paralleled Lodge's, and emphasised the depth of research he had undertaken before forming his conclusions.

> It is treacherous and difficult ground, where fraud lurks and self-deception is possible and falsehood from the other side is not unknown. There are setbacks and disappointments for every investigator. But if one picks one's path one can win through and reach the reward – a reward which includes great spiritual peace, an absence of fear in death, and an abiding consolation in the death of those whom we love.[177]

On the 'No' side was Edward Clodd. Aged 77, Clodd was an ardent rationalist, atheist and evolutionist, and had just completed a book on spiritualism, *The Question: 'If a Man Die, Shall He Live Again?'*. His response was emphatic. He believed that spiritualism could not be subjected to the rigour of scientific investigation. Such experiments as had been conducted disproved the subject.

Clodd's views were not about to dissuade the converted, and the immediate post-war period saw a flurry of arguments and studies about spiritualism in popular magazines. Although Doyle's next book, *The Vital Message*, was serialised in *Nash's – Pall Mall Magazine* (May to October 1919), almost all of Doyle's articles on psychic matters would appear in *The Strand*.[178]

---

[177] Doyle, *Strand*, July 1917, p. 51.
[178] *The Vital Message* covered much of the same material Doyle had already explored in *The Strand*. He had sold the American rights to *Hearst's International Magazine*, and the British *Nash's* was owned by Hearst.

This began with an interview conducted by journalist Hayden Church in the March 1919 *Strand*. Among Doyle's various observations, he said 'Nearly every woman is an undeveloped medium,' but admitted, 'There are true men and there are frauds – blasphemous frauds, the most horrible of all frauds!' Doyle advised that people might find a reliable medium via what was then the London Spiritualist Alliance,[179] of which Doyle became President in 1925. Church prodded Doyle into giving examples of experiences which he had found unquestionable. Those he cited were almost certainly via Lily Loder-Symonds which, as she lived with the Doyles, did not make her a reliable example.

Doyle was fascinated with anything unusual that suggested spiritual or psychic influence. The August 1920 *Strand* published an uncredited article on 'The Sideric Pendulum', and Doyle contributed an introductory note. A sideric pendulum is one that swings in a circle or ellipse rather than side to side, as many people may have seen if they simply hold a weight suspended from a thread and watch what happens. In his note Doyle says that although he cannot see the matter as bearing directly upon spiritualism he did see it as supporting the likelihood of forces beyond our scientific knowledge.[180]

★

In 1919 Doyle began a series called 'The Uncharted Coast', which was later incorporated into his book *The Edge of the Unknown* (1930). Doyle revisited previously recorded cases of inexplicable events to see if they could be explained by a new understanding of spiritualism and whether any scientific or psychic laws could be inferred. The first three articles, 'The Law of the Ghost' (December 1919), 'A New Light on Old Crimes' (January 1920) and 'The Shadows on the Screen' (May 1920), considered in what ways spirits may communicate with the living, and under what circumstances. They ranged from coffins which refused to stay still to the famous case of the murder in the Red Barn where the mother

---

[179] Known as the College of Psychic Studies since 1970.

[180] Even this relatively harmless note caused a New Zealand reader to over-react. G. M. Thomson wrote to his local paper stating that the article, and by association Conan Doyle, was a 'wicked thing' causing 'a good deal of mischief among credulous women'. Doyle responded that he could not understand why the correspondent was so rude and that he could conduct a simple experiment and demonstrate the sideric pendulum for himself. (*Otago Daily Times*, 21 December 1920.)

dreamed about the location of her daughter's body, to a woman who, halfway down her stairs, always felt a slight push.

In the first case Doyle believed that the spirits were objecting to being buried in a vault rather than in the ground, and once the coffins were properly interred all problems ceased. In the second case a sensitive person may be open to channels from a murdered individual, which might manifest in dreams, which only happens within a limited time after death. He recommended that if the police have problems finding a missing person or resolving a murder they should consult a medium at the earliest opportunity. In the third case Doyle believed that following an emotionally dramatic moment the surroundings may absorb some spiritual intensity and that someone with the right psychic sensitivity could pick this up.

Doyle related some personal experiences of his own in these essays. In the first, for instance, he told of a message received through automatic writing from the agitated spirit of a man concerned about a note he had left in a cupboard. Doyle's investigation and a subsequent séance helped settle the spirit's concerns, and there were no further disturbances. Such examples were always interesting because of Doyle's direct involvement.

The majority of the examples, though, were drawn from books citing old cases, and these were the weakest part of the series because Doyle simply drew his conclusions without investigating further. The case of the moving coffins in the first article is a good example. His source was *West Indian Tales* by Algernon Aspinall published in 1912. This referred not only to the oft-reported case of the coffins in the family vault in Barbados, but to two similar cases – one in Suffolk, England, and the other in the Baltic town of Ahrensburg.

Had Doyle undertaken some research he would have discovered that his friend Andrew Lang had given a talk on this very subject, which was printed in the December 1907 issue of *Folk-Lore*.[181] Lang provided further detail than Aspinall's account. While Lang does not doubt that something odd happened in Barbados, he notes that written accounts of the events differed and there was no record of the coffin disorder in the contemporary church records. Moreover, there was no supporting evidence for the similar events in Suffolk or Ahrensburg, and Lang speculated that

---

[181] Lang's talk, 'Death's Deeds', was delivered to the Folk-Lore Society on 19 June 1907.

one event had become grafted on to others. So whereas Lang remained curious but sceptical, Doyle felt the accounts were authentic and accepted them without question.

The fourth article, 'An Old Story Re-told' (September 1920) dealt with the Fox sisters, Margaret and Kate, who between them in effect started the spiritualist movement. The Fox family lived in a village near Rochester, New York, and in 1848 the house became plagued by a series of knockings. What proved striking was that the younger sister, Kate, aged twelve, seemed unafraid and began to communicate with whatever was making the noises. The two sisters became famous, toured the country and stimulated interest in contact with the dead. Many rumours spread, one being that beneath the floor of their house bones had been found, and it was believed a murder had been committed there some years before. The children even identified the murderer. In fact the bones were not found until after the girls died, and they proved to be animal bones.

The sisters kept up the pretence for forty years but in 1888 the elder sister, Margaret, confessed it had all been a hoax. Although she later recanted, by then their credibility had plummeted and they sank into poverty and alcoholism.

It has long been accepted that the girls were frauds who had started it as a clever joke and, when everyone took it seriously, did not dare confess. However, supporters claim that the only reason Margaret confessed is that she was desperate for money and was bribed by a journalist. Although their activities started the interest in spiritualism, just about all authorities have discredited them.

Doyle, though, was a staunch supporter. His essay refers to the excavations beneath the house and the discovery of bones as happening quite early in the children's activities. He believed that one reason Margaret admitted the hoax was because she had converted to Catholicism, but as she was also desperately in need of money she was prepared to do anything. Doyle believed that though the children had been fraudulent in later years, they nevertheless had a genuine talent which they wasted, succumbing to human weakness.

★

For his next essay in the series, 'The Absolute Proof' (November 1920), Doyle turned to the contentious subject of spirit photographs. He dealt mostly with evidence from France and Germany, in particular the 1914

THOUGHT-FORM OR APPA-
RITION IN FRONT OF EVA,
BUILT UP OF ECTOPLASM.

An image from the book *Les phénomènes dits de Matérialisation* which was reproduced in the November 1920 issue of *The Strand* as part of Doyle's irrefutable proof of spiritualistic mediums.

book *Les phénomenàs dit Matérialisation,* compiled by the German scientist and physician Albert von Schrenck-Notzing from notes and photographs taken by Juliette Alexandre-Bisson. The photographs were of the medium Eva Carriàre, showing the manifestation of spirits formed from ectoplasm that emanated from her mouth and other orifices. Doyle saw this as undisputed proof, especially as the séances were conducted under highly controlled conditions. Schrenck-Notzing went to extreme lengths to reduce the possibility of fraud, including the medium being naked, inspected by doctors and then dressed in an outfit of gauze. Moreover, Doyle was not relying solely on the book for details. He had attended a séance with Eva in France earlier that year (1920). Schrenck-Notzing compiled a second book dealing with another medium, which Doyle also discussed.

Schrenck-Notzing's controlled conditions were more convincing than the photographs, which look contrived. Eva's abilities were exposed as fraudulent as early as 1913, and when Harry Houdini saw her perform he knew immediately how she hid and regurgitated the ectoplasm. The photographs were even easier to discredit because the faces appearing on the manifestations were recognised by some as having been cut out of French magazines.

Once again, Doyle dismissed any challenges to the medium's abilities, yet it is surprising he accepted the photographs without question. Doyle was an accomplished photographer, and had several contributions in the *British Journal of Photography* in the early 1880s. His friend William Ransford had helped Doyle produce the mocked-up photographs of Professor Challenger and his colleagues for *The Strand*, so Doyle was well aware of how photographs could be doctored. Yet he refused to believe this. In 1919 he had attended a séance held by William Hope, founder of the Crewe Circle spiritualist group in Cheshire. Hope produced a photograph showing Doyle's son Kingsley, and despite the similarity between it and a pre-existing photograph, Doyle accepted it as genuine. He later wrote to the *Daily Express* seeking to silence critics of spirit photography and referred to his own experience:

> I am convinced that if your correspondents were to examine the literature on spirit photography they would treat it more seriously than most of them seem inclined to do. It might occur in some cases that a plate used twice would show some trace of the former exposure, but as the extra faces are as often as not in front of the sitters such an explanation becomes impossible. In both the photographs which were taken of me, under rigid test conditions, by Mr Hope, at Crewe, the psychic figures were in front, and on one occasion they cloud me altogether.[182]

---

[182] Doyle, letter, *Daily Express*, 20 December 1919.

Doyle argued that a spirit photograph is not a photograph in the usual sense but is a 'psychograph', which he maintained was 'a transference by abnormal means of something which exists elsewhere.'[183] He believed this accounted for any discrepancy. Nevertheless, William Hope was unmasked as a fraud by Harry Price at a session in January 1922 where Price used marked plates to show that Hope substituted these for false ones. Doyle refused to believe this and argued, in *The Case for Spirit Photography*, published in December 1922, that it was the investigators who had perpetrated the trickery.

Although Doyle accepted that not all mediums were genuine, he refused to believe that all were fakes, or that in all instances he had himself been tricked. This obstinacy came to a head in the most famous hoax in which Doyle was involved, that of the Cottingley Fairies.

Doyle had been planning an article about fairies for *The Strand*, when in May 1920 he heard about two photographs taken of fairies in the north of England. Following up various leads, Doyle contacted the theosophist Edward Gardner, who had acquired copies of the photographs through his local Lodge. It transpired that the pictures had been taken by two girls: thirteen-year-old Elsie Wright and her ten-year-old cousin Frances Griffith at the Wrights' family home in Cottingley, near Shipley, Yorkshire. Elsie's mother, Polly, was interested in spiritualism, had started to attend her local Theosophical Lodge and took the photographs with her. That was how they came to the attention of Edward Gardner, who showed them to a local photographer, Harold Snelling, to confirm their authenticity.

The girls had taken the photographs in a favourite spot at the bottom of the garden where the local beck trickled through.[184] It was often muddy and Mrs Wright would scold the girls, so they made an excuse for why they played there. Elsie had a talent for drawing and copied on to stiff cards images of fairies and gnomes from *Princess Mary's Gift Book* (which had been published for Christmas 1914), and then cut them out. Together with her sister she fixed the pictures into the ground or on to bushes with hatpins. Borrowing her father's camera, Elsie then took a

---

[183] *Ibid.*

[184] It was pertinent that only two months earlier, in May 1917, *Punch* had published Rose Fyleman's poem, 'There are Fairies at the Bottom of our Garden'. The photographs seem to illustrate Fyleman's poem closely.

photo of Frances with these fairies dancing in front of her. The first photo, taken in July 1917, was treated as something of a joke, and Elsie's father did not take it seriously, either then or when they took a second photo a few weeks later. The second shows a gnome dancing besides a seated Elsie, and is a more effective photo.

When Doyle learned of the pictures he asked whether the girls could take some more, which they did in August 1920. The girls were now three years older and the photos are even more intriguing. Doyle reimbursed them with £20-worth of War Bonds.

In writing his initial report, 'Fairies Photographed' (December 1920), Doyle disguised the children's names to protect them and their family. Elsie became Iris Carpenter, and Frances became Alice. Doyle and Gardner checked the photographs further, taking them to Kodak for verification. Doyle reports that two experts agreed the photographs were genuine but they would not vouch for the veracity of the content. Gardner also explored the younger girl's ability to draw and compared her fairy drawings with those in the picture, deducing that the girl had not faked them. Doyle's report, which, to be fair, showed some caution, was accompanied by a report by Gardner that showed rather more conviction.

Doyle then went back to the article he had originally drafted and revised it as 'The Evidence for Fairies' for the March 1921 issue. This covered the whole subject of fairy-folk and gave a diverse set of examples in which authors and psychics had claimed seeing fairies or similar creatures, but the 'evidence' is thin on the ground. Greenhough Smith's introduction ends on a slightly ambiguous note, but implies that Smith may also have been a believer:

> This article was written by Sir A. Conan Doyle before actual photographs of fairies were known to exist. His departure for Australia prevented him from revising the article in the new light which has so strikingly strengthened his case. We are glad to be able to set before our readers two new fairy photographs, taken by the same girls, but of more recent date than those which created so much discussion when they were published in our Christmas number, and of even greater interest and importance. They speak for themselves.[185]

---

[185] *The Strand*, March 1921, p. 199.

IRIS AND THE DANCING GNOME.
(An untouched enlargement from the original negative.)
THIS PICTURE AND THE EVEN MORE EXTRAORDINARY
ONE OF THE FAIRIES ON PAGE 465 ARE THE TWO
MOST ASTOUNDING PHOTOGRAPHS EVER PUBLISHED.
HOW THEY WERE TAKEN IS FULLY DESCRIBED IN SIR
A. CONAN DOYLE'S AMAZING ARTICLE.
(See page 466.)

The second of the fairy photographs taken by Elsie Wright and Frances Griffith
and published in *The Strand*, December 1920.

Apart from the two new photographs, Doyle said nothing more about the cousins from Cottingley. He provided a theory about fairy-folk, suggesting that they exist in a different medium separated from us by a different rate of vibration[186] and that by changing that rate creatures might shift from one medium to another.

Two years later Doyle returned to the Cottingley Fairies in a short 'Epilogue' published in the February 1923 *Strand*. The magazine reprinted facsimiles of two undated notes sent by Frances (her real name is now revealed and misspelled) to a friend in South Africa, which referred to the fairies. The notes were almost certainly written towards the end of 1917 and don't reveal anything new, but Doyle felt that because they were written before the story 'broke', they were proof of its veracity.

Doyle's weakness was in believing the children. He pronounced, 'The only theory which I would not discuss was the honesty of the children, for that I considered to be well attested.'[187] Unfortunately, like the Fox sisters, they were playing a prank to which they confessed in 1983.[188] Both girls admitted that they could not confess to the hoax at the time for fear of upsetting Doyle. Elsie, who had married and was then Mrs Elsie Hill, said:

> I was feeling sorry for Conan Doyle because the Press had been giving him stick about the supernatural. I knew that he had lost his son in the War and I felt he was trying to comfort himself through unworldly things. It would have been terrible for him to have been destroyed by two little village kids.[189]

Doyle's inner convictions would have likely allowed him to overcome the children's confession at that time as, with other hoaxers, he would suspect them of claiming a hoax in order to hide the truth. There is a certain irony, though. It was not until 1978 that it was realised that the

---

[186] The idea that vibrations were the basis of existence dates back to various Eastern religious beliefs and was codified in the concept of theosophy by Helena Blavatsky. She believed we are all created by 'vibration' through the Divine Resonance that brought us and the universe into existence. Professor Crookes built on this idea and suggested that vibrations in the ether could account for telepathy and other psychic communication.

[187] Doyle, 'The Cottingley Fairies, An Epilogue', *Strand*, February 1923, p. 105.s

[188] See 'Cottingley Fairies a Fake' by David Hewson, *The Times*, 18 March 1983, p. 3.

[189] See 'Secrets of Two Hoaxers' by David Hewson, *The Times*, 4 April 1983, p. 3.

illustrations for the fairies came from *Princess Mary's Gift Book*, and yet Doyle should have known because that volume reprinted his story 'The Début of Bimbashi Joyce'.

There is another factor to bear in mind when considering Doyle's belief in fairies. The young Doyle had grown up surrounded by illustrations of fairies not only by his uncle Richard, but by his father, whose pictures were often surreal or sinister. It would be a salve to Doyle's memories of his father to believe that they may have been inspired by genuine fairy visions rather than an increasing mental instability.

★

Doyle concluded his 'Uncharted Coast' series with 'A Worker of Wonders' (May 1921), about medium Daniel Dunglas Home. Born in Scotland in 1833, Home had emigrated to America in his youth with his aunt and first displayed his skills there in 1851. He returned to Britain in 1855 and became famous for his levitation trick. The most noted example was at the home of Lord Adare in 1868, when he levitated out of one window and back through another.[190] Doyle knew of Home while the medium was still alive because he referred to him in his 1883 story 'The Winning Shot', about a stranger with strong mesmeric power over others. Doyle's description of the Adare incident repeats the basic account, though Howard Elcock's accompanying illustration grossly misrepresents it.

Doyle had every opportunity to understand how tricks could be performed by mediums because he had become friends with Harry Houdini. They first met in April 1920 while Houdini was on a tour of Britain. Houdini had sent Doyle a copy of his book *The Unmasking of Robert Houdin*, about the French magician upon whom Houdini had modelled himself. It included a section on the American mediums Ira and William Davenport, in which Houdini explains how they performed their spirit-cabinet trick. Doyle went to see Houdini perform and asked the magician to visit him at Windlesham. Doyle was impressed by Houdini's abilities and believed he must have supernatural assistance.

Doyle met Houdini again two years later when Doyle was on a lecture tour of North America. Houdini invited him to his New York home and

---

[190] The illusion was exposed by many. See Ivor Ll. Tuckett, *The Evidence for the Supernatural*, (London: Kegan, Paul, Trench, Trübner, 1911), pp. 31–35.

showed him a new illusion, which convinced Doyle even more of Houdini's supernatural abilities. Doyle continued his tour but met Houdini again in Atlantic City, and this time Doyle invited Houdini to attend a séance at which Jean would demonstrate her skills at automatic writing. At one point Jean wrote down a message purporting to come from Houdini's mother. Houdini kept quiet at the time but in later writings he maintained that he had never witnessed a genuine medium and stated that the message could not have been from his mother as she did not know a word of English. Doyle was affronted by this sleight on his wife and the relationship between the two rapidly soured. Houdini remained the pragmatist, and had demonstrated to Doyle how such tricks could be performed, but Doyle refused to accept anything that challenged his beliefs.

After Houdini's tragic death in October 1926, Doyle wrote a long article entitled 'Houdini the Enigma', which ran in the August and September 1927 issues of *The Strand*. Doyle began by considering Houdini's good points, regarding him as courageous, charitable, a good companion (when he was in the right mood) and devoted to his mother. Doyle also believed that Houdini's campaign against mediums was good to the degree that it exposed frauds, but he felt Houdini became intolerant and even offensive towards others whom Doyle believed were genuine. He cited the notable case of Mina 'Margery' Crandon, who is regarded as the toughest opponent Houdini encountered. This arose when the *Scientific American* offered a prize of $2,500 to any medium accepted as genuine by an independent committee agreed by the magazine. Doyle suggested they investigate Mrs Crandon. Houdini was one of the committee, even though Doyle objected to his presence because of his impartiality. At the outset the rest of the committee investigated Margery without telling Houdini, who was furious when he discovered what was happening. The committee were about to accept Margery's abilities when Houdini became involved in late 1924.

This was a true battle of wills, a skilled magician against an equally adept medium. Houdini used several tricks of his own to restrict Margery's abilities, including building a special box in which she was padlocked and into which Houdini surreptitiously hid a ruler so that he could later claim she was going to use this to ring the spirit bell. However, Margery's spirit guide, her dead brother Walter, called Houdini's bluff, even though

Houdini had been sure no one else knew the ruler was there (apart from his own assistant) and that the séance was being held in total darkness. Doyle, who received details direct from Mr Crandon, described this as 'the most dangerous moment of their careers'.[191]

In the end the only way Houdini could discredit them was by showing the committee how he could achieve the same results, without any psychic abilities. It was sufficient to deny the Crandons the prize-money (which had risen to $5,000) but failed to satisfy everyone that they were not genuine. Doyle, of course, fully supported them, going so far as to say:

> The Crandons are themselves the most patient and forgiving people in the world, treating the most irritating opposition with a good-humoured and amused tolerance. But there are other forces which are beyond human control, and from that day the shadow lay heavy upon Houdini.[192]

During the struggle between Houdini and Margery, the spirit-guide, Walter, had threatened Houdini, saying, 'Some day you've got to die.' Doyle mentioned this and other spiritualist warnings that Houdini ignored, including a presentiment of his own death. Doyle was convinced that Houdini was a psychic medium, despite his public denials, and that many of Houdini's remarkable escapes were through supernatural intervention. He recalled how Houdini told him that when he was undertaking an especially dangerous trick he would not do it until an inner voice told him it was safe. Most would interpret that as meaning his own intuition or instinct after years of experience, but Doyle regarded it as a 'psychic element'.

Doyle also recounted the episode in Atlantic City where his wife had presented a message to Houdini from his mother obtained through automatic writing. Doyle noted that Houdini seemed 'deeply moved, and there is no question that at the time he entirely accepted it'.[193] Doyle then considered Houdini's subsequent objections. First, the notepaper on which Dame Jean recorded the message had a cross placed at the top, and Houdini argued that his mother would never use a cross as she was a devout Jew. Doyle maintained that all mediums place a cross on their notes as a holy symbol. As for the main argument that Houdini's mother

---

[191] Doyle, 'Houdini the Enigma', *Strand*, August 1927, p. 137.
[192] *Ibid.*
[193] Doyle, 'Houdini the Enigma', *Strand*, September 1927, p. 266.

did not know a word of English, Doyle stated that the message comes to the medium in 'a flood of thought and of emotion', which the medium then translates.

After Houdini's death there were many reports of attempts to contact his spirit. Houdini had agreed with his brother Theo that they would have a ten-word code known only to them and if any medium claimed to be in touch with whichever of the two had died first, they had to identify the code. According to Houdini's biographer, Ruth Brandon, even ten years after Houdini's death the brother had 'not had as much as a peep from Houdini'.[194]

Doyle reported differently. He claimed he had learned of several messages from Houdini and, although none contained the 'conclusive proofs' upon which he insisted, there was one of particular interest. A New York medium, Mrs Wood, had already received a warning message before Houdini's death alerting him to possible danger. Now, some time after his death, she reported that Houdini materialised at a séance and said plainly, 'You were right and I was wrong', and instructed that the message be passed to Doyle.[195] Coincidentally, after Doyle's friend Jerome K. Jerome died in June 1927 he also sent a spirit message for Doyle saying, 'You were right and I was wrong.'[196]

★

Since the end of the war, Doyle's crusade to promote and vindicate spiritualism meant that he had written little by way of fiction apart from several Sherlock Holmes stories.[197] The few others he contributed to *The Strand*, besides the boxing ghost story 'The Bully of Brocas Court' (November 1921), were relatively minor. Despite its title, 'The Nightmare Room' (December 1921) is a parody of cinematographic performances disguised at first as a ghost story. 'The Lift' (June 1922) concerns a man who has occasional premonitions of disaster, and has another just before he and his girlfriend venture into a lift up a building like the Blackpool Tower. Neither story has any of the old Conan Doyle magic.

---

[194] Brandon, *Houdini* (292).
[195] Doyle, 'Houdini the Enigma', *Strand*, September 1927, p. 270.
[196] Kalush & Sloman (545).
[197] Doyle was even quoted by the American newspapers as saying that he was not going to write any more fiction, as he had 'Other Work to Do'. See *The Pittsburgh Sun*, 19 April 1923.

However, his determination to demonstrate the veracity of spiritualism and to show the treatment meted out to genuine mediums led to him to return to Professor Challenger for the first time in twelve years with a new novel, *The Land of Mist*. It was serialised in *The Strand* from July 1925 to March 1926 with the subtitle 'The Quest of Edward Malone'. Doyle sends his reporter hero from *The Lost World* and 'The Poison Belt' on an investigation into the true nature of spiritualism. Challenger's wife has died, and this has caused him to wither slightly, but he is still as obstinate and argumentative as ever. On occasions Malone is accompanied by Challenger's daughter, Enid.[198] He admonishes Malone and his daughter for even considering investigating spiritualism, but the two persevere regardless. Enid does not always accompany Malone, but among others who do is Lord John Roxton.

It is a very episodic novel, as Doyle takes the reader methodically through the various aspects of spiritualism from a church service, to a séance, to the persecution and trial of a genuine medium, to various meetings and discussions and to the investigation of a haunted house. That investigation, set in Dorset, is the most atmospheric episode in the whole novel and shows that Doyle retained his storytelling abilities, though elsewhere they have become benumbed by his exhortations to the reader that they must take spiritualism seriously as it will be the salvation of mankind.

Doyle had started writing *The Land of Mist* at a frantic pace, telling Greenhough Smith that he had written almost 15,000 words in three days. He wrote fast because the book was intensely important to him and he feared he might pass away before it was finished. At first Doyle believed that Smith was uncertain about the novel, perhaps because of the lack of action. He wrote to Smith, saying:

> I was glad to get your note for it showed that you had not regretted the serial but I was sorry for I hate not to meet your wishes. A sensational scene in a long reasoned narrative is one thing, and a succession of sensational scenes for sensation's sake is another. I fear it would not do.[199]

---

[198] The existence of a daughter may come as a surprise to those who had read 'The Poison Belt', for that story makes no reference to any children. One would think Challenger would ensure his daughter would be included with his wife and friends in the oxygenated room to survive as long as possible. One must deduce, therefore, that Enid was born after the adventures in that novel and that more than twenty years have passed.

[199] Letter, Doyle to Smith, 20 September 1925 [UVa050–1].

THE CIRCLE OF WOOD, IN THE FULL LIGHT OF THE CANDLE, ROSE UPON EDGE AND STOOD THERE SHAKING, AS IF TRYING TO KEEP ITS BALANCE.

Frontispiece by Francis E. Hiley to 'The Land of Mist', *The Strand*, August 1925.

In introducing the story in *The Strand*, Greenhough Smith wrote:

Many of the almost incredible scenes and incidents which he depicts have, he assures us, either occurred to himself or to those whose testimony cannot be doubted. We venture to think that, whatever are the conclusions of the public, they will be amazed at the adventures which are still to be encountered in this workaday world.

Doyle had amassed a significant collection of books and artefacts over the years, and in January 1925 he had opened the Psychic Bookshop and Library opposite Westminster Abbey. Beneath the bookshop he kept on display his collection in what he called 'The World's Happiest Museum'.[200] Much of what was mentioned in 'The Land of Mist' could be found there.

Unfortunately the story loses credibility when Challenger, the ultimate sceptic, concedes at the end when Enid proves herself to be a medium and provides Challenger with information that exonerates him from what he had believed was a terrible wrong in his youth. Clearly Doyle was prepared to sacrifice Challenger in the need to vindicate spiritualism.

Yet whether the public saw that is another matter. The book received reasonable reviews, though W. L. Courtney in the *Daily Telegraph* called it 'one of the best ghost stories with which I am familiar'. Doyle must have winced, as he was not trying to write a ghost story. None of his writings about spiritualism were intended to prove the supernatural. He wanted to establish that there are laws which we have yet to formulate that govern the psychic realm, just as scientific laws govern this world. His passion was to understand those laws and encourage others to explore them. Yet his gullibility in the minds of many over the Cottingley Fairies and spirit photography only undermined his case. *The Strand* gave him a significant public forum and Doyle made good use of it, but the passage of time suggests that Doyle's spiritualist crusade failed.

---

[200] See 'The World's Happiest Museum' by Leonard Crocombe, *The Strand*, May 1927, pp. 451–458

14

Memories in The Strand

DURING 1923 DOYLE WROTE his autobiography, *Memories and Adventures*. Most of it was serialised in *The Strand* from October 1923 to July 1924, though the final book version included some material published elsewhere.[201] We have already covered much of his life as reflected in *Memories and Adventures*, and have seen how it related to his writings, but there were other experiences remembered in both his autobiography and other contributions to *The Strand*.

This was particularly true of sport. In addition to his interest in boxing, discussed in Chapter 5, Doyle was adept at cricket, football, shooting, golf, skiing, riding – the list goes on. His chapter about sport in *Memories and Adventures* overlapped an earlier article in the September 1909 *Strand* also called 'Some Recollections of Sport'. In his typically forthright manner, Doyle began the earlier article at the risk of alienating some readers by suggesting what did not qualify as sport, such as flat-racing. 'Sport is what a man does, not what a horse does,' he remarked. He conceded that there was more skill required for steeplechasing, but did not agree with the gambling that went along with it. He later revealed that Dr Watson spent over half his army pension on the races![202] While he agreed that shooting wild birds for food was acceptable, as well as fox-hunting

---

[201] The only contemporary part of his autobiography that did not run in *The Strand* was his early psychic experiences, which appeared in *Pearson's Magazine*.
[202] See 'The Adventure of Shoscombe Old Place', *Strand*, April 1927.

(because foxes kill, and 'to slay one is to save many') he did not believe
we had the moral right to kill creatures for amusement. He still held
that view twenty years later, because this part of the article was reprinted
in the May 1928 *Strand* at the start of a symposium, 'Blood Sports –
Should They Be Abolished?'

He stretched the truth when it came to fishing, boasting that he had
caught a fish greater in weight than any other fisherman's daily total –
200 tons. He was, though, talking about his experiences on a Greenland
whaler in 1880, an adventure which was doubtless the making of him

**"I USED IN MY EARLY GOLFING DAYS TO PRACTISE ON THE VERY RUDIMENTARY LINKS
IN FRONT OF THE MENA HOTEL, JUST UNDER THE PYRAMIDS."**

Doyle gaining some golfing practice whilst in Egypt (illustration by Arthur
Twidle from *The Strand*, September 1909).

with its mental, physical and spiritual challenges. He did not, of course, catch the whale single-handedly, but he did spend one occasion in the lancing boat which is where the final capture and kill happens.

He regarded boxing as the 'finest single-man sport' while Rugby football was the best 'collective' sport. He had played as a forward in the Edinburgh University team, but felt his understanding of the sport was inadequate and changed to Association football. When he arrived in Portsmouth in 1882 he immersed himself in local activities and was an early member of Portsmouth Football Club in its amateur days. He wrote:

> Even then we could put a very fair team in the field, and were runners up for the County Cup the last season that I played. In the same season I was invited to play for the county. I was always too slow, however, to be a really good back, though I was a long and safe kick.[203]

His slowness may have been due to his weight. He wrote to his mother some time in 1884 commenting that football gave much-needed exercise, as he was growing stout – 15 stone 8lb.[204] That may account for why he became their goalkeeper playing, for some reason, under the alias A. C. Smith.

It is rugby rather than football that features in the Sherlock Holmes story 'The Adventure of the Missing Three-Quarter' in the August 1904 *Strand*. Holmes professes to know nothing about the game but nevertheless holds the view that amateur sport 'is the best and soundest thing in England.' Doyle may also have paid a nod to his old football club though, for in their search for the missing player Holmes uses a draghound called Pompey, and by 1904 Pompey was the nickname of the now professional Portsmouth Football Club.

★

Doyle believed he was a better player of billiards than golf, but then he did have a billiards table at home. It was while playing golf with

---

[203] Doyle, 'Some Recollections of Sport', *Strand*, September 1909, p. 275.

[204] We also know that Doyle was 6 feet 1 inch tall, as portrayed in 'Inches and Eminence' by Beckles Willson (*Strand*, August 1904), which gave profiles of many celebrities according to their height.

Fletcher Robinson that the two plotted *The Hound of the Baskervilles*. But he proclaimed that cricket was the game that gave 'more pleasure during my life than any other branch of sport'. There were times when it seemed that writing got in the way of cricket. His business diaries contain very little personal information apart from his writing income and his cricket scores. Wherever he lived he made sure he was involved with the local cricket club – he even played cricket on his honeymoon in Ireland in August 1885. Although he was only ever an amateur, he did enter the higher ranks in August 1900 when he played a first-class three-day cricket match for the MCC (Marylebone Cricket Club), and on the first day had the triumph of his career – he dismissed the great W. G. Grace:

> Alas! there was nothing in the ball to make the deed memorable. It was a little short of a half-volley outside the off-wicket. But that is just where luck comes in. Four first-class professionals had done nothing against Grace's impenetrable defence because he was on his guard against them. But this innocuous ball was above suspicion. He tried to pull it, and getting under it sent it up to an amazing height into the air. My heart seemed to go about as high as I saw Storer[205] run from the wickets to get under it, but it was very safe in the hands of the Derbyshire crack. That moment of supreme good fortune atoned for many a missed chance and many a day's pounding on a hard wicket.[206]

Grace had his revenge the following year at Lord's Cricket Ground when he bowled Doyle out. Doyle told this story frequently and included it in a tribute, 'W. G. Grace, A Memory' in the July 1927 *Strand*, where he called Grace 'the very impersonation of cricket, redolent of fresh air, of good humour, of conflict without malice, of chivalrous strife, of keenness for victory by fair means and utter detestation of all that were foul.'[207] Such a description pretty much sums up Doyle's attitude to life.

---

[205] William Storer, an accomplished all-rounder, who played first-class cricket for Derbyshire from 1887 to 1905.

[206] Doyle, 'Some Recollections of Sport', *Strand*, September 1909, p. 277.

[207] Doyle, 'W. G. Grace, A Memory', *Strand*, July 1927, p. 90.

"THE MOST SINGULAR BALL I HAVE EVER RECEIVED."

The incident that inspired 'The Story of Spedegue's Dropper' illustrated by
Arthur Twidle (from *The Strand*, September 1909).

Doyle's most ignominious defeat in a non-first-class match came
when he fell victim to a 'donkey-drop' ball delivered by 'Bunny' Lucas.
Doyle called it:

> …the most singular ball that I have ever received. He propelled it like a
> quoit into the air to a height of at least thirty feet, and it fell straight and
> true on to the top of the bails. […] I tried to cut it off my stumps with
> the result that I knocked down my wicket and broke my bat, while the
> ball fell in the midst of this general chaos. I spent the rest of the day won-
> dering gloomily what I ought to have done – and I am wondering yet.[208]

After thirty years or more brooding over it, he turned it into a classic
cricket story, 'The Story of Spedegue's Dropper', in the October 1928
Strand. Local player Tom Spedegue suffers from asthma and a bad heart
but has been practising a new way of delivering the ball, a lob or donkey-
drop where the ball goes high into the air and drops straight on to the
bails. Witnessed by a retired cricketer, Spedegue suddenly finds himself in

[208] *Ibid.*

Doyle (third from left top row) and W. G. Grace (fourth from left, seated) in
the London County and MCC match in 1900 (from *The Strand*, July 1927).

the England team against Australia at Lords. Nervous at first, and no one
knowing what to expect, Spedegue perfects his delivery and wins England
the Ashes. Tongue-in-cheek, Doyle calls the event 'the greatest joke in the
history of cricket', but it is a typical Doyle story of how, through invention,
determination, skill and courage, the common man can come up trumps.

Doyle was full of cricket stories, such as the time when a ball from a
fast bowler was delivered so fast that Doyle didn't see it. It struck him
on the thigh and seemed rather more painful than he would have expected. Then he realized he had a box of matches in his pocket and the
ball had set them ablaze.

Generally Doyle had few mishaps in his sporting life, though he was
nearly stabbed in a bout of fencing and disabled his knee during one
cricket match. Doyle was, though, game for almost anything, and even
took part in the International Road Competition, organised by Prince

Henry of Prussia in 1911 with the aim of pitting British cars against German ones. The British team won, but Doyle did not see it as a success in developing international friendship. Once back in London he promptly ensured that a firm of which he was a director withdrew £30,000 from the bank in Berlin. Doyle had a feeling the two nations would soon be at war, when all thought of fair play faded.

★

The prospect that Doyle might have become a Member of Parliament came close, not once, but twice. He stood as a Liberal Unionist candidate in two general elections: the first in Edinburgh Central in October 1900, and the second in Hawick Burghs in February 1906. Although the Liberal Unionists were an offshoot of the Liberal Party, their fundamental difference over Irish Home Rule allied them to the Conservative Party, with whom they formed a government in 1900.

When he came to write about his experiences twenty years later Doyle was uncertain quite why he had stood for Parliament, as he was not a political animal and could not imagine himself 'fettered to a party'; being something of a fatalist, though, Doyle felt he should give it a go to see whether or not it was really in his blood. He was sure he had been put on the Earth for some great purpose, and was searching to find what that was. It was only later that he decided it was for the support of spiritualism, and he learned much about the process of communicating with crowds and understanding their needs while promoting his own during his two election campaigns.

It was believed at one point in the 1900 campaign that Doyle might win. He certainly had a more robust series of meetings than his opponent.[209] However, towards the end of the campaign it was put about that Doyle was a Roman Catholic, and since at that time there was much opposition to any representation by Catholics, Doyle's support dwindled – though he still polled nearly 45 per cent of the votes cast.

Though less successful, probably because Thomas Shaw was the incumbent MP, the Hawick result was of greater interest. Doyle was comparatively well known in the area, which includes the towns of Selkirk

---

[209] Ironically, Brown was head of the publishing firm of Thomas Nelson, which would later publish new editions of two of Doyle's books.

Table 5: Arthur Conan Doyle's election results

	Candidates	1900 Election Edinburgh Central	Candidates	1906 Election Hawick Burghs
Liberal	George Mackenzie Brown	3,028	Thomas Shaw	3,125
Liberal Unionist	Arthur Conan Doyle	2,459	Arthur Conan Doyle	2,444
Majority		569		681

and Galashiels. He had put himself forward as the prospective future candidate for the constituency in November 1903 when he advocated Tariff Reform. The towns, which had been prosperous in the wool trade, were noticing the effect of German imports. Doyle later wrote, 'I really expended a good deal of work as well as money upon the attempt.'[210] He maintained a presence in the area, and several of his stories were reprinted at that time in the *Hawick News and Border Chronicle*. He played cricket there with an MCC eleven, he lectured there, and he became Vice-President of both the Border Amateur Athletic Association and the Hawick and Wilton Cricket Club. As a patron of the Border Amateur Football League he donated the Conan Doyle Cup in 1905. He also took part in the annual 'common riding' festival[211] in June 1904 where, mounted on a hunter, he had to gallop through the town over a measured course of about half a mile. It was something he was determined not to repeat, though he remembered the bravery and fighting skills of the locals in *Sir Nigel*.

Doyle was also involved in a campaign to raise money to rebuild the bridge at Selkirk, which had been destroyed in a flood in 1902. He opened the fund-raising bazaar at Selkirk on 12 December 1903 and his name is present in a booklet issued to help raise funds, called *The Book o' the Brig*. Intriguingly that booklet contains a Holmes pastiche, called, rather clumsily, '"Sherlock Holmes" Discovering the Border Burghs, and, by deduction, the Brig Bazaar'. It is not known who wrote the spoof, and the rediscovery of the booklet in February 2015 raised the question of whether it was in fact Doyle. But if so, he would most certainly have

---

[210] Doyle, 'Memories and Adventures', *Strand*, March 1924, p. 244.
[211] This has been held since 1515 and celebrates the heroism of the village townsfolk in capturing an English flag from a raiding party during the conflicts between England and Scotland.

signed and promoted it, and the story is not written in Doyle's style nor with his skill and ability. Nevertheless it demonstrated his acceptance of pastiches, especially if they helped raise much-needed funds.

Although Doyle never did become a Member of Parliament – something for which he later admitted he was grateful – this did not stop him holding strong views on all manner of subjects, such as Britain's defence, as we have already encountered. He contributed (often reluctantly) to several of the symposia that *The Strand* ran, in which they garnered the views of various eminent people on specific issues. The September 1911 issue asked, if you had absolute power, 'What Reform is Most Needed?'. There were a variety of radical responses, ranging from Andrew Carnegie's abolishing war and disbanding the armed forces, to Justin McCarthy granting Home Rule to Ireland. Doyle reflected one of his recent concerns:

> The divorce laws are so arranged at present that divorce is practically impossible for a poor man, that people are tied without hope of release to lunatics, drunkards and criminals and great numbers (more than two hundred thousand individuals) are separated by law and yet are not free to marry again – a fact that cannot be conducive to public morality.[212]

Doyle had become President of the Divorce Law Reform Union in 1909 and produced for them a leaflet, *Divorce Law Reform: An Essay*. He continued to fight for reform over the next decade, just one of many causes he championed. He was appointed chairman of a Royal Commission to consider the subject and in July 1917 presided over a meeting comprised mostly of members of both Houses of Parliament in drafting a Matrimonial Causes Bill which would allow a marriage to be dissolved following a separation of three years. Unfortunately the proposal was not supported, least of all by the Church of England, and the necessary reforms were not implemented during Doyle's lifetime.

Doyle promoted his feelings in a Sherlock Holmes story. In 'The Adventure of the Devil's Foot' (*Strand*, December 1910) we find Dr Sterndale explaining the circumstances that led to his crime:

---

[212] Doyle, *Strand*, September 1911, p. 270.

I could not marry her, for I have a wife who has left me for years and yet whom, by the deplorable laws of England, I could not divorce. For years Brenda waited. For years I waited. And this is what we have waited for.

For which reason, Holmes excuses him.

During the First World War *The Strand* ran another symposium, 'What Will England be Like in 1930?' (August 1917). Doyle's response was cautiously optimistic depending on the outcome of the war. He had no doubt that Britain would win, but it depended on the extent of that victory and how much military force needed to be maintained to contain Germany. Doyle hoped the victory would be sufficient that Britain's military forces could be reduced and that money spent on increasing old-age pensions, encouraging education, subsidising scientific research, temperance legislation and drastic reforms for poverty and disease. He also hoped there would be greater profit-sharing between the Labour and capitalist extremes. Without that working agreement, Doyle argued, 'the country will be convulsed by never-ending troubles', by which he foresaw the Depression of the 1920s.

He ended his essay by saying that he believed the last twenty years had been 'the most wicked epoch of the world's history; so that all changes are likely to be for the better'. For someone with such a keen interest in history his view about 'the most wicked epoch' is debatable, but he would nevertheless cling to that optimism, despite the death of his son, Kingsley, a year later.

Among other symposia to which Doyle contributed was 'The Most Useful Invention or Discovery since 1850' in the August 1918 *Strand*. This reproduced a postcard from Doyle stating that he believed it was Sir Ronald Ross's discovery 'that the mosquito carries the germ of malaria. It has made great regions habitable which were practically barren before…'.

★

Doyle contributed to several other symposia, although he seldom enjoyed them. He sent a postcard to Smith on 1 May 1913 saying 'Down with flu — when is that blessed symposium?' In the end Doyle did not contribute, though the irony is that it was related to one of the great mysteries that Doyle had helped perpetuate — that of the *Marie Celeste*.

The symposium, 'The Greatest Mystery of the Sea. Can You Solve It?', ran in the July 1913 issue. The ship's name was properly the *Mary Celeste*, a brigantine discovered on 4 December 1872 off the coast of the Azores, with none of its crew on board and no lifeboat. The last entry in the log-book had been ten days before, and contained no suggestion of any problem. The fate of the crew has never been resolved.

Doyle had used the incident as the basis for his story 'J. Habakuk Jephson's Statement', published anonymously in the January 1884 *Cornhill Magazine*. He fictionalised everything in the story. It was Doyle who changed the name to the *Marie Celeste*. He invented names for the captain and crew as well as adding passengers. The basis of his story is that one of the crew had a hatred of white men and encouraged the others to kill the captain and flee to West Africa. Jephson survived because he possessed a magic charm.

Doyle was delighted that the story was purchased by *The Cornhill*, and even more delighted at the fuss it caused in various newspapers, some of which attributed it to Robert Louis Stevenson, Doyle's idol. Delight turned to surprise when the *Boston Herald* ran the story in its 3 April 1885 edition as a possible true account. As a consequence, some of Doyle's story has fused with the real facts in the public consciousness to embellish the mystery.

It is unfortunate that Doyle did not contribute to the symposium so that we could learn what he really believed. Barry Pain suggested the crew had been kidnapped by an unknown ship. Morley Roberts suspected an insurance scam. Horace Annesley Vachell wondered whether an underwater explosion had vomited poisonous gas into the air, causing the crew to abandon ship. Arthur Morrison suggested that one of the crew was a religious fanatic who killed everyone and then jumped overboard.

The symposium generated yet another purportedly true account, 'Abel Fosdyk's Story', in the November 1913 issue. It had been submitted by A. Howard Linford, Headmaster of Peterborough Lodge, a public school in Hampstead. He claimed it was a document that had been given to him by an old servant, though he could not vouch for its accuracy. There were sufficient errors in the story for it to be regarded as a literary hoax but it continued the chain of such stories, which Doyle had started thirty years earlier.

★

Doyle's recollections in some symposia suggest that he was either forgetful or chose not to recall certain facts. For instance, in 'The Book I Most Enjoyed Writing' he said that he had 'never written to order ... or sold any work until it was well on the way to completion'.[213] He had clearly forgotten that he had sold *Uncle Bernac* before he had started it, and agreed to the series of Sherlock Holmes stories for *Collier's Weekly* before starting those, and in both cases struggled to complete them.

His frustration at contributing to the symposia is often shown by the brevity of his answer. When asked which character in fiction he would most like to have created, he said:

> I think Colonel Newcome as the ideal English gentleman would have my vote.[214]

Another symposium asked whether the contributors were haunted by a recurring dream. Doyle responded that he had never had a recurring dream but he did have prophetic dreams, though he did not enlarge upon this, merely saying:

> In sleep the soul is freed and has enlarged knowledge. This it endeavours to pass on to the body, but it seldom succeeds.[215]

Doyle did subsequently report a dream in his essay 'The Dreamers' (June 1928), compiled from his correspondence files. After recording the dreams of others he ended with one of his own. At a séance he was told he would visit another sphere in his sleep, and he begged that he might remember everything. He recalled that the dream began with him in a town or city among dilapidated stone villas. He was aware someone was with him, but he could not see them. He was suddenly elsewhere, in a large hall with coloured frescoes, standing near a man in Elizabethan dress – each was aware of the other. He shifted again to being inside a vehicle moving in a

---

[213] Doyle, 'The Book I Most Enjoyed Writing', *Strand*, March 1922, p.240.

[214] Doyle, 'The Great Characters of Fiction', *Strand*, December 1927, p.642. Colonel Newcome is the primary character in the family saga, *The Newcomes*, by William Makepeace Thackeray. Another contributor, E. Philllips Oppenheim, wrote 'I would choose to have been the creator of Sherlock Holmes.' He believed that the character of Holmes was 'a perfect exposition of the writer's craft.' (p.646)

[215] Doyle, 'Haunting Dreams', *Strand*, April 1923, p. 371.

" Well, if you fellows are going to dress like that, we poor moderns have no chance."

Image from Doyle's dream of his spirit visiting another sphere and time.
Illustration by Percy Spence for *The Strand*, June 1928.

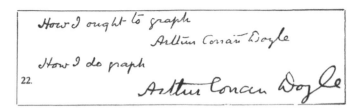

Doyle's double autograph signed for Signor Boriani of the Pall Mall Restaurant (from *The Strand*, October 1912).

hurry past ruins, to the top of a hill where below him was a vast city. He then awoke but the next day a psychic message told him that the vision was of a probationary city, though he explained no more.

From dreams to humour: there was one instance among the symposia when brevity was the whole point. Signor Arnolfo Boriani, proprietor of the Pall Mall Restaurant in the Haymarket, had amassed a collection of autographs by his clientele. *The Strand* ran a number of them with commentary and noted that Doyle 'must be credited with the cleverest pun in the book'. He had signed twice, the first saying 'How I ought to graph', and the second 'How I do graph'.[216] Boriani evidently caught him on a good day!

★

Considering the pressure on his time it is surprising that Doyle agreed to be one of the judges in a short story competition that *The Strand* announced in its December 1919 issue. The first prize, for a story under 6,000 words, was £250 (around £9,000 today), with runner-up prizes of £100 and £50. The fellow judges were H. Rider Haggard and H. G. Wells, plus the editors of *The Strand* and its companion magazines *The Grand* and *John o' London's Weekly*.[217] It was reported that some 3,500 stories were submitted, and a shortlist, with the authors' names removed, was prepared for the judges to read. The May 1920 issue gave the final results, and also listed the top three of each individual judge. It is interesting that while the winner, 'Redemption' by Oswald Wildridge, was

---

[216] See 'Autographs After Dinner', *Strand*, October 1912, p. 449.
[217] Charles Garvice was also named as a judge, but he died in March 1920 before the final selection was settled.

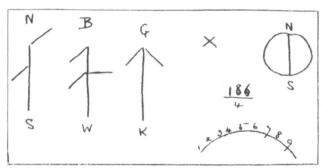

THE ABOVE DIAGRAM ACCOMPANIED A BURIED TREASURE
PROBLEM WHICH WAS SENT TO SHERLOCK HOLMES.
CAN YOU SOLVE IT ?

Among the mysteries sent to Sherlock Holmes was this treasure map which
related to the wreck of an East Indiaman ship off the South African coast in
1782. Doyle wrote about the map in the December 1917 *Strand* but did not
name the ship, though he was almost certainly referring to the *Grosvenor*,
whose treasure had already become a legend by that time and has continued
to raise interest and investigation. Doyle did not try to solve the treasure map
and it is not clear whether anyone else has.

given first place by four of the judges and second place by H. G. Wells,
Doyle didn't rank it at all. It may have been because it was a sea story
and the author was no sailor, whereas Doyle had had some nautical experience. Doyle's vote went to 'The Flower-Show at Kwaliz' by Herbert
Tremaine (the alias of Maude Deuchar), a charming oriental fantasy
which Doyle called 'very beautiful and original'.[218] Wells also voted it
into first place, while Haggard placed it second. Although neither judge
knew the identities of the authors, Doyle and Wells made a sound choice.
While the winner, Oswald Wildridge, has long been forgotten, Maude
Deuchar has been rediscovered more recently thanks to her vivid
wartime play *The Handmaidens of Death*.

★

Among Doyle's memories were those of the notable people he met, and
his storytelling skills bring many incidents vividly to life. He met the Prime
Minister, David Lloyd George, in April 1917 for breakfast at 10 Downing

---

[218] The story was published in the June 1920 *Strand*.

Street, and as it was just the two of them, Lloyd George poured the tea and Doyle served the bacon and eggs. One time Doyle was visiting Lord Burnham's house, Hall Barn at Beaconsfield, in which was installed a Turkish bath. He insisted Doyle take advantage of the facilities and, as Doyle was sitting in the drying-room draped only in a towel, who should walk in but Arthur Balfour, soon to be Prime Minister. Doyle recorded, 'There were no explanations, and I felt that he went away with the impression that this was my usual costume.'[219]

Other memories include teaching Rudyard Kipling golf at his home in Brattleboro', Vermont, much to the consternation of the locals who had not seen the game. With H. G. Wells, whose 'many-sided genius' Doyle admired, Doyle discovered he had unknowingly met Wells's father, who once had been a professional cricketer, and had become a groundsman at a cricket ground Doyle had played at in Hampshire. With J. M. Barrie, Doyle wondered if he had sown the seed for what became his play *The Admirable Crichton*, completed in 1902. He recalled that the two were walking together at Barrie's home in Kirriemuir when Doyle related a thought that had come to him the previous night of a king, shipwrecked on an island, with the only other survivor being a very capable sailor. He suspected that before long the roles would be reversed.

Doyle never met Robert Louis Stevenson, but they corresponded when Stevenson lived in Samoa. Stevenson apparently narrated the Sherlock Holmes stories to his native servants, who had no idea what they were about but were nevertheless amazed. Doyle was asked by Stevenson's executors to complete his last novel, *St. Ives*, but he did not feel equal to the task.

Needless to say Sherlock Holmes provided plenty of anecdotes and Doyle included several in 'Some Personalia About Mr Sherlock Holmes' in the December 1917 issue. Doyle received many letters addressed to Holmes. A local workman believed that when Doyle was knighted he changed his name to Sherlock Holmes, and sent him a bill in that name. Another woman addressed the newly knighted author as 'Good Lord'.

---

[219] Doyle, 'Memories and Adventures', *Strand*, April 1924, p. 339. Doyle does not date this meeting but refers to Balfour as the Prime Minister. Lellenberg, *Letters* (501), dates it to June 1902, which is a month before Balfour became Prime Minister. Andrew Lycett dates it as September 1905, when Balfour was Prime Minister, but there is no record that Doyle was at Hall Barn at that time.

Doyle also referred to the many letters he received asking if Holmes could help with a problem and he selected one in particular. A man had been missing for a week. He had been staying at a London hotel, and had drawn out forty pounds that day and visited the music-hall that evening. He returned to the hotel to change his clothes but then vanished, and no one saw him leave. Doyle correctly deduced that he had indeed left, and because the hour was close to midnight had caught a train that would run through the night with him arriving somewhere in the morning, which would not seem unusual. He suggested either Edinburgh or Glasgow, and was subsequently proved correct.[220]

★

Doyle's memories and anecdotes gave him a fund of stories for luncheon parties and after-dinner speeches. He concluded 'Memories and Adventures' with a variety of miscellaneous memories such as once saving a potential suicide from jumping off the Thames Embankment, and of raising a fund which amounted to £300 for the Italian marathon runner who should have won, but was disqualified because he was helped over the line, at the 1908 Olympic Games. But there is a comment at the end which is telling. Doyle's life was full, often frantic, as he bounded from one meeting to the next, one cause to the next, one story, lecture or essay to the next. So when, at the start of the First World War he signed up for the Civilian Reserve, he found the life of a private soldier delightful. 'To be led and not to lead was most restful …'[221] It says much about Doyle's life that it needed a war for him to find a moment's respite.

---

[220] *The Strand* ran no detailed accounts of either the George Edalji or Oscar Slater cases during Doyle's life. Doyle did write about them in the book edition of *Memories and Adventures*, but these had first appeared in *The Great Stories of Real Life*, a fortnightly partwork edited by Max Pemberton and published by Newnes, in 1924.

[221] Doyle, 'Memories and Adventures', *Strand*, July 1924, p.24.

15

Final Days

THE LAST SHERLOCK HOLMES STORY by Arthur Conan Doyle, 'The Adventure of Shoscombe Old Place', appeared in the April 1927 *Strand*. Doyle showed he could still present a decent mystery that taxed the brain, even though it continued to follow the tried-and-tested formula. Again we have Holmes informed of a sudden and eccentric change in an individual's habits, which Holmes then follows through to the somewhat bizarre conclusion.

Several of these stories, collected as *The Case-Book of Sherlock Holmes*, include eccentric plots. 'The Adventure of the Creeping Man' (March 1923) is borderline science fiction because it deals with the extreme effects of a serum extracted from monkey glands. It's one of the last cases before Holmes's retirement, and sadly Watson feels he has become one of Holmes's habits. 'The Adventure of the Sussex Vampire' (January 1924) is not about a real vampire – Holmes has no truck with the supernatural and says to Watson, 'No ghosts need apply' – but still boasts a macabre atmosphere. It also refers to perhaps the most quoted unwritten case, the Giant Rat of Sumatra, 'a story for which the world is not yet prepared.' 'The Adventure of the Lion's Mane' (December 1926) is set after Holmes's retirement so is narrated by Holmes himself and involves yet another little-known deadly hazard. Doyle still sustained credibility, even though it was evident he was searching far and wide for something original to tell.

Doyle was still paid £100 per thousand words for Holmes, so 'Shoscombe' brought in £628 from *The Strand* (less Watt's commission) and £875 from the American publication in *Liberty* – the two equal to over £80,000 today. Although the value of £100 had almost halved between 1893 and 1927, Doyle was still one of the magazine's highest-paid contributors.

Having finished the last story, Doyle wrote a brief piece about Holmes in order to introduce a competition. Doyle referred to the fear he had long held that Holmes would become stale over the years or, as he put it, 'one of those popular tenors who, having outlived their time, are still tempted to make repeated farewell bows to their indulgent audiences. This must cease and he must go the way of all flesh, material or imaginary'.[222]

The competition was for readers to list what they thought were the twelve best Sherlock Holmes short stories (not in any order). The one that was closest to Doyle's selection, already in Greenhough Smith's hands, would win £100 and an autographed edition of *Memories and Adventures*. Although all of the stories had run in *The Strand*, because *The Case-Book* collection had not yet appeared Doyle limited the selection to the previous forty-four.

Doyle explained how he reached his final selection in the June issue. He discussed his choice more or less in order of publication so it is not possible to say categorically which was his top favourite. The stories, with his reasons are shown below.

Table 6: Arthur Conan Doyle's selection of the twelve best Sherlock Holmes stories

Story	Doyle's reason for selection
'The Adventure of the Speckled Band'	That, I am sure, will be on every list.
'The Red-Headed League'	The originality of plot.
'The Dancing Men'	The originality of plot.
'The Adventure of the Final Problem'	Deals with the only foe who ever really extended Holmes.
'A Scandal in Bohemia'	It opened the path for others and has more female interest than usual.
'The Empty House'	Explains away the alleged death of Holmes.
'The Five Orange Pips'	It has a certain dramatic quality of its own.
'The Second Stain'	The better of the two that deal with high diplomacy and intrigue.
'The Devil's Foot'	It is grim and new.
'The Priory School'	For the dramatic moment when Holmes points his finger at the Duke.
'The Musgrave Ritual'	Has a historical touch which gives it a little added distinction. It is also a memory from Holmes's early life.
'The Reigate Squire'	Of the others the one in which Holmes shows the most ingenuity.

---

[222] Doyle, 'Mr Sherlock Holmes To His Readers', *Strand*, March 1927, p. 281.

The winner of the contest selected ten of Doyle's twelve, but we do not learn where he differed. Of the ones omitted perhaps the most surprising is 'The Adventure of Silver Blaze', but Doyle disqualified it on the grounds that the racing detail was 'very faulty'. Ten years earlier, the American librarian, anthologist and novelist Burton Egbert Stevenson had contributed an article to *The Strand* called 'Supreme Moments in Detective Fiction' (January 1917) and he selected what he felt were the five most outstanding stories.

Story	Stevenson's reason for selection
'The Adventure of Silver Blaze'	Holmes's greatest feat, unquestionably.
'The Naval Treaty'	The most ingenious.
'The Man With the Twisted Lip'	Close second to 'The Naval Treaty' in ingenuity.
'The Adventure of the Speckled Band'	The most *outré* of the Sherlock Holmes stories.
'The Red-Headed League'	Has the best start.

There is some overlap. Doyle almost chose 'The Naval Treaty', settling instead on 'The Second Stain'. This shows, not surprisingly, that the Holmes stories contain something for everyone, which is why they remain popular today. In making his list, Doyle said, 'Whatever their merit – and I make no claim for that – they are all as good as I could make them.'[223]

Doubtless many readers believed that Holmes would be back, as he had been so often before. There certainly was no outpouring of grief as there had been in 1893, but then times had changed. Holmes was no longer unique, nor as distinctive as he had been in the 1890s. His existence had brought detective fiction to a new level, sufficient for it to be regarded as a separate genre and thereby to grow and flourish. Most of Holmes's immediate imitators in *The Strand* had long fallen by the wayside, but the abundance of new popular-fiction magazines provided ample fertile soil in which new detectives could blossom. 'The Old Man in the Corner', in the stories by Baroness Orczy, proved highly popular in *The Royal Magazine*. G. K. Chesterton's Father Brown delighted readers of *The Story-teller*. R. Austin Freeman's tales of Dr John Thorndyke fascinated readers of *Pearson's Magazine*. Elsewhere there were the Max

---

[223] Doyle, 'How I Made My List', *Strand*, June 1927, p. 612.

Carrados stories by Ernest Bramah, the Arsène Lupin stories by Maurice Leblanc and, of course, by the 1920s Agatha Christie with Hercule Poirot and Dorothy L. Sayers with Lord Peter Wimsey. The list could fill this book. They all owe something to Doyle in creating the market and establishing the genre, but beyond that they owe little, establishing themselves as original and distinctive fictional detectives in their own right.

The Strand published its own share of new detectives such as the Scarlet Runner series by husband-and-wife team C. N. and A. M. Williamson; the lip-reader Judith Lee in the stories by Richard Marsh; several of the Philip Trent stories by E. C. Bentley, and many stories by Edgar Wallace, H. C. McNeile (as 'Sapper'), F. Britten Austin, E. Phillips Oppenheim and the rest. It was easy to be satiated on detective fiction and clever mystery stories and hardly notice the absence of Sherlock Holmes. And yet, on those occasions when the Holmes stories did appear during the 1920s there was always a respectful reverence for them, alongside a comforting nostalgia. Somehow, because the stories were no longer contemporary but existed in a pre-war era, there was a feeling that Holmes lived on forever in that lost past. Doyle felt some of that. In saying farewell to Holmes and in thanking his readers, he remarked:

> I thank you for your constancy, and can but hope that some return has been made in the shape of that distraction from the worries of life and stimulating change of thought which can only be found in the fairy king-dom of romance.[224]

★

After the final Holmes story, Doyle continued to appear in the *The Strand*. Apart from his contributions to symposia and his articles on Houdini and dreams he had ten more stories, one of which was a five-part serial. Besides his cricketing story about Spedegue's Dropper, the stories for the next two years were all science fiction.

Readers of the September 1927 *Strand* saw an announcement pro-claiming for the next issue the start of Doyle's 'thrilling new adventure'

---

[224] Doyle, 'Mr Sherlock Holmes to His Readers', *Strand*, March 1927, p. 284.

'The Maracot Deep'; 'greater even than "The Lost World"!' The first episode was dramatically illustrated on the cover. The serial, which ran until February 1928, introduces us to Professor Maracot who, though like Challenger in his hatred of the press and his devotion to science, is physically very different. Thin, emotionless, gaunt, like an 'animated mummy', he is aloof, absent-minded and secretive. As a consequence his colleagues on the voyage of the SS *Stratford* have no idea of his intentions until the expedition is well under way.

In Doyle's traditional storytelling mode, the story is a first-person narrative told through letters and messages, just as in *The Lost World*. Here the narrator is the zoologist Cyrus Headley. Maracot's purpose is to explore the bottom of the Atlantic Ocean and in particular the area around a deep cleft he had discovered and called the Maracot Deep. He has invented a pressurised capsule (which we now call a bathysphere), and here Doyle was at the cutting edge of exploration. At the time Doyle was writing 'The Maracot Deep' two scientists, William Beebe and Otis Barton, were building what would become the world's first bathysphere, which made its first test descent in May 1930. Science-fiction authors had, of course, long preceded Doyle. To some extent he was reworking Jules Verne's *20,000 Leagues Under the Sea* (1870), and H. G. Wells had used a bathysphere in 'In the Abyss' (1896). Doyle's adventure tale is an effective tribute to both Verne and Wells.

Professor Maracot descends in his capsule along with Headley and engineer Bill Scanlan. The cable supporting the sphere is cut by a giant crayfish and descends over five miles into the abyss. The three adventurers almost die of asphyxiation before they realise they have landed near a vast underwater building, almost buried by centuries of detritus. They are rescued by the inhabitants of this world, who turn out to be descendants of survivors from Atlantis who have continued to exist through developing science and technology inherited from their ancestors. One of their inventions is a thought-transference machine by which they are able to communicate, though they also discover that they have a common language in ancient Greek. They have found how to split the atom, and power their city by atomic energy.

Headley becomes romantically attached to a young Atlantean woman, Mona, and they discover they were lovers in a previous life.

With fierce gestures and cries the priests of the Temple drove us roughly out of their sacred shrine.

Tom Peddie's striking frontispiece to the December 1927 episode of 'The Maracot Deep'

The Atlanteans have developed a form of transparent diving suit that allows them to explore the ocean depths. Maracot and his colleagues discover the wreck of the ship from which they had descended, which had been destroyed in a hurricane.

Doyle reintroduced his gas 'levigen', which is nine times 'lighter' than hydrogen and which had amused him when Greenhough Smith challenged him about it in *The Lost World*. Headley finds a way to communicate with the surface by sending a message inside a silica globe filled with the gas. This also becomes the method for their return to the outer world.

Doyle had not finished with this submarine world, though. A year later he returned with a two-part serial, 'The Lord of the Dark Face' (April and May 1929), which recounts an episode Headley had left out of his previous message because he felt it would not be believed. It should have been left out again, as the story suffers from Doyle introducing some of his occult beliefs. Maracot and his colleagues continue to explore the ocean bed near the home of their rescuers and, in particular, the ruins of an old temple, which had evidently been part of the original Atlantis. Here they encounter Baal-Seepa, Lord of the Dark Face, who is the epitome of evil (though he doesn't act like he is). The temple is not his home but is a focal point he can visit. He spends most of his time on the upper Earth. Having lived for at least 11,000 years we may regard him as the Satan-like influence of all evil. However, somewhat stupendously, Maracot draws upon occult knowledge that no one knew he had and manages to destroy Baal-Seepa. The story is a most unlikely and pointless appendage to 'The Maracot Deep', which stood well enough on its own.

Unfortunately 'The Lord of the Dark Face' was like two other stories Doyle wrote at the time; both ingenious ideas spoiled by an absurd development. 'When the World Screamed' (April to May 1928) is a new Professor Challenger story. As there is no reference to his daughter or to his psychic adventures we may presume it takes place before *The Land of Mist*, except that the events are so momentous one would have expected them to be referred to in that serial. Challenger believes the Earth is a living organism with its own nervous system and a degree of sentience. This was not a concept that originated with

Doyle; it had been considered by several Victorian philosophers and scientists in developing the theory of animism, as expressed by Sir Edward Tylor in his 1871 book *Primitive Culture*. Tylor had based his conclusions on his study of spiritualism. In 'When the World Screamed' Doyle sought to explore this theory by scientific means. Challenger drills deep into the Earth's crust in order to stimulate the Earth's sensory apparatus. The work is conducted in the Sussex Weald (near Doyle's home at Crowborough) and proves highly effective, for as the drill penetrates the Earth's nervous system it emits a 'howl in which pain, anger, menace, and the outraged majesty of Nature all blended into one hideous shriek'.[225]

Doyle ends the story at that moment, with Challenger's triumph as the first human 'whom Mother Earth had been compelled to recognize'. Even though this is such a stupendous discovery, Doyle does not pursue it. As with many of his past stories the thrill is in the idea and its culmination, not in its cataclysmic aftermath. As Doyle approached his seventieth birthday, he was satisfied to post the concept and let the reader's imagination do the rest.

The last Professor Challenger story is the weakest. 'The Disintegration Machine', in the January 1929 issue, is again narrated by Malone. He and Challenger take up an invitation from scientist Theodore Nemor, who has invented a machine that can split the molecules of any object or living being so that it completely disappears. He can then reverse the process. He demonstrates this on Challenger, having a joke so that when Challenger reappears it is at first without his hair and beard. Realising the destructive power of this invention, Challenger tricks Nemor into sitting in the machine and disintegrates him, leaving his molecules dispersed. Malone hesitates but Challenger is resolute. The device is too dangerous and he tells Malone, 'The first duty of the law-abiding citizen is to prevent murder … I have done so.'[226] In fact Challenger has just committed murder, but that does not enter the argument and Challenger moves on to 'matters of more importance'.

It is sad to have ended Challenger's adventurous if bombastic career in such a shameful way, and yet Challenger was never a pleasant character;

---

[225] Doyle, 'When the World Screamed', *Strand*, May 1928, p. 450.
[226] Doyle, 'The Disintegration Machine', *Strand*, January 1929, p. 10.

apart from *The Lost World*, the stories explore the power of science over nature and humanity, rather than the reverse. Doyle uses Challenger to develop an interesting idea, but also always to glorify him and that may be why, apart from *The Lost World*, the other Challenger stories have been forgotten.

There was an interesting coda to the Challenger series. An occasional writer, John Henry Symons, who earned a living as a master draper, believed that Doyle had plagiarised two of his stories and he drew this to the attention of publisher and former politician Horatio Bottomley, who reported it in his short-lived weekly scandal-sheet, *John Blunt*. Symons claimed that *The Land of Mist* was copied from his 1925 novel *A Splendid Angel*, and 'The Disintegration Machine' from *The End of the Marriage Vow*, published in 1928. Doyle brought a libel action against Bottomley and established that his works were already with *The Strand* before Symons's books were published. In October 1929, Bottomley and Symons withdrew their allegations, paid damages and apologised unreservedly. Doyle must have had a feeling of *déjà vu*, thinking of the earlier allegations of plagiarism by J.-H. Rosny *aîné*. He may have felt there was nothing in the world of science fiction that had not already been covered – and indeed, even as long ago as 1929 that was almost true.

Yet his last story of science fiction was his most original. It was highly distinctive, powerful and effective, and certainly his best. This was 'The Death Voyage' in the October 1929 *Strand*, which is a thought experiment in alternative history. It is set in November 1918 in the final days of the First World War. In our history Kaiser Wilhelm II abdicated on 9 November and fled into exile in the Netherlands. In Doyle's story the Kaiser refuses to resign. Instead he hurries to Kiel where the Navy has already mutinied, takes control of his forces and sets sail with his fleet for one final battle against the Allies. Doyle provides the Kaiser with a heroic rather than an ignominious fate, and even has the British fleet fly its flags at half-mast in tribute to a brave man. The story raises the question of whether it would have been better for the Kaiser to have died heroically than in exile. At the time Doyle wrote the story the Kaiser was still alive in the Netherlands, and would remain so until his death in 1941.

Although there were a few earlier alternate histories, the concept would not establish itself until J. C. Squire compiled his volume of essays *If It Had Happened Otherwise* in 1931. Doyle was probably aware

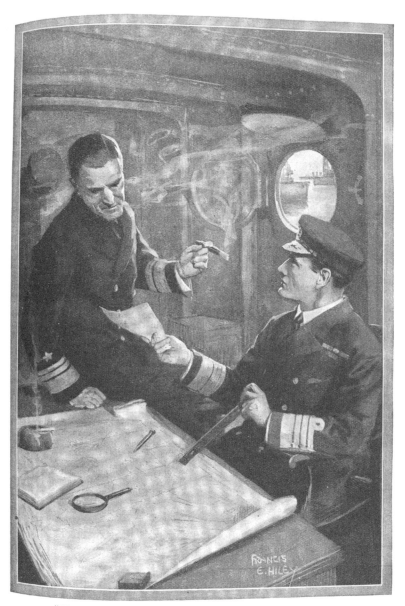

"What do you make of that, Bradman?" he asked.
"Say, it's just fine on the face of it!" the American answered.

A scene from Doyle's alternate history story 'The Death Voyage', illustrated by Francis Hiley and published in *The Strand*, October 1929. It was the last new story he would see published.

of the essay that inspired Squire's volume – 'If Napoleon Had Won the Battle of Waterloo' by the historian G. M. Trevelyan in *Westminster Gazette* in 1907. He even considers that idea as part of the story. But there had been few alternate histories before Doyle wrote 'The Death Voyage', and the story deserves to be better known as one of his more intriguing ideas.

★

Sadly 'The Death Voyage' was the last new story that Doyle saw in print. He had written three others, all of which appeared posthumously in *The Strand*. Doyle died at his home in Windlesham on 7 July 1930, his final words being to his wife, Jean: 'You are wonderful.' He was buried four days later in his garden next to his writing hut. Among the attendees was Sir Frank Newnes as representative of *The Strand*. Two days later, on 13 July, there was a Memorial Service at the Albert Hall, London, organised by the Marylebone Spiritualist Alliance. Estimates vary but it is believed that around 6,000 attended.

Two weeks after the service, but too soon for *The Strand* to have included an announcement, the August issue published 'The Parish Magazine'. This was a humorous story of a group of townsfolk who play a practical joke on the local printer by having him publish a supplement to the Parish Magazine in such a hurry that he fails to read it and then discovers it is full of libellous and scandalous allegations.

The September issue ran an obituary, 'The Passing of Conan Doyle', by Greenhough Smith. News had come through just as the magazine was going to press, and Smith reserved the right to say more later. He still filled four pages, mostly with material already stated elsewhere, but among his personal comments he said:

> Of my own long personal relationship with the late Sir Arthur I can only say, in this hurried note, how much I admired the personal character of the man. His interests were widespread, and whatever he did, he did with utmost sincerity of heart, and abundant enthusiasm.[227]

That same issue reprinted the first Holmes story, 'A Scandal in Bohemia'. The next issue, for October, ran a longer feature by Smith, 'Some Letters

---

[227] H. Greenhough Smith, 'The Passing of Conan Doyle', *Strand*, September 1930, p. 227.

of Conan Doyle', with a selection of excerpts. Smith now had time to comment on Doyle the writer. Some critics had remarked that Doyle's style of writing was commonplace and undistinguished and Smith rushed to his defence.

> Now I take it that the mark of a good style — as it is of the medium of every art — is its capacity to achieve the purpose for which it was intended. Conan Doyle was one of the great story-tellers of the world, and his purpose was to tell a story; and this his style, simple, clear and easy-flowing, never drawing off the reader's notice by any frills or gewgaws of its own, achieves to absolute perfection.[228]

Doyle's story, 'The End of Devil Hawker', announced for the September issue, at last appeared in November. It was a return to his love of historical fiction. Set in the Regency period and again featuring former boxer Tom Cribb, after he had retired and was running his inn, it tells of Sir John Hawker, a known bully who wins £6,000 at cards through sleight of hand and is then blackmailed by a rascal called Jakes. Hawker waits for the right opportunity to attack Jakes and is then alarmed when Jakes resorts to justice through Hawker's own gentleman's club. It's a clever story showing Doyle in good form, combining historical atmosphere with the study of evidence. It would have been a fitting final farewell.

There was, though, one last story, in many ways uncharacteristic; 'The Last Resource' in the December 1930 *Strand*. It had already appeared in the American magazine *Liberty* on 16 August 1930, a suitable venue as it dealt with an American gangster, Kid Wilson, who had fled into hiding in London. It's narrated for the most part by the gangster himself, and so contains many slang Americanisms that do not feel at home in *The Strand*. It explains how Wilson came to London after he had a vision of other gangsters taking their revenge on him, rather like the St Valentine's Day massacre that had happened in Chicago just the year before, in February 1929.

That was the end, in more ways than one. Not only was it the last appearance by Doyle in *The Strand*, it was the last issue edited by Greenhough

---

[228] H. Greenhough Smith, 'Some Letters of Conan Doyle', *Strand*, October 1930, p. 390.

Smith. He was already semi-retired and George Blake had served as Acting Editor since 1928. Smith was, after all, older than Doyle and close to his seventy-sixth birthday. It was a good time to go. He was succeeded by Reeves Shaw, who had already been editing the companion *Grand Magazine*.

If ever there was an end of an era, this was it. Smith lived another five years, dying on 14 January 1935, just after his eightieth birthday. Between them, Smith and Doyle left behind a formidable legacy. They had made the new form of popular-fiction magazine a huge success, and this had ushered in an era of short fiction and established detective fiction as a genre in its own right. They worked together for forty years, a partnership unequalled in the world of British magazine publishing.

16

After Life

REGINALD POUND, WHO TOOK OVER editorship of *The Strand* in June 1942, wrote two books about the magazine. In one he wrote:

> Sir A. Conan Doyle's death in 1930 may not have deprived *The Strand* of any of its later circulation, for by then his was a waning power. But it broke another link in the line of narrative writing which had distinguished the magazine through many years.[229]

It was that break in the chain that would become significant as *The Strand* entered its fifth and sixth decades. It had been a magazine of regular contributors. It was not just Doyle and Greenhough Smith that provided that continuity. One who contributed even more material than Doyle for almost as long had been W. W. Jacobs, whose light-hearted stories, often about sailors on land or at sea, had become almost as iconic for the magazine as the Holmes stories. P. G. Wodehouse sold all his stories between 1905 and 1939 to *The Strand* and it was here that Jeeves and Wooster, Lord Emsworth, Mr Mulliner and others first appeared. Other frequent contributors included Anthony Armstrong, F. Britten Austin, Gilbert Frankau, Denis Mackail, Roland Pertwee, H. de Vere Stacpoole, Sapper and Horace Annesley Vachell, all of whom gave the magazine a comforting familiarity.

But one by one these writers passed away and few are remembered today. By the start of the 1940s, when the magazine celebrated its fiftieth

---

[229] Pound, *Maypole* (11).

anniversary, most had gone. With the outbreak of World War II, paper rationing took its toll. Over twenty of Newnes's magazines were sacrificed in order that the survivors had sufficient paper. Even so the page count of *The Strand* reduced and, from October 1941, it shrank in size to pocketbook format. Reeves Shaw resigned in disgust, and after R. J. Minney held the editorial reins for a few months, Reginald Pound took over. That the magazine survived at all was out of regard to its former prestige and history. 'From the economic standpoint,' Pound recalled, 'its viability seemed to be just about exhausted.'[230] The magazine had shown no significant profit since the early 1930s and it was effectively trading on its old reputation.

If that is what it needed during those dark wartime years, that is what Pound would provide and so *The Strand* looked back to Doyle and Holmes in celebration of its heyday and to keep the spirit alive.

There had always been trivial and miscellaneous pieces where *The Strand* traded on the name of Sherlock Holmes. As early as the March 1899 issue Gertrude Bacon had presented a series of sketches of pigs in 'Pigs of Celebrities'. She remarked that Doyle's very matchstick-like porcine figure had a close resemblance to 'the immortal and lamented Sherlock Holmes', and that the pig 'is evidently "on the Scent" of some baffling mystery'.[231]

A piece about Bedouin trackers in the August 1913 issue was called '"Sherlock Holmes" in Egypt'. A similar article in the November 1914 issue about aboriginal trackers in Australia was called 'Black "Sherlocks"'. In a light-hearted vein, the August 1915 issue printed reader Adelaide Adcock's image of Sherlock Holmes drawn by using a typewriter.

This type of frippery continued in *The Strand* in the 1940s. A filler about a deerstalker hat that disappears from a shop window is headed 'The Latest Sherlock Holmes Mystery' (April 1943), while a photograph of two policemen staring at something is labelled 'Why, There's Sherlock Holmes' (May 1943). In '"I gave it the chop, Pop"' (December 1943), Parke Cummings looked at the vogue of ending a sentence in a word that rhymes with the previous word. He suggests that Holmes might

[230] Pound, *Strand* (165).
[231] Gertrude Bacon, 'Pigs of Celebrities', *Strand*, March 1899, p. 341.

have turned to Watson stoking the fire on a wintry night and said, 'My
dear Watson – lots on.'

Thankfully there were more substantial articles reminding readers of
the glories of the past and alerting them to new discoveries. In the August 1943 issue Hesketh Pearson gave notice of his full-length biography
of Doyle with an article, 'Sherlock Holmes and "The Strand"'. It revealed
that in researching for the biography Pearson had found both a 'scenario
for an unwritten Sherlock Holmes story', and a complete story, 'The
Man Who Was Wanted'. Pearson did not think much of the story, calling
it 'not up to par' and 'feeble', but he added:

> …when my discovery was announced in America the threat of its sup-
> pression almost created an international 'incident', one Holmes fan going
> so far as to suggest that the future relationship between the two countries
> might be imperilled if this addition to the Sherlock saga were not given
> to the world.[232]

Pearson provided an extract from the story in his biography, but the
full story remained unpublished for five years. The American magazines
relentlessly pursued the estate and *The Strand* later reported that 'the fantastic sum of 20,000 dollars has been offered by one magazine for the
serial rights'.[233] Eventually it was published in Hearst's *Cosmopolitan* for
August 1948 for an undisclosed sum, the cover proclaiming:

> FOUND! The Last Adventure of SHERLOCK HOLMES, a hitherto
> unpublished story by Sir Arthur Conan Doyle.

Imagine the embarrassment and indignation of the Doyle estate, particularly the two sons Adrian and Denis, when the true author of 'The
Man Who Was Wanted' stepped forward after the story appeared in the
British newspaper, *Sunday Despatch*, in January 1949. His name was
Arthur Whitaker. He revealed that in 1910, while unemployed, he had
tried to earn some money by writing several detective stories. He sent
'The Man Who Was Wanted' to Doyle, hoping he might use the story as
a collaboration. Doyle responded that he did not collaborate, but that
the story was not bad, and he paid Whitaker ten guineas in case he

---

[232] Hesketh Pearson, 'Sherlock Holmes and "The Strand"', *Strand*, August 1943, p. 46.
[233] See *The Strand*, August 1944, p. 25.

should ever use the basic idea. Since that's close to £900 in today's terms, Whitaker could count his blessings.

Doyle did not use the story, so its rediscovery and publication rather disturbed Whitaker, by then just turned sixty and not in the best of health. Hoping to put the matter right he made contact with Doyle's estate. The two sons suspected Whitaker of trying to get a share of the money from the publication, but when Whitaker produced the letter from Doyle they paid him off with £150.[234]

The Strand did not publish 'The Man Who Was Wanted', probably all to the good, but it did publish the first authorised new Sherlock Holmes story in the February 1947 issue. 'The Adventure of the First Class Carriage' was by Monsignor Ronald Knox and illustrated by Tom Purvis, 'In Loving Memory of Sidney Paget'. Knox was already a noted writer of detective novels, and had an enviable reputation as an expert on Sherlock Holmes. In 1912 he had delivered a paper to Oxford University's Bodley Club called 'The Mind and Art of Sherlock Holmes', which provided a detailed analysis of all of the Holmes stories to that date. Knox sent a copy to Doyle, who was amazed that anyone could spend so much time on what he regarded as a relatively minor subject. Doyle told Knox that he clearly knew more about the subject than Doyle did.

In writing his pastiche Knox entered into the spirit of the game, starting the story by referring to yet other recorded but unpublished cases such as the 'Missing Omnibus' and the 'Luminous Cigar-Box' before settling down, in time-honoured tradition, to have a domestic servant relate her tale of the disappearance of Nathaniel Swithinbank. Being a railway mystery it is inevitably compared to Doyle's own 'The Man With the Watches', and there are indeed some similarities, but Knox's story, though a little too short to create the full Holmesian atmosphere, was nevertheless a delight to encounter as *The Strand*'s first new Sherlock Holmes story in twenty years.

Ronald Knox's brother Edmund, who had just stepped down as editor of *Punch*, provided the next material about Holmes in the December 1948 *Strand*, with a lengthy obituary, 'The Passing of Sherlock Holmes'. It was,

---

[234] That is worth about £4,000 in today's terms, so with the original payment from Doyle, Whitaker received the equivalent of close on £5000 for the story and a degree of literary immortality. Unfortunately he did not live to enjoy it as he died in July 1949.

THE MESSAGES WERE IN THE SAME HANDWRITING AS THAT WITH WHICH
MRS. HENNESSY'S FIND HAD MADE US FAMILIAR

Sherlock Holmes was resurrected in *The Strand* in February 1947 with new artwork by Tom Purvis.

of course, a humorous piece but a clever one. Holmes, who had been born in 1855, had died in his ninety-third year after being stung by one of his bees. In his dotage he would listen quietly to the wireless – the Third Programme and Home Service, of course: he held the Light Programme, and especially the *Dick Barton* serial in 'profound contempt'. He reveals that Holmes had two middle names, 'Spencer Tracy'. Knox tells of how Holmes became a detective just in time for the 'unprecedented wave of crime' that washed over England in the 1890s. He lists many of his cases, most of which are still kept under wraps in the British Museum. Dr Watson had become Lord Watson and had died the previous year after a violent attack in the House of Lords while studying provisions of the National Health Bill. Knox lists Holmes's various monographs and other achievements, and concludes by saying of Holmes:

> A sturdy moralist, if not a devout Churchman, he was also an ardent Democrat, a believer in the close union of the English-speaking races, a hater of the colour bar, and a despiser of the trappings of pomp and power.[235]

The very next issue of *The Strand* (January 1949) featured 'Conan Doyle, Detective' by John Dickson Carr. Carr had just completed his biography of Doyle and this was an advance publication of his chapter dealing with the Edalji Case. It was the first opportunity readers of *The Strand* had to discover the full details of the case in their magazine. Carr provided a full outline, from the initial killing of several horses, sheep and cows during the spring and summer of 1903, to the arrest of solicitor George Edalji, his trial and imprisonment. He reproduced some of the letters that Doyle received when he took up the crusade to clear Edalji's name. Although Doyle did establish Edalji's innocence, enabling him to be restored to his profession, there was no compensation paid for Edalji's three-year imprisonment.

In an article in the January 1946 *Strand*, Jim Marshall had called Holmes the 'world's most durable detective', and he considered not only the many films starring Holmes but also his dedicated followers in the American-based society, the Baker Street Irregulars. His essay contradicted Knox's later obituary by stating that Holmes was born on 6 January 1854. He revealed that in the agreement between Universal Pictures and the Doyle estate the studio had agreed to pay £40,000 for the film rights to just twenty-two stories, and that the price for the rights rose each year! He also revealed

---

[235] E. V. Knox, 'The Passing of Sherlock Holmes', *Strand*, December 1948, p. 82.

that Eille Norwood, who played the character of Holmes for the silent
screen in 47 films, upon retiring turned to creating crossword puzzles as a
hobby. Having spent many years contributing to the *Daily Express*, he was
now compiling them for *The Strand*.[236]

There was more minutiae about Holmes in two further articles.
'Sherlock Holmes in America' by Paul Gore-Booth in the March 1949
issue was an extended review of four issues of the *Baker Street Journal*, published in New York by Ben Abramson. It provided some history of the
Baker Street Irregulars and revealed that there were at least two people
alive in the United States who had been christened Sherlock Holmes. The
second piece could have initiated a regular column, 'Holmesiana', for
which Ernest Short provided plans of Holmes's rooms at 221B Baker
Street as well as a map of the street showing the location of 221B.

Alas there was to be no more 'Holmesiana'. That feature appeared
in the March 1950 issue, which was the very last edition of *The Strand*.
It was issue number 711, but there had been a combined number for
May/June 1947, so there had been 710 individual issues. Doyle had
appeared in 269 of them up to the end of 1930, and there were a further eighteen issues with features about him or Holmes. Doyle is thus
represented in 40 per cent of the magazine's total run. If we count to
the end of 1930, when there had been 480 issues, Doyle was present
or represented in 279 issues, 58 per cent of the run. Doyle was therefore in over half of the issues of *The Strand* published during his lifetime; an impressive figure considering all of his other commitments
and activities.

The end of *The Strand* was a relatively sudden decision. It was still
advertising a year's subscription as a Christmas present at the start of
November 1949, but on 13 December 1949 a press release told of its
planned demise with the March 1950 issue. The main reason was the
cost of paper, which was three times its pre-war level. It maintained it
still had a circulation of 'well over 100,000' which it had a few years

---

[236] There was a heavily illustrated feature about Eille Norwood's portrayal of Holmes in 'Sherlock
Holmes on the Film' by Fenn Sherie, *Strand*, July 1921, pp. 72–78. Doyle was delighted with Norwood's portrayal of Holmes, though he criticised the films for including telephones and motorcars,
'luxuries of which the Victorian Holmes never dreamed'. (*Strand*, January 1924, p. 96.)

before, but Reginald Pound disclosed that by the end it had dropped to 95,000 and was still falling.[237]

Lord Rothermere offered to take over publication under the Amalgamated Press but received no response. In theory the magazine did not end but was merged with *Men Only*, at that time another pocketbook magazine of short fiction and light articles. But there was no continuity of tradition. *The Strand* had gone.

There were many tributes paid to the magazine, all of them placing Doyle and Sherlock Holmes at the head of the list of major names. There were efforts to perpetuate the legacy. That had already been attempted by the *London Mystery Magazine*, a digest-size magazine published by Hulton Press and edited by Michael Hall. He had persuaded the Post Office to assign 221B Baker Street as the magazine's editorial address, which both raised the magazine's profile and resulted in sacks-full of correspondence. The magazine did not otherwise prevail on the memory of Doyle or Holmes, except that the pseudonymous 'Sagittarius' (writer Olga Miller) wrote two Holmesian poems. 'Hedunit' in the first issue (June 1949) celebrates how everyone follows the Sherlock trail. In the third issue (April 1950) 'Doctor ...?' asks who Dr Watson really was, and how he came to have so much free time.

The *London Mystery Magazine* changed publisher after issue number fifteen in April 1952 and lost the Baker Street address, but it was an indication that Holmes had a life in print after *The Strand*, rather than just in films and radio (and, soon, television).

There was an attempt to revive *The Strand* as *The New Strand* in 1961. It had nothing to do with Newnes or the original magazine, but was published by a company set up by crime writer John Creasey with Ernest Kay, the editor of *John o'London's*. It was edited by South African journalist Noni Jabavu – the first black African woman to edit a British literary magazine. She made sure the magazine had a diverse range of contents, and kept a connection to Sherlock Holmes with a regular column, 'Baker Street and Beyond', by Lord Donegall, editor of the *Sherlock*

---

[237] See Pound, *Strand* (193), also the editorial to the March 1950 issue, and the report in *The Times*, 14 December 1949, p. 4.

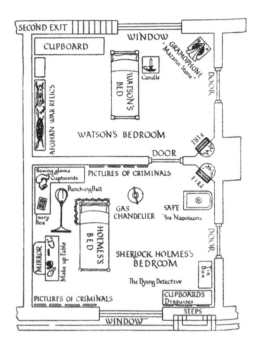

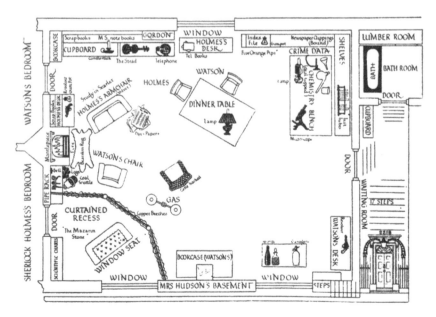

The final issue of *The Strand*, dated March 1950, featured a column, 'Holme-siana', with several plans by Ernest Short. These show 221B Baker Street in painstaking detail, keeping the world of Sherlock Holmes alive.

Holmes Journal. Unfortunately *The New Strand* only ran for fifteen issues, folding in February 1963.

The Strand was resurrected again, at least in name, in America in the autumn of 1998 by Andrew F. Gulli who has made it primarily a mystery fiction magazine, and it usually publishes a Sherlock Holmes story each issue. The name and legacy are thus kept alive, at least so far as mystery fiction is concerned, but the general fiction magazine publishing a diversity of material and able to sustain the careers of major writers has long gone.

★

Doyle was not a great writer, not in the same league as his contemporaries Rudyard Kipling or Joseph Conrad, but he was a great storyteller and the distinction is important. Although Doyle's desire was to write historical fiction, he wanted first and foremost to produce works which were enjoyable and popular; exactly the type of books he enjoyed reading, such as those by Walter Scott and Robert Louis Stevenson. He was not writing for a literary elite but for a popular market. It was his good fortune that the popular market was itself evolving during his early years towards the more sophisticated but less highbrow illustrated magazines that published highly competent but easily accessible fiction. Doyle's talent was that he could add an original twist and a new idea to old plots and his preference to write the stories as first-person narratives meant that he cast the reader into the midst of the action. The reader became the storyteller and Doyle would bring his world alive so that the reader saw, heard and almost tasted it. No one who has read Watson's description of the Hound of the Baskervilles, or of the young Nigel Loring's gallop across the Surrey Hills, or of the capture of the tourists of the *Korosko*, or Malone's journey across the Lost World, or any of a hundred scenes in Doyle's fiction will ever forget them.

He once wrote:

> In short stories it has always seemed to me that so long as you produce your dramatic effect, accuracy of detail matters little. I have never striven for it and have made some bad mistakes in consequence. What matter if I can hold my readers?[238]

---

[238] Doyle, 'How Our Novelists Write Their Books', *Strand*, December 1924, p. 644.

And hold his readers he did. It made him one of the most popular and best-remembered writers of the period.

It is remarkable how George Newnes, Greenhough Smith and Doyle came together at that right moment in 1891: a true meeting of minds, each determined to provide the best fiction to the largest possible readership. It resulted in a magazine that changed the face of popular fiction, creating a huge market that lasted for nearly fifty years – and in establishing detective and mystery fiction as a distinct genre. It changed the literary world but, as we have seen, it also became a very personal venue for Doyle to further not just his career as a writer, but to explore his beliefs, his interests and his ideals. For forty years *The Strand* and Arthur Conan Doyle were inseparable, and popular fiction in Britain was all the better for it.

Appendix 1

Arthur Conan Doyle's appearances in The Strand Magazine

This lists all of Doyle's appearances in the English edition of *The Strand*, along with other items of interest relevant to Doyle or Sherlock Holmes.

All items are fiction unless identified as interview (iv), non-fiction (nf), pictorial feature (pic), poem (pm) or contribution to symposium (sym).

1891

March, 'The Voice of Science'
July, 'The Adventures of Sherlock Holmes, I: A Scandal in Bohemia'
August, 'The Adventures of Sherlock Holmes, II: The Red-Headed League'
September, 'The Adventures of Sherlock Holmes, III: A Case of Identity'
October, 'The Adventures of Sherlock Holmes, IV: The Boscombe Valley Mystery'
November, 'The Adventures of Sherlock Holmes, V: The Five Orange Pips'
December, 'The Adventures of Sherlock Holmes, VI: The Man With the Twisted Lip'; also 'Portraits of Celebrities at Different Times of Their Lives: A. Conan Doyle'

1892

January, 'The Adventures of Sherlock Holmes, VII: The Adventure of the Blue Carbuncle'
February, 'The Adventures of Sherlock Holmes, VIII: The Adventure of the Speckled Band'
March, 'The Adventures of Sherlock Holmes, IX: The Adventure of the Engineer's Thumb'
April, 'The Adventures of Sherlock Holmes, X: The Adventure of the Noble Bachelor'

May, 'The Adventures of Sherlock Holmes, XI: The Adventure of the Beryl Coronet'

June, 'The Adventures of Sherlock Holmes, XII: The Adventure of the Copper Beeches'

August, 'A Day with Conan Doyle' (iv) by Harry How

December, 'The Adventures of Sherlock Holmes, XIII: The Adventure of Silver Blaze'

1893

January, 'The Adventures of Sherlock Holmes, XIV: The Adventure of the Cardboard Box'

February, 'The Adventures of Sherlock Holmes, XV: The Adventure of the Yellow Face'

March, 'The Adventures of Sherlock Holmes, XVI: The Adventure of the Stockbroker's Clerk'

April, 'The Adventures of Sherlock Holmes, XVII: The Adventure of the 'Gloria Scott''

May, 'The Adventures of Sherlock Holmes, XVIII: The Adventure of the Musgrave Ritual'

June, 'The Adventures of Sherlock Holmes, XIX: The Adventure of the Reigate Squire'

July, 'The Adventures of Sherlock Holmes, XX: The Adventure of the Crooked Man'

August, 'The Adventures of Sherlock Holmes, XXI: The Adventure of the Resident Patient'

September, 'The Adventures of Sherlock Holmes, XXII: The Adventure of the Greek Interpreter'

October, 'The Adventures of Sherlock Holmes, XXIII: The Adventure of the Naval Treaty' Part 1

November, 'The Adventures of Sherlock Holmes, XXIII: The Adventure of the Naval Treaty' Part 2

December, 'The Adventures of Sherlock Holmes, XXIV: The Adventure of the Final Problem'

1894

July, 'The Lord of Château Noir'

December, 'The Medal of Brigadier Gerard' and 'An Alpine Pass on "Ski"' (nf)

1895

April, 'The Exploits of Brigadier Gerard, I: How the Brigadier Held the King'

May, 'The Exploits of Brigadier Gerard, II: How the King Held the Brigadier'

June, 'The Exploits of Brigadier Gerard, III: How the Brigadier Slew the Brothers of Ajaccio'

July, 'The Exploits of Brigadier Gerard, IV: How the Brigadier Came to the Castle of Gloom'

August, 'The Exploits of Brigadier Gerard, V: How the Brigadier Took the Field Against the Marshal Millefleurs'

September, 'The Exploits of Brigadier Gerard, VI: How the Brigadier was Tempted by the Devil'

December, 'The Exploits of Brigadier Gerard, VII: How the Brigadier Played for a Kingdom'

1896

January, 'Rodney Stone', part 1
February, 'Rodney Stone', part 2
March, 'Rodney Stone', part 3
April, 'Rodney Stone', part 4
May, 'Rodney Stone', part 5
June, 'Rodney Stone', part 6
July, 'Rodney Stone', part 7
August, 'Rodney Stone', part 8
September, 'Rodney Stone', part 9
October, 'Rodney Stone', part 10
November, 'Rodney Stone', part 11
December, 'Rodney Stone', part 12

1897

January, 'Life of a Greenland Whaler' (nf)
May, 'The Tragedy of the Korosko', part 1
June, 'The Tragedy of the Korosko', part 2
July, 'The Tragedy of the Korosko', part 3
August, 'The Tragedy of the Korosko', part 4
September, 'The Tragedy of the Korosko', part 5
October, 'The Tragedy of the Korosko', part 6
November, 'The Tragedy of the Korosko', part 7
December, 'The Tragedy of the Korosko', part 8

1898

June, 'Round the Fire, I: The Story of the Beetle-Hunter'
July, 'Round the Fire, II: The Story of the Man with the Watches'
August, 'Round the Fire, III: The Story of the Lost Special'
September, 'Round the Fire, IV: The Story of the Sealed Room'
October, 'Round the Fire, V: The Story of the Black Doctor'
November, 'Round the Fire, VI: The Story of the Club-Footed Grocer'
December, 'Round the Fire, VII: The Story of the Brazilian Cat'

1899

January, 'Round the Fire, VIII: The Story of the Japanned Box'
February, 'Round the Fire, IX: The Story of the Jew's Breast-Plate'
March, 'Round the Fire, X: The Story of B24'; also 'Pigs of Celebrities' by
    Gertrude Bacon
April, 'Round the Fire, XI: The Story of the Latin Tutor'
May, 'Round the Fire, XII: The Story of the Brown Hand'
October, 'The Croxley Master', part 1
November, 'The Croxley Master', part 2
December, 'The Croxley Master', part 3

1900

January, 'The Crime of the Brigadier'
February, helped complete 'The Episode of the Dead Man Who Spoke' by
    Grant Allen
March, 'Playing With Fire'
September, 'A Glimpse of the Army' (nf)

1901

March, 'Strange Studies from Life, I: The Holocaust of Manor Place' (nf)
April, 'Strange Studies from Life, II: The Love Affair of George Vincent
    Parker' (nf)
May, 'Strange Studies from Life, III: The Debatable Case of Mrs Emsley' (nf)
June, 'A British Commando: An Interview with Conan Doyle' (iv) by Philip
    Trevor
August, 'The Hound of the Baskervilles', part 1
September, 'The Hound of the Baskervilles', part 2
October, 'The Hound of the Baskervilles', part 3
November, 'The Hound of the Baskervilles', part 4
December, 'The Hound of the Baskervilles', part 5. Also 'Mr William Gillette as
    Sherlock Holmes', Harold J. Shepstone and letter 'Where Sherlock Holmes
    Died', Hubert J. Mason

1902

January, 'The Hound of the Baskervilles', part 6
February, 'The Hound of the Baskervilles', part 7
March, 'The Hound of the Baskervilles', part 8
April, 'The Hound of the Baskervilles', part 9
August, 'The Adventures of Etienne Gerard, I: How Brigadier Gerard Lost
    His Ear'
November, 'The Adventures of Etienne Gerard, II: How the Brigadier Saved
    the Army'

December, 'The Adventures of Etienne Gerard, III: How the Brigadier Rode to Minsk'

1903

January, 'The Adventures of Etienne Gerard, IV: Brigadier Gerard at Waterloo', part 1, 'The Adventure of the Forest Inn'

Feb 'The Adventures of Etienne Gerard, V: Brigadier Gerard at Waterloo', part 2, 'The Adventure of the Nine Prussian Horsemen'

March, 'The Adventures of Etienne Gerard, VI: The Brigadier in England'

April, 'The Adventures of Etienne Gerard, VII: How the Brigadier Joined the Hussars of Conflans'

May, 'The Adventures of Etienne Gerard, VIII: How the Brigadier Said Good-bye to His Master'

June, 'The Leather Funnel'

October, 'The Return of Sherlock Holmes, I: The Adventure of the Empty House'

November, 'The Return of Sherlock Holmes, II: The Adventure of the Norwood Builder'. Also 'The New Sculpturing Machine' by M. Dinorben Griffiths in which Doyle is mentioned

December, 'The Return of Sherlock Holmes, III: The Adventure of the Dancing Men'

1904

January, 'The Return of Sherlock Holmes, IV: The Adventure of the Solitary Cyclist'

February, 'The Return of Sherlock Holmes, V: The Adventure of the Priory School'

March, 'The Return of Sherlock Holmes, VI: The Adventure of Black Peter'

April, 'The Return of Sherlock Holmes, VII: The Adventure of Charles Augustus Milverton'

May, 'The Return of Sherlock Holmes, VIII: The Adventure of the Six Napoleons'

June, 'The Return of Sherlock Holmes, IX: The Adventure of the Three Students'

July, 'The Return of Sherlock Holmes, X: The Adventure of the Golden Pince-Nez'

August, 'The Return of Sherlock Holmes, XI: The Adventure of the Missing Three-Quarter'. Also 'Inches and Eminence' by Beckles Willson, recording Doyle's height

September, 'The Return of Sherlock Holmes, XII: The Adventure of the Abbey Grange'

December, 'The Return of Sherlock Holmes, XIII: The Adventure of the Second Stain'

1905

December, 'Sir Nigel', part 1. Also 'The Funniest Picture I Have Ever Published' reproducing a Sherlock Holmes cartoon by Lyonel Feininger (nf)

1906

January, 'Sir Nigel', part 2
February, 'Sir Nigel', part 3
March, 'Sir Nigel', part 4
April, 'Sir Nigel', part 5
May, 'Sir Nigel', part 6
June, 'Sir Nigel', part 7
July, 'Sir Nigel', part 8. Also anonymous article 'The Forerunners of Sherlock Holmes'
August, 'Sir Nigel', part 9
September, 'Sir Nigel', part 10
October, 'Sir Nigel', part 11
November, 'Sir Nigel', part 12
December, 'Sir Nigel', part 13

1908

March, 'The Pot of Caviare'
August, 'The Silver Mirror'. Also 'The Undoing of Archibald', composite story extracted from works by fifty novelists including a paragraph from a Sherlock Holmes story
September, 'A Reminiscence of Mr Sherlock Holmes, I: The Singular Experience of Mr John Scott Eccles'
October, 'A Reminiscence of Mr Sherlock Holmes, II: The Tiger of San Pedro' [Note: these two episodes are usually combined and published as 'The Adventure of Wisteria Lodge']
December, 'The Adventure of the Bruce-Partington Plans'

1909

April, 'Bendy's Sermon: A Story in Verse' manuscript facsimile (pm)
August, 'The Lord of Falconbridge: A Legend of the Ring'
September, 'Some Recollections of Sport' (nf)
December, 'The Home-Coming'

1910

August, 'The Terror of Blue John Gap'
September, 'The Marriage of the Brigadier'
December, 'A Reminiscence of Sherlock Holmes: The Adventure of the Devil's Foot'

1911

March, 'A Reminiscence of Sherlock Holmes: The Adventure of the Red Circle', part 1

April, 'A Reminiscence of Sherlock Holmes: The Adventure of the Red Circle', part 2

August, 'One Crowded Hour'. Also 'The S.P.B. (Society for the Propagation of the Beard' by J. Willsher (nf)

September, 'What Reform is Most Needed?' (sym)

December, 'The Disappearance of Lady Frances Carfax'. Also 'The Twenty-First Birthday of the Strand Magazine' (sym)

1912

April, 'The Lost World', part 1

May, 'The Lost World', part 2

June, 'The Lost World', part 3

July, 'The Lost World', part 4

August, 'The Lost World', part 5. Also 'Twelve-Object Pictures: A Puzzle for Artists' (pic) nine artists depict Sherlock Holmes in bizarre circumstances

September, 'The Lost World', part 6

October, 'The Lost World', part 7. Also 'Autographs After Dinner' (sym)

November, 'The Lost World', part 8

December, 'The Fall of Lord Barrymore'

1913

January, photograph of Professor Challenger statuette, with caption (pic)

March, 'The Poison Belt', part 1

April, 'The Poison Belt', part 2

May, 'The Poison Belt', part 3

June, 'The Poison Belt', part 4

July, 'The Poison Belt', part 5. Also 'The Greatest Mystery of the Sea: The 'Marie Celeste'' (sym)

August, 'Sherlock Holmes in Egypt', Greville H. Parker

September, 'How It Happened'

November, 'The Horror of the Heights'

December, 'The Adventure of the Dying Detective'

1914

July, 'Danger! Being the Log of Captain John Sirius'

September, 'The Valley of Fear', part 1. Sherlock Holmes depicted on cover

October, 'The Valley of Fear', part 2

November, 'The Valley of Fear', part 3

December, 'The Valley of Fear', part 4

1915

January, 'The Valley of Fear', part 5
February, 'The Valley of Fear', part 6. Also, 'How I Broke Into Print' (sym)
March, 'The Valley of Fear', part 7
April, 'The Valley of Fear', part 8
May, 'The Valley of Fear', part 9
August, 'Sherlock Holmes Drawn by a Typewriter' by Adelaide Adcock
October, 'An Outing in War-Time' (nf)
December, 'Stranger Than Fiction' (nf)

1916

January, 'The Prisoner's Defence'
April, 'The British Campaign in France: The Battle of Mons' part 1 (nf)
May, 'The British Campaign in France: The Battle of Mons' part 2 (nf)
June, 'The British Campaign in France: The Battle of Le Cateau' (nf)
July, 'The British Campaign in France: The Battle of the Marne' (nf)
August, 'The British Campaign in France: The Battle of the Aisne' (nf)
September, 'The British Campaign in France: The La Bassée-Armentières
    Operations' (nf)
October, 'The British Campaign in France: The First Battle of Ypres', part 1 (nf)
November, 'The British Campaign in France: The First Battle of Ypres', part 2 (nf)
December, 'The British Campaign in France: Neuve Chapelle and
    Hill 60' (nf)

1917

January, 'The British Campaign in France: The Second Battle of Ypres',
    part 1 (nf)
February, 'The British Campaign in France: The Second Battle of Ypres',
    part 2 (nf)
March, 'The British Campaign in France: The Battle of Richebourgh-
    Festubert' (nf)
April, 'The British Campaign in France: The Battle of Loos', part 1 (nf)
May, 'The British Campaign in France: The Battle of Loos', part 2 (nf)
June, 'The British Campaign in France: The Battle of Loos', part 3 (nf)
July, 'Is Sir Oliver Lodge Right?: "Yes"' (debate)
August, 'What Will England Be Like in 1930?' (sym)
September, 'His Last Bow: The War Service of Sherlock Holmes'. Sherlock
    Holmes depicted on cover
December, 'Some Personalia About Mr Sherlock Holmes' (nf)

1918

April, 'Three of Them, I: A Chat About Children, Snakes, and Zebus; II: About
    Cricket'

May, 'The Battle of the Somme', part 1 (nf)
June, 'The Battle of the Somme', part 2 (nf)
July, 'Three of Them, III: Speculations'
August, 'Three of Them: IV: The Leatherskin Tribe'. Also 'The Most Useful Invention or Discovery since 1850' (sym)
October, 'The Battle of Arras: The Greatest British Victory in Three Years' (nf)
November, 'The Battle of Messines' (nf)
December, 'Three of Them, V: About Naughtiness and Frogs and Historical Pictures'

1919

January, 'Cambrai: The Most Dramatic Battle in the War'
February, 'Cambrai: The Second Phase'
March, 'Life After Death: An Interview with Sir Arthur Conan Doyle' (iv) by Hayden Church
September, 'Tanks' by Sir Albert Stern, which reproduces correspondence from Doyle
December, 'The Uncharted Coast, I: The Law of the Ghost' (nf)

1920

January, 'The Uncharted Coast, II: A New Light on Old Crimes' (nf)
May, 'The Uncharted Coast, III: The Shadows on the Screen' (nf). Also the result of £250 short story competition with comment by Doyle who was one of the judges (nf)
August, Introduction to 'The Sideric Pendulum: A New Step into the Unknown' (nf)
September, 'The Uncharted Coast, IV: An Old Story Re-told' (nf)
November, 'The Uncharted Coast, V: The Absolute Proof' (nf)
December, 'Fairies Photographed: An Epoch-Making Event' (nf)

1921

March, 'The Evidence for Fairies' (nf)
May, 'The Uncharted Coast, VI: A Worker of Wonders' (nf)
July, 'Sherlock Holmes on the Film: An Interview with Eille Norwood' by Fenn Sherie (nf)
October, 'The Adventure of the Mazarin Stone'
November, 'The Bully of Brocas Court: A Legend of the Ring'
December, 'The Nightmare Room'

1922

February, 'The Problem of Thor Bridge', part 1
March, 'The Problem of Thor Bridge', part 2. Also 'The Book I Most Enjoyed Writing' (sym)

April, 'The Youth of Sherlock Holmes' by Hayden Church (nf)
June, 'The Lift'
July, 'Now Then, Smith!' (pm)
December, 'Billy Bones'

1923

February, 'The Cottingley Fairies' (nf)
March, 'The Adventure of the Creeping Man'. Sherlock Holmes depicted on cover
April, 'Haunting Dreams' (sym)
August, 'Three of Them, VI: The Forbidden Subject' (ss)
October, 'Memories and Adventures, I' (nf). Arthur Conan Doyle depicted on cover
November, 'Memories and Adventures, II' (nf)
December, 'Memories and Adventures, III' (nf)

1924

January, 'Memories and Adventures, IV' (nf) and 'The Adventure of the Sussex Vampire'. Sherlock Holmes depicted on cover
February, 'Memories and Adventures, V' (nf)
March, 'Memories and Adventures, VI' (nf)
April, 'Memories and Adventures, VII' (nf)
May, 'Memories and Adventures, VIII' (nf)
June, 'Memories and Adventures, IX' (nf)
July, 'Memories and Adventures, X' (nf)
December, 'How Our Novelists Write Their Books' (sym)

1925

January, 'The Adventure of the Three Garridebs'. Sherlock Holmes depicted on cover
February, 'The Adventure of the Illustrious Client', part 1. Sherlock Holmes depicted on cover
March, 'The Adventure of the Illustrious Client', part 2. Sherlock Holmes depicted on cover
July, 'The Land of Mist or, The Quest of Edward Malone', part 1. Professor Challenger depicted on cover
August, 'The Land of Mist or, The Quest of Edward Malone', part 2
September, 'The Land of Mist or, The Quest of Edward Malone', part 3
October, 'The Land of Mist or, The Quest of Edward Malone', part 4
November, 'The Land of Mist or, The Quest of Edward Malone', part 5
December, 'The Land of Mist or, The Quest of Edward Malone', part 6

1926

January, 'The Land of Mist or, The Quest of Edward Malone', part 7
February, 'The Land of Mist or, The Quest of Edward Malone', part 8
March, 'The Land of Mist or, The Quest of Edward Malone', part 9
October, 'The Adventure of the Three Gables'. Sherlock Holmes depicted on cover
November, 'The Adventure of the Blanched Soldier'. Sherlock Holmes depicted on cover
December, 'The Adventure of the Lion's Mane'

1927

January, 'The Adventure of the Retired Colourman'. Sherlock Holmes depicted on cover
February, 'The Adventure of the Veiled Lodger'. Sherlock Holmes depicted on cover
March, 'A Sherlock Holmes Competition: Mr Sherlock Holmes to His Readers' (contest)
April, 'The Adventure of Shoscombe Old Place'. Sherlock Holmes depicted on cover
May, 'The World's Happiest Museum' (iv) by Leonard Crocombe
June, 'The Sherlock Holmes Prize Competition Result: How I Made My List' (nf)
July, 'W. G. Grace – A Memory' (nf). Also 'How We Hold Things' by Claude F. Luke with a photograph of Doyle's hand writing with a pen
August, 'Houdini the Enigma', part 1 (nf)
September, 'Houdini the Enigma', part 2 (nf)
October, 'The Maracot Deep: The Lost World Under the Sea', part 1. Also illustrated on cover
November, 'The Maracot Deep', part 2
December, 'The Maracot Deep', part 3. Also 'The Great Characters of Fiction: Which Should I Most Liked to Have Created?' (sym)

1928

January, 'The Maracot Deep', part 4
February, 'The Maracot Deep', part 5
April, 'When the World Screamed', part 1
May, 'When the World Screamed', part 2; also, 'Blood Sports – Should They Be Abolished?' (sym)
June, 'The Dreamers: Notes from a Strange Mail-Bag' (nf)
October, 'The Story of Spedegue's Dropper'

1929

January, 'The Disintegration Machine'. Professor Challenger depicted on cover
April, 'The Lord of the Dark Face, I: The Dangers of the Deep'

May, 'The Lord of the Dark Face, II: The Crisis'
October, 'The Death Voyage: The Kaiser and His Fleet'

1930

August, 'The Parish Magazine'
September, 'The Passing of Conan Doyle' by H. Greenhough Smith (obituary).
    Also a reprint of 'A Scandal in Bohemia'
October, 'Some Letters of Conan Doyle' by H. Greenhough Smith (nf)
November, 'The End of Devil Hawker'
December, 'The Last Resource'

1935

March, Obituary of H. Greenhough Smith

1943

August, 'Sherlock Holmes and The Strand', Hesketh Pearson (nf)

1946

January, 'Durable Detective', Jim Marshall (nf)

1947

February, 'The Adventure of the First Class Carriage' by Ronald A. Knox (ss)

1948

December, 'The Passing of Sherlock Holmes' by E. V. Knox (nf)

1949

January, 'Conan Doyle, Detective' by John Dickson Carr (nf)
March, 'Sherlock Holmes in America' by Paul Gore-Booth (nf)

1950

March, 'Holmesiana' by Ernest Short (nf)

Appendix 2

Arthur Conan Doyle's appearances in the American edition of The Strand Magazine

All items are fiction unless identified as interview (iv), non-fiction (nf), pictorial feature (pic), poem (pm) or contribution to symposium (sym).

1891

March, 'The Voice of Science'
July, 'The Adventures of Sherlock Holmes, I: A Scandal in Bohemia'
August, 'The Adventures of Sherlock Holmes, II: The Red-Headed League'
September/October, 'The Adventures of Sherlock Holmes, III: A Case of Identity'
November, 'The Adventures of Sherlock Holmes, IV: The Boscombe Valley Mystery'
December, 'The Adventures of Sherlock Holmes, V: The Five Orange Pips'

1892

January, 'The Adventures of Sherlock Holmes, VI: The Man With the Twisted Lip'; also 'Portraits of Celebrities at Different Times of Their Lives: A. Conan Doyle'
February, 'The Adventures of Sherlock Holmes, VII: The Adventure of the Blue Carbuncle'
March, 'The Adventures of Sherlock Holmes, VIII: The Adventure of the Speckled Band'
April, 'The Adventures of Sherlock Holmes, IX: The Adventure of the Engineer's Thumb'
May, 'The Adventures of Sherlock Holmes, X: The Adventure of the Noble Bachelor'
June, 'The Adventures of Sherlock Holmes, XI: The Adventure of the Beryl Coronet'

July, 'The Adventures of Sherlock Holmes, XII: The Adventure of the Copper Beeches'

September, 'A Day with Conan Doyle' (iv) by Harry How

1893

January, 'The Adventures of Sherlock Holmes, XIII: The Adventure of Silver Blaze'

February, 'The Adventures of Sherlock Holmes, XIV: The Adventure of the Cardboard Box'

March, 'The Adventures of Sherlock Holmes, XV: The Adventure of the Yellow Face'

April, 'The Adventures of Sherlock Holmes, XVI: The Adventure of the Stockbroker's Clerk'

May, 'The Adventures of Sherlock Holmes, XVII: The Adventure of the 'Gloria Scott''

June, 'The Adventures of Sherlock Holmes, XVIII: The Adventure of the Musgrave Ritual'

July, 'The Adventures of Sherlock Holmes, XIX: The Adventure of the Reigate Squire'

August, 'The Adventures of Sherlock Holmes, XX: The Adventure of the Crooked Man'

September, 'The Adventures of Sherlock Holmes, XXI: The Adventure of the Resident Patient'

October, 'The Adventures of Sherlock Holmes, XXII: The Adventure of the Greek Interpreter'

November, 'The Adventures of Sherlock Holmes, XXIII: The Adventure of the Naval Treaty', part 1

December, 'The Adventures of Sherlock Holmes, XXIII: The Adventure of the Naval Treaty', part 2

Christmas, 'The Adventures of Sherlock Holmes, XXIV: The Adventure of the Final Problem'

1894

July, 'The Lord of Château Noir'

December, 'The Medal of Brigadier Gerard' and 'An Alpine Pass on "Ski"' (nf)

1895

April, 'The Exploits of Brigadier Gerard, I: How the Brigadier Held the King'

May, 'The Exploits of Brigadier Gerard, II: How the King Held the Brigadier'

June, 'The Exploits of Brigadier Gerard, III: How the Brigadier Slew the Brothers of Ajaccio'

July/August, 'The Exploits of Brigadier Gerard, IV: How the Brigadier Came to the Castle of Gloom'

September, 'The Exploits of Brigadier Gerard, V: How the Brigadier Took the Field Against the Marshal Millefleurs'
October, 'The Exploits of Brigadier Gerard, VI: How the Brigadier was Tempted by the Devil'

1896

January, 'The Exploits of Brigadier Gerard, VII: How the Brigadier Played for a Kingdom'
July, 'Portraits of Celebrities at Different Times of Their Lives: A. Conan Doyle'

1897

June, 'The Tragedy of the Korosko', part 1
July, 'The Tragedy of the Korosko', part 2
August, 'The Tragedy of the Korosko', part 3
September, 'The Tragedy of the Korosko', part 4
October, 'The Tragedy of the Korosko', part 5
November, 'The Tragedy of the Korosko', part 6
December, 'The Tragedy of the Korosko', part 7

1898

January, 'The Tragedy of the Korosko', part 8
July, 'Round the Fire, I: The Story of the Beetle-Hunter'
August, 'Round the Fire, II: The Story of the Man with the Watches'
September, 'Round the Fire, III: The Story of the Lost Special'
October, 'Round the Fire, IV: The Story of the Sealed Room'
November, 'Round the Fire, V: The Story of the Black Doctor'
December, 'Round the Fire, VI: The Story of the Club-Footed Grocer'

1899

January, 'Round the Fire, VII: The Story of the Brazilian Cat'
February, 'Round the Fire, VIII: The Story of the Japanned Box'
March, 'Round the Fire, IX: The Story of the Jew's Breast-Plate'
April, 'Round the Fire, X: The Story of B24'; also 'Pigs of Celebrities' by Gertrude Bacon
May, 'Round the Fire, XI: The Story of the Latin Tutor'
June, 'Round the Fire, XII: The Story of the Brown Hand'
November, 'The Croxley Master', part 1
December, 'The Croxley Master', part 2

1900

January, 'The Croxley Master', part 3
March, helped complete 'The Episode of the Dead Man Who Spoke' by Grant Allen

April, 'Playing With Fire'
October, 'A Glimpse of the Army' (nf)

1901

April, 'Strange Studies from Life, I: The Holocaust of Manor Place' (nf)
May, 'Strange Studies from Life, II: The Love Affair of George Vincent Parker' (nf)
June, 'Strange Studies from Life, III: The Debatable Case of Mrs Emsley' (nf)
July, 'A British Commando: An Interview with Conan Doyle' (iv) by Philip Trevor
September, 'The Hound of the Baskervilles', part 1
October, 'The Hound of the Baskervilles', part 2
November, 'The Hound of the Baskervilles', part 3
December, 'The Hound of the Baskervilles', part 4

1902

January, 'The Hound of the Baskervilles', part 5. Also 'Mr William Gillette as Sherlock Holmes', Harold J. Shepstone and letter 'Where Sherlock Holmes Died', Hubert J. Mason
February, 'The Hound of the Baskervilles', part 6
March, 'The Hound of the Baskervilles', part 7
April, 'The Hound of the Baskervilles', part 8
May, 'The Hound of the Baskervilles', part 9
September, 'The Adventures of Etienne Gerard, I: How Brigadier Gerard Lost His Ear'
December, 'The Adventures of Etienne Gerard, II: How the Brigadier Saved the Army'

1903

January, 'The Adventures of Etienne Gerard, III: How the Brigadier Rode to Minsk'
February, 'The Adventures of Etienne Gerard, IV: Brigadier Gerard at Waterloo', part 1, 'The Adventure of the Forest Inn'
March, 'The Adventures of Etienne Gerard, V: Brigadier Gerard at Waterloo', part 2, 'The Adventure of the Nine Prussian Horsemen'
April, 'The Adventures of Etienne Gerard, VI: The Brigadier in England'
May, 'The Adventures of Etienne Gerard, VII: How the Brigadier Joined the Hussars of Conflans'
June, 'The Adventures of Etienne Gerard, VIII: How the Brigadier Said Good-bye to His Master'
June, 'The Leather Funnel'
December, 'The New Sculpturing Machine' by M. Dinorben Griffiths in which Doyle is mentioned

1904

September, 'Inches and Eminence' by Beckles Willson, recording Doyle's height

1906

June, 'The Funniest Picture I Have Ever Published' reproducing a Sherlock
    Holmes cartoon by Lyonel Feininger
August, anonymous article 'The Forerunners of Sherlock Holmes'

1908

April, 'The Pot of Caviare'
September, 'The Silver Mirror'. Also 'The Undoing of Archibald' composite
    story extracted from works by fifty novelists including a paragraph from
    a Sherlock Holmes story

1909

May, 'Bendy's Sermon: A Story in Verse' manuscript facsimile (pm)
September, 'The Lord of Falconbridge: A Legend of the Ring'
October, 'Some Recollections of Sport' (nf)
December, 'The Home-Coming'

1910

September, 'The Terror of Blue John Gap'. Also life-size portrait of Sir Arthur
    Conan Doyle (not in British edition)
October, 'The Marriage of the Brigadier'

1911

January, 'A Reminiscence of Sherlock Holmes: The Adventure of the Devil's
    Foot', part 1. Sherlock Holmes depicted on cover
February, 'A Reminiscence of Sherlock Holmes: The Adventure of the Devil's
    Foot', part 2
April, 'A Reminiscence of Sherlock Holmes: The Adventure of the Red Circle',
    part 1. Sherlock Holmes depicted on cover
May, 'A Reminiscence of Sherlock Holmes: The Adventure of the Red Circle',
    part 2
October, 'What Reform is Most Needed?' (sym)

1912

January, 'The Twenty-First Birthday of the Strand Magazine' (sym)
September, 'Twelve-Object Pictures: A Puzzle for Artists' (pic) nine artists depict
    Sherlock Holmes in bizarre circumstances

1913

January, photograph of Professor Challenger statuette, with caption (pic)
April, 'The Poison Belt', part 1. Also 'Arthur Conan Doyle. A Study of the Man
    and His Books' by A. St. John Adcock (from *The Bookman*; not in British
    edition)
May, 'The Poison Belt', part 2. Professor Challenger depicted on cover
June, 'The Poison Belt', part 3. Professor Challenger depicted on cover
July, 'The Poison Belt', part 4. Professor Challenger depicted on cover
August, 'The Poison Belt', part 5. Also 'The Greatest Mystery of the Sea: The
    "Marie Celeste"' (sym)
September, 'Sherlock Holmes in Egypt', Greville H. Parker
October, 'How It Happened'

1914

December, 'The War. A Statement of the British Case' (not in British edition)

1915

September, 'Sherlock Holmes Drawn by a Typewriter' by Adelaide
    Adcock

1916

January, 'Stranger Than Fiction' (nf)

Bibliography

In addition to my own complete run of *The Strand Magazine*, and other popular fiction magazines of the period, the following books and essays have either been consulted in the preparation of this volume or are recommended for further reading. Footnote references within the main text are to the author below, with page reference. If the author has more than one title listed the footnote cites the key word from the title, e.g. Pound, *Maypole* or Pound, *Strand*.

Ashley, Mike, *The Age of the Storytellers*, London: British Library, 2006.

Bergem, Phillip G., *A Doylean and Sherlockian Checklist of The Strand Magazine*, Andover, Minnesota: privately printed, 2007 (with updates).

Bergem, Phillip G., *The Family and Residences of Arthur Conan Doyle*, St. Paul, Minnesota: privately printed, 2003 (second edition).

Blackbeard, Bill, *Sherlock Holmes in America*, New York: Harry N. Abrams, Inc., 1981.

Booth, Martin, *The Doctor, The Detective & Arthur Conan Doyle*, London: Hodder & Stoughton, 1997.

Brandon, Ruth, *The Life and Many Deaths of Harry Houdini*, London: Secker & Warburg, 1993.

Bunson, Matthew E., *The Sherlock Holmes Encyclopedia*, London: Pavilion Books, 1995.

Carr, John Dickson, *The Life of Sir Arthur Conan Doyle*, London: John Murray, 1949.

Chan, Winnie, *The Economy of the Short Story in British Periodicals of the 1880s*, London: Routledge, 2014.

Cooper, Joe, *The Case of the Cottingley Fairies*, London: Robert Hale, 1990.

Dark, Sidney, *The Life of Sir Arthur Pearson, Bt. G.B.E.*, London: Hodder & Stoughton, 1922.

Dirda, Michael, *On Conan Doyle*, Princeton: Princeton University Press, 2012.

Doyle, Georgina, *Out of the Shadows: The Untold Story of Arthur Conan Doyle's First Family*, Ashcroft, British Columbia: Calabash Press, 2004.

Duncan, Alistair, *The Norwood Author: Arthur Conan Doyle & The Norwood Years (1891–1894)*, London: MX Publishing, 2010.

Duncan, Alistair, *An Entirely New Country*, London: MX Publishing, 2011.

Edwards, Owen Dudley, *The Quest for Sherlock Holmes*, Harmondsworth: Penguin Books, 1984.

Edwards, Owen Dudley, 'Introduction', *The Exploits of Brigadier Gerard*, Edinburgh: Canongate Press, 1991.

Edwards, Owen Dudley, 'Introduction', *The Haunted Grange of Goresthorpe*, Ashcroft, British Columbia: Calabash Press on behalf of The Arthur Conan Doyle Society, 2000.

Friederichs, Hulda, *The Life of Sir George Newnes, Bart.*, London: Hodder & Stoughton, 1911.

Garrick-Steele, Rodger, *The House of the Baskervilles*, Bloomington, Indiana: 1st-Books Library, 2004.

Gibson, John Michael & Green, Richard Lancelyn (editors), *The Unknown Conan Doyle: Uncollected Stories*, London: Secker & Warburg, 1982.

Goldfarb, Clifford S., *The Great Shadow: Arthur Conan Doyle, Brigadier Gerard and Napoleon*, Ashcroft, British Columbia: Calabash Press, 1997.

Green, Richard Lancelyn, 'Introduction', *The Uncollected Sherlock Holmes*, Harmondsworth: Penguin Books, 1983.

Green, Richard Lancelyn & Gibson, John Michael, *A Bibliography of A. Conan Doyle*, Boston: Hudson House, 2000 (revised edition).

Hardwick, Michael, *The Complete Guide to Sherlock Holmes*, London: Weidenfeld & Nicolson, 1986.

Hines, Stephen (editor), *The True Crime Files of Sir Arthur Conan Doyle*, New York: Berkley Prime, 2001.

Hollyer, Cameron, 'Author to Editor: Arthur Conan Doyle's Correspondence with H. Greenhough Smith', *ACD: The Journal of the Arthur Conan Doyle Society*, volume 3, 1992.

Jackson, Kate, *George Newnes and the New Journalism in Britain, 1880–1910*, Aldershot: Ashgate, 2001.

James, Louis, *Fiction for the Working Man*, London: Oxford University Press, 1963.

Jerome, Jerome K., *My Life and Times*, London: Hodder & Stoughton, 1925.

Kalush, William & Sloman, Larry, *The Secret Life of Houdini*, New York: Atria, 2006.

Law, Graham, *Serializing Fiction in the Victorian Press*, Basingstoke: Palgrave, 2000.

Lellenberg, Jon, *Nova Fifty-Seven Minor*, Bloomington: Gaslight Productions, 1990.

Lellenberg, Jon, Stashower, Daniel & Foley, Charles (editors), *Arthur Conan Doyle, A Life in Letters*, London: HarperPress, 2007.

Lycett, Andrew, *Conan Doyle: The Man Who Created Sherlock Holmes*, London: Weidenfeld & Nicolson, 2007.

McDonald, Peter D., 'The Adventures of the Literary Agent: Conan Doyle, A. P. Watt, Holmes and The Strand in 1891', *Victorian Periodicals Review* 30:1 (spring 1997), reprinted in *ACD: The Journal of the Arthur Conan Doyle Society*, volume 8 (1998).

Marshall, Archibald, *Out and About: Random Reminiscences*, London: John Murray, 1933.

Miller, Russell, *The Adventures of Arthur Conan Doyle*, London: Harvill Secker, 2008.

Morton, Peter, *'The Busiest Man in England', Grant Allen and the Writing Trade, 1875–1900*, Basingstoke: Palgrave, 2005.

Pearson, Hesketh, *Conan Doyle: His Life and Art*, London: Methuen, 1943.

Pemberton, Sir Max, *Sixty Years Ago and After*, London: Hutchinson, 1936.

Pound, Reginald, *A Maypole in the Strand*, London: Ernest Benn, 1948.

Pound, Reginald, *The Strand Magazine, 1891–1950*, London: Heinemann, 1966.

Press, Charles, *A Bedside Book of Early Sherlockian Parodies and Pastiches*, London: MX Publishing, 2014.

Pugh, Brian W., *A Chronology of the Life of Sir Arthur Conan Doyle*, London: MX Publishing, 2014 (third edition).

Pugh, Brian W. & Spiring, Paul R., *Bertram Fletcher Robinson: A Footnote to the Hound of the Baskervilles*, London: MX Publishing, 2008.

Sillars, Stuart, *Visualisation in Popular Fiction, 1860–1960*, London: Routledge, 1995.

Starrett, Vincent, *221B: Studies in Sherlock Holmes*, New York: Macmillan, 1940.

Stashower, Daniel, *Teller of Tales: The Life of Arthur Conan Doyle*, London: Allen Lane, 2000.

Stavert, Geoffrey, *A Study in Southsea: The Unrevealed Life of Arthur Conan Doyle*, Horndean: Milestone Publications, 1987.

Stock, Randall, 'Revealing "A Scandal in Bohemia": Its History and Manuscript' in *Bohemian Souls*, edited by Otto Penzler, New York: The Baker Street Irregulars in association with The Harry Ransom Center at The University of Texas at Austin, 2011, pp. 105–124.

Usborne, Richard, *Wodehouse at Work to the End*, London: Barrie & Jenkins, 1976.

Whyte, Frederic, *A Bachelor's London*, London: Grant Richards, 1931.

Index

References to pictures are in *italics*. Titles of books and plays are in *italics*, whilst titles of short stories, essays, poems and serials are in 'single quotes'. References in footnotes are listed as 'n', e.g. 61n.